Draping

LAURENCE KING

Published in 2013
by Laurence King Publishing Ltd
361–373 City Road
London EC1V 1LR
United Kingdom
Tel. +44 20 7841 6900
E-mail enquiries@laurenceking.com
www.laurenceking.com

Reprinted 2014, 2016, 2017, 2018, 2019

A catalogue record for this book is available from
the British Library

ISBN 978 1 78067 286 1

Design by The Urban Ant Ltd
Picture research by Heather Vickers
Photography by Sia Aryai Photography, www.siaaryai.com
Line art by Briana Boyko
Technical diagrams and Photoshop enhancement
by Mikiela Salgado

Printed in China

Draping

The Complete Course

Karolyn Kiisel

Laurence King Publishing

Contents

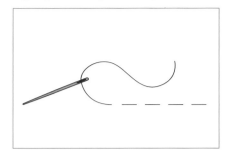

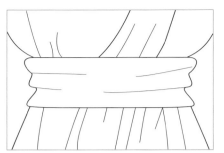

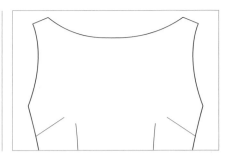

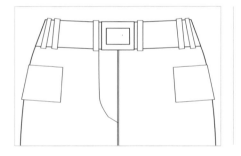

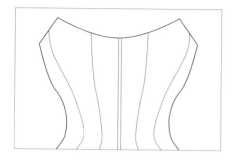
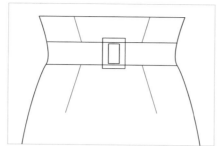

PART 2: Intermediate Draping

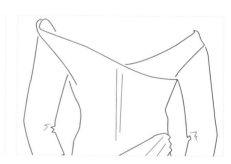

Introduction
Draping is an art

'Draping' is the term for using fabric to create a design directly on a mannequin or dress form. It is an essential skill for a fashion designer.

The French word for draping is *moulage*, meaning 'to mould or sculpt'. Fashion designers are artists, giving physical expression to concepts as they work with form, space and energy flow. Impact and emotion enter with the use of colour and surface detail, but first a silhouette must be sculpted.

Learning to drape, or model on the stand, involves training the eye to recognize balance, symmetry and a graceful line, and training the hand to dexterity in cutting, pinning and joining complex curves.

Ultimately, success for designers and artists lies in finding their own unique style of expression. Draping is a skill that helps the individuality of the designer's creative vision to emerge.

In this book, you will be draping ancient forms of clothing, historical garments from art works, costumes from films, contemporary designer pieces and styles from past decades.

At the beginning of each chapter are examples of early forms of clothing, often simple woven panels of cloth wrapped, tied or draped over the body. Understanding how a modern blouse or jacket evolved from these basic shapes makes it easier to conceptualize how to drape one. It is less intimidating when you understand that, for thousands of years, people have created beautiful, practical, transformational shapes from a simple length of woven cloth.

Many of the designs in the book are taken from the 'Golden Age of Draping'. From the late 1930s through the 1960s, Hollywood costume designers had unlimited resources from the studios to clothe their stars. After

World War II, in Europe and New York, the couture ateliers were blossoming. Balenciaga, Dior, Givenchy and, later, Yves Saint Laurent were only a few of the many designers using new fabrics and techniques to produce beautifully draped and impeccably tailored couture clothing. Learning to drape these iconic styles teaches important basic techniques and hones observational skills.

Studying modern and contemporary clothing helps to focus on the subtleties of shape and form. To create a silhouette that is truly new, one must know what has come before.

The value of learning to drape

When draping, the toile is a work in progress, continuing to evolve until it is taken off the mannequin and turned into a pattern for a garment.

Draping a new design, rather than drafting a flat pattern for it, is, for many, an easier way to develop the important skill of visualizing how a two-dimensional sketch moves into a three-dimensional form. As the contours of the garment can be seen taking shape during the draping process, it eliminates some of the guesswork involved with pattern drafting.

When drafting, it is not until the pattern is finished and the garment is cut and sewn that one can see the three-dimensional result. Becoming proficient at pattern drafting takes a lot of experience. With a few basic skills, draping can be done by anyone, even as our ancestors did with their simple tunics and robes.

Creating a signature look

The ultimate goal of training in the skills of draping is to strengthen original expression while creating new silhouettes.

Clothes are marketed today less by their fit and finesse than by a 'designer's statement'. In fashion, it is crucial for a designer to develop their own style. Having this 'signature look' sets a designer apart. Further, it helps the women who wear it define their own personal styles.

Today's woman wants clothes that not only fit comfortably but that help her express her attitudes and sensibilities. She wants her clothing to say something to the world about who she is. Like the actress who can't get into character without her costume, a woman needs her clothes to help her excel in the corporate world, relax into a yoga posture or feel glamorous for a special event.

The first step in creating a signature look is to anchor a creative vision before beginning to drape. The inspiration can come from a sunset, a painting, a photograph of another design, or simply a feeling or attitude that you want to express.

Top: Creating beautifully draped clothing requires developing an eye for perfect composition. In Sir Lawrence Alma-Tadema's *The Frigidarium* (1890),

details are adjusted to bring the proportions into balance.

Above: Yves Saint Laurent, a master of draping skills, created a new and unique fashion sense for women. His signature look is still sought after today.

If you have the skills to execute your creative vision, your personal flair becomes apparent, driven by your decisions on proportion and line, scale and volume, subtleties of shape and placement of details.

Refining the drape and adjusting the final proportion becomes very personal; you work on it until you arrive at a balance that *you* like. When it pleases your eye, it is done. When you continue to pursue and express the looks you connect with and that attract you, your own style inevitably emerges.

Form follows function

'Form follows function' is basic design theory. If the designer is clear on the function or purpose of their design, the many choices to be made during the draping process will flow more naturally.

Clothing has many functions, from basic warmth and protection to attraction and seduction. It is important to understand the garment's physical as well as non-physical purpose. How a garment makes a woman feel is as important as how it will make her look.

A crucial draping skill is understanding grainline placement. A simple tunic cut on the bias will have a totally different feel to one cut with straight grains placed vertically. The designer must be able to control the deeper energetic flow of the form they are creating and how it will affect the wearer. In this book, you will practise discerning the emotional tenor of a design and explore ways of making sure that mood or tone is present in the finished garment.

In the clothing created by the Inuit, the design purpose is clear: to keep out the cold.

Draping today

Basic draping techniques have remained constant since the development of the padded mannequin and its continued popularization by the Wolf Form Company in the early 1900s.

However, in design studios around the world, technology is embraced to save time and money. Design firms have master pattern 'blocks' that reflect their specific fit and sizing. These are used to produce new collections in which the width of a pair of trousers or the scale of a jacket is changed by simply manipulating these blocks. Digital pattern cutting allows companies to churn out dozens of variations in short order.

So what, then, is the enduring value of draping by hand in this brave new world of digital fashion?

The challenge is for designers to go beyond the rote process of developing a pattern that fits well and to use the basic concepts of darting and seaming as a springboard for creating new and unique forms.

Much of contemporary design is not about the perfection of the classic couture of the 1960s. It's about twisting, wrapping, tucking and cutting asymmetrically, reminding us sometimes of early forms of clothing.

When a designer is aspiring towards an innovative silhouette, they need to experiment with focal points to create emphasis and attitude, and work with proportions and scale to sculpt a shape that evokes a specific emotion.

To create something truly fresh and new, the intimate, hands-on relationship between designer, toile and mannequin is invaluable in facilitating the expression of the designer's personal vision.

It is now possible to have the best of both worlds: the inspiration that comes from the purity of the simple draped panels together with the classic draping skills that were perfected in the Parisian ateliers. Both serve to turn the art of sculptural draping into something magical and new.

 When you see this icon, refer to the DVD that accompanies the book for video demonstrations of draping techniques.

Tools and preparation

Draping, as with any artisans' skill, has its tools of the trade. It is a worthwhile investment to find tools that are of good quality and that fit your physical size. Having the right tools increases efficiency and will help the skills to become second nature so you can focus on the creative rather than the technical.

The mannequin

The primary piece of equipment needed to begin draping is the mannequin, or dress form. Many variations are available. Choosing the right one will depend on your circumstances and needs. The best of these covered mannequins are solidly mounted on heavy metal stands. Be careful of mannequins that are covered in fabric that is too tightly woven, as pins will not easily penetrate.

Standard mannequins usually follow the measurement specifications of commercial sizing. In a professional design studio, a small to medium size is often used. When the clothing is finished, it can easily be graded up or down for larger or smaller sizes.

The Wolf Form Company mannequins pictured in this book are high-quality linen-covered 'cocktail dress' mannequins, which have more bust and hip definition than standard mannequins. They are adjustable, meaning they are easy to move up and down, and the shoulders collapse inwards to allow garments to be put on over the top. They roll and turn easily.

Before using the mannequin, you will need to define the bust, waist and hips. The best way is to use a cotton twill tape, 0.5–1.5 cm (¼–½") wide, and pin it around the mannequin as follows:

- **Bust tape** Start at a side seam and wrap the tape around the fullest part of the bust (the 'bust point'), pinning every 7.5–10 cm (3" or so) all the way into the mannequin. Allow the tape to follow the mannequin at the centre front. Keep the tape high in the back, parallel to the floor.

- **Waist tape** The waistline will usually have a seam in the fabric, making it easy to identify; but if not, simply find the smallest part and wrap the tape tightly around the waistline, pinning as you go.

- **Hip tape** Hip measurements are usually taken 18 cm (7") below the waist. Starting at a side seam, pin the tape horizontally keeping it parallel to the floor, at 18 cm (7") below the waist.

Preparatory skills

To make full use of the information in this book, it is recommended that you have mastered some basic sewing skills (see 'Terminology'), and have some experience with pattern drafting, which is used in the 'Marking and Truing' sections of each chapter to create the pattern for the garments draped.

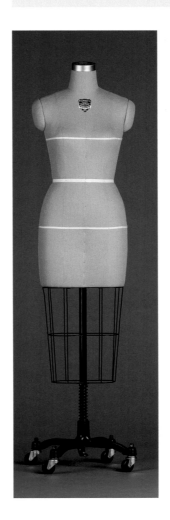
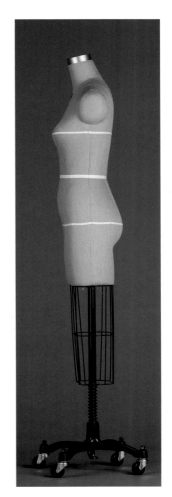

Understanding your mannequin's measurements

Measure your mannequin and keep the measurements at hand. That way, if you are working on a garment for a specific size, or customizing it for an individual, you can determine how you may need to adjust your mannequin. If you are draping something for a larger size than your mannequin, it is possible to pad the mannequin to reach the desired measurements. The best way to do this is to simply cut strips of cotton felt approximately 12.5 cm (5") wide and wrap and shape the mannequin until it reaches the measurements you need.

If the size you need is smaller than your mannequin, you must allow for that by draping the mannequin more tightly or make the adjustments later in the truing stage.

The bifurcated neck-to-ankle mannequin

The bifurcated neck-to-ankle mannequin is necessary for draping trousers. Some mannequins are available with only one leg, which makes it a little easier to drape the crotch area, but harder ultimately to see the full drape.

This style of mannequin is also useful for full-length designs where the shape of the leg needs to be considered.

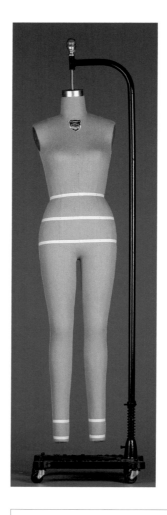 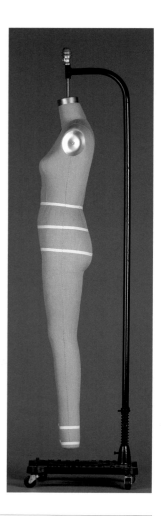

Draping in front of a mirror

It is very useful to drape in front of a mirror. As you learn how to study your silhouette and shape, it becomes important to see it from a distance. With a mirror, it is easy to glance up and observe your drape from about 1.5 m (4–5') away. It is a good perspective check, allowing you to view your drape with fresh eyes and again compare it to the sketch or photograph you are working from.

Calico

Calico is the traditional garment industry standard used for toiles, or fitting prototypes. It drapes differently from the final fabrics of most of the garments being made in this book, but it has other very positive qualities.

First and foremost, calico has a stable grainline that can be easily seen. Where more loosely woven fabrics will stretch and pull out of shape when draping, the calico's grainlines will remain perpendicular. It is light and supple, easy for cutting and folding and creasing with your hands. The crispness makes it clear to see how the pieces are fitting together and when they are balanced.

Fairly inexpensive, it is your artists' medium; it is good to think of it as paper. It is not too precious – don't get too attached to it, or worry about ruining it. You can tear it and mark it and experiment with it. Have enough on hand so that if something is just not working, you can discard it and start over.

An important skill for a designer to master is the ability to visualize. This means being able to see what a sketch will look like as a finished garment, and what a calico drape will look like in the final fabric. Silk charmeuse has a lovely, soft hand, for example, yet is difficult to handle in draping. If the design is first draped in calico, the balance can be achieved more easily. With some practice, you will learn to visualize how the garment will look in the charmeuse after it is draped in calico.

There are four different types of fabric used throughout this book. While it is not necessary to work with such a variety, it is helpful to understand their different qualities. Where possible, use a fabric type that will drape as closely as possible to the way your final garment fabric will drape.

Standard calico This medium-weight and fairly crisp fabric works well for most garments. It is light enough to manipulate easily and holds shape as you work with bodices, skirt shapes and sleeves. Observe how in the centre of the folds there are little 'breaks' in the fold where it makes a sharp turn rather than a smooth roll. A softer fabric might not do that, but then it will not allow you to achieve as defined a silhouette as this crisper fabric.

Cotton twill This softer but weightier twill reacts quite differently from calico. Observe how the folded edges are rolling more smoothly and the entire piece looks more substantial. It does not have the crispness that calico has, but because it is heavier, it will hold a larger silhouette. This is a perfect choice for garments such as coats and jackets.

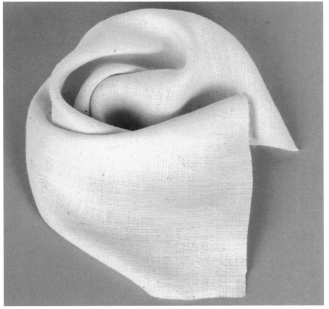

Muslin The lightest of the fabrics used in the book, muslin is loosely woven, semi-transparent and has a very crisp hand. Used in Chapter 2.2: Blouses, it is the perfect weight for the large puffed sleeve. Thin and light, it has enough body to hold shape and works well where multiple layers of fabric are being used.

Silk/hemp blend This cloth, while slightly heavier than the cotton twill, has a softer, smoother drape, which is evident in the way the folds do not 'break' at all. It is loosely woven and perfect for garments where the grainline needs to be visible, such as the corsets in Chapter 1.3. In Chapter 3.3: Draping on the Bias, it smoothes and shapes over the curves of the mannequin very easily because it has such a heavy drape.

General supplies

Tape measure Helpful to use in visualizing volume for calico pieces and also to check measurements of the toile while draping.

Scissors Your most important tool. Choose carefully: you want a scissor that is light enough to be comfortable, yet heavy enough to deftly cut through the calico as you drape.

Metre rule Important for finding and marking the grainlines.

Right-angled ruler Necessary for checking that the straight and horizontal grains are at right angles.

Clear grading ruler The transparency and grids of this ruler are helpful when marking grainlines and seam allowances on the calico.

Soft lead pencil Test the pencil on the calico you are using and choose one that is soft enough to make a clear, visible grainline, yet not so soft that it smudges the fabric.

Draping supplies

Pins and wrist cushion A generous supply of pins will increase efficiency, and a wrist cushion is helpful in keeping the pins at hand rather than reaching for them while you are holding on to the calico.

Twill tape – black and white Used for marking necklines, armholes, style lines, etc.

Sticky tape – black and red Used as above, but with a more temporary use. Red is used for correction lines.

Elastic Having elastic on hand in a few different widths – 0.5, 1.5 and 2.5 cm (¼, ½ and 1") – will help when gathering sections of calico.

Hem gauge For measuring hems in relation to the cage of the mannequin, and for checking sections of a garment that call for uniform size.

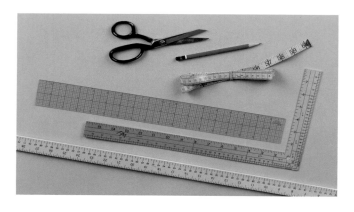

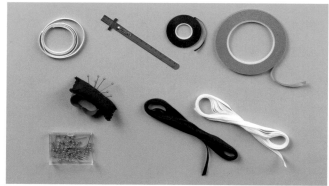

Marking and truing supplies

Chalk – two colours Used for marking seams when turning fronts over backs, hems, etc. Having two colours will help you to colour-code if you adjust fit and re-mark a seam.

Pencils – regular, red and blue Used for drawing on the toile after it is taken apart. The first line drawn is with regular pencil. A correction line will be in red, and a further correction will be in blue.

Carbon paper Used in truing up when lines need to be traced through to a second piece of calico or onto the reverse side of the calico.

Tracing wheel For use with carbon paper to trace lines onto a second piece of calico or onto the reverse side of the calico.

Needle and thread When marking a toile, sometimes a pencil is not enough and a basted line needs to be made using a needle and thread to allow for a more precise marking.

Additional rulers

Small grading rulers Useful for marking seam allowances. Their transparency makes it easy to see the sew lines as you mark the cut lines.

Clear French curve Because this curve goes from convex to concave, it is essential for areas, such as the waistline, that follow that trajectory. This curve is also useful for truing up armholes and small curves.

Hip curve Traditionally used to follow the curve from the waist along the hipline, its universal shape is useful in many other areas.

Hem curve This curve is the general shape of a skirt hem as it travels from the centre front in a soft curve up towards the side seam.

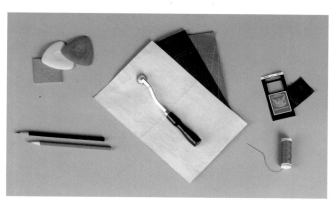

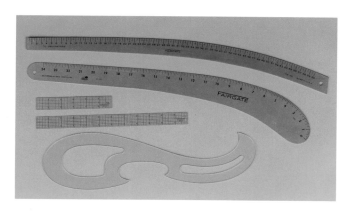

Terminology

The following are terms used throughout the book. Brief definitions are given here, and many will be explained further elsewhere in the book.

Abbreviations

CF = centre front

CB = centre back

Calico

Grainlines These refer to the direction of the threads. Woven fabrics consist of two threads interlaced at right angles. The vertical or 'warp' threads run parallel to the selvedge. The horizontal or 'weft' thread runs crosswise.

Straight grain The warp thread direction, sometimes called the lengthgrain.

Horizontal grain The weft thread direction.

Bias line This runs at 45° to the straight grain and is the part of the fabric that has the most give.

Selvedge edge The bound edges on either side of the fabric. Most fabrics are woven at 115–150 cm (45–60") wide.

Blocking the calico To stretch, pull and press the calico until the warp/vertical and weft/horizontal threads of the weave are perpendicular and the edges are straight.

Diagrams

Calico-preparation diagrams The charts at the beginning of each project with the measurements of the pieces of calico to be cut. If the measurements of the mannequin you are using are different from the standard mannequin used here, simply adjust the dimensions of the calico pieces up or down. The measurements of the pieces have an allowance of several extra centimetres, so unless your mannequin is 7.5 cm (3") different, the pieces will work.

Flat sketches The two-dimensional line drawings that are made from photographs as a blueprint for construction and grainline configuration.

Fit and figure

Ease The extra fabric allowed in the fit of a garment. For example, if the waistline measurement is 66 cm (26") and the skirt waistband measurement is 68.5 cm (27"), then there is 2.5 cm (1") ease in the skirt/waist fit.

Bust point The fullest part of the bust.

Waistline The narrowest part of the waist area on the mannequin.

Hip line The fullest part of the hip, usually considered to be 18 cm (7") down from the waist.

High hip line This measurement is taken about 5–7.5 cm (2–3") down from the waist at the hipbone where casual trousers, such as jeans, often sit.

Princess line The vertical line that divides the torso in half from centre front to side seam. Usually it begins at the centre of the shoulder, but it can also curve out from the armhole.

Stitching

Sew line This is referred to in draping and in truing up, and is simply the stitching line that will be used to join the seams.

Baste (tack) To hand-sew a stitch line to hold a seam together temporarily.

Thread trace A hand-sewn straight stitch line used to mark seams or edges during draping or the marking and truing-up process.

Herringbone stitch A useful stitch for holding together two pieces of calico during draping in areas that may have some pressure pulling on them.

Tailor tack A stitch used to mark a single point on the fabric during draping and the marking and truing-up process.

Step 1   Step 2

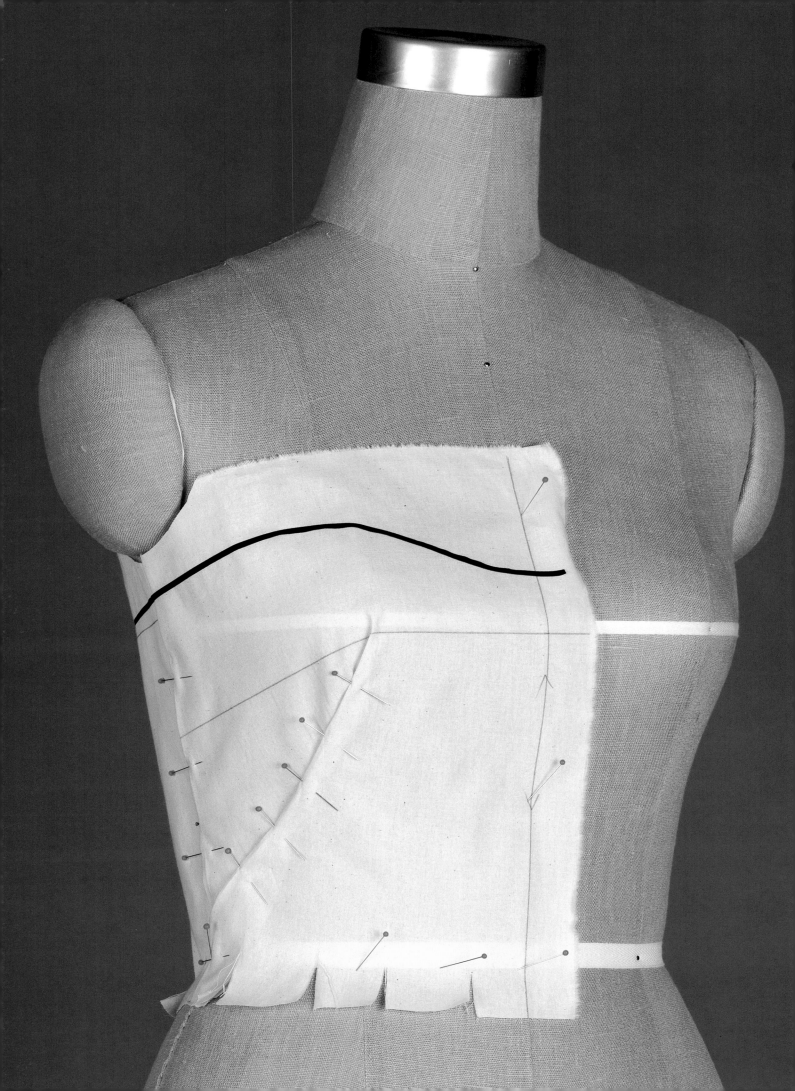

1 Beginning Draping

1.1 Draping the Woven Panel
1.2 Dresses
1.3 Corsets

Section 1 works to develop your skills of observation as each fashion design is studied in terms of its composition – the specific balance of silhouette and proportion.

Photographs of the draping projects will be analysed in terms of grainline placement and construction, then translated into working 'blueprints' – flat sketches from which to drape.

Basic draping skills are introduced, such as preparing the mannequin and calico, pinning, trimming, clipping, marking and truing, and presenting a finished toile.

You will learn to identify a designer's intended mood and tone and further define the attitude of a garment by using a muse to place the design in a social context.

1.1

Draping the Woven Panel

History

The earliest clothing was probably made from leaves, grasses and bark or, in colder climates, animal skins and furs.

The development of weaving must have heralded a giant leap in the sophistication of a civilization. As the techniques developed, woven panels were wrapped, draped and tied over the body. Simply creating the fabrics would have required so much time and effort that cutting the cloth was unrealistic.

Since few ancient fabrics have survived to the present day, only the artistic renderings of garments on pottery fragments and murals suggest what early clothing might actually have looked like. Some of the oldest garments that we can see and study are those depicted on ancient Greek and Roman sculptures and vases.

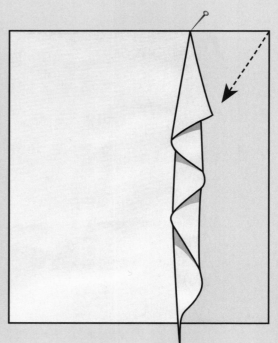

These early garment forms – the chiton and peplos of the Greeks, and the toga worn in Rome – were simple basic shapes; many were woven panels of varying sizes. However, the draping was sometimes elaborate. It is thought that a nobleman in full dress would have been accompanied by a servant to help keep the drapes properly adjusted. In all their variety, these garments appear to be very comfortable, their relaxed, elegant style echoing the Greek ideal of freedom. The fabrics of flax (linen) and wool must have been very fine to drape with the beautiful folds seen in sculptures and paintings.

Garments became increasingly complicated as craftsmanship and technology developed and new fabrics became available. Yet from time to time there has been a return to simplicity, a refreshing revival of this more natural style.

In the modern era, garments made from draped square-cut panels appear in the artwork of Alphonse Mucha and Maxfield Parrish. Isadora Duncan, the founder of modern dance, was famous for wearing her version of a tunic. In the first half of the twentieth century, the great Italian textile and clothing designer Mariano Fortuny made exquisite, timeless garments from two rectangles of pleated silk.

The draping projects in this chapter are variations of these classic tunic forms and, because of their simplicity, are excellent exercises for developing an eye for proportion and balance. Finding the symmetry and adjusting the gathers of these pieces teaches sensitivity to handling fabric, a skill that takes practice.

Far left: This huipil from the Triki, a mountain-dwelling tribe in Oaxaca, Mexico, is a square-cut garment that exhibits a traditional weaving style over two centuries old. It consists of three rectangles, finished and ornamented with coloured ribbon. The drape is symmetrical and graceful.

Left: Preserving the integrity of the square-cut woven panel gives the most natural form to a drape. There is a majestic quality in its simplicity.

A contemporary design using the simplicity of two rectangles by Karolyn Kiisel for Tara West Spa-wear, made of hemp/silk.

Exercises
Preparing the calico

All woven fabrics consist of two threads interlaced at right angles. The vertical (warp) threads run parallel to the selvedge edge and are called the 'straight grain', or sometimes the 'lengthgrain'. The horizontal (weft) thread runs crosswise on the fabric and is called the 'horizontal grain', or 'crossgrain'.

In the weaving process, the warp threads are usually set up tightly on the loom first and then the weft threads criss-cross back and forth, filling in the fabric. The warp threads, therefore, are usually stronger, and the fabric has the strongest drape when hung vertically.

Tearing the calico

To prepare the calico for draping, the pieces are torn to predetermined measurements. Tearing the calico is more accurate than measuring and cutting with scissors because the original perpendicular grid of the warp and weft threads of the calico often becomes distorted during shipping. Even when measuring from the selvedge edges, it is not possible to be certain that the threads are running parallel to the edges of the fabric.

Understanding grainlines

It is important to understand how the set of the grainlines can affect the look of a garment. Their direction determines the energy flow. The reason square-cut garments like tunics look so elegant and regal is because the grainlines are perfectly balanced.

Calico preparation

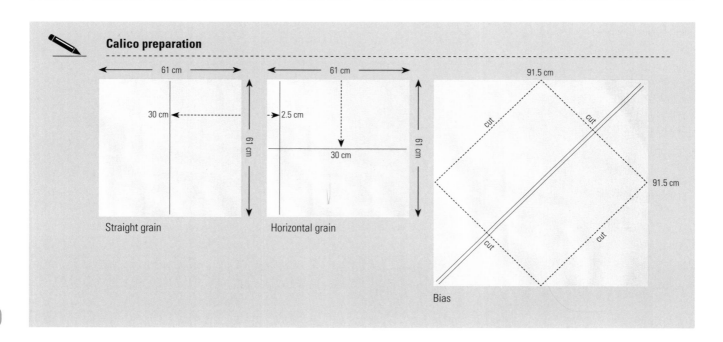

61 cm

30 cm

61 cm

Straight grain

61 cm

2.5 cm

30 cm

61 cm

Horizontal grain

91.5 cm

cut

cut

cut

cut

91.5 cm

Bias

Step 1

First the selvedge edge must be removed. When the fabric is finished on the loom, the tighter weave of the edges, while serving to keep it from unravelling, will sometimes restrict the drape of the fabric. If the fabric is steamed and/or pressed, the edges pull in and cause the fabric to pucker.

- Tear selvedge edge off by clipping in about 1.5 cm (½"), grasping edge firmly and pulling it sharply down length of fabric.

- Now mark desired measurements of the calico, clip edge and tear both the straight grain and horizontal grain directions.

- It is helpful to first draw a small straight grain for reference so that you do not lose track of the direction.

Step 2

After the fabric is torn to specific measurements, it must be 'blocked'. Blocking the fabric is the means by which the warp and weft threads are pulled back into their original shape, exactly perpendicular to each other.

- Create a grid by drawing vertical and horizontal lines on graph paper. You do not need to draw the exact size of the piece; a right angle will suffice to align the fabric and check that it is square.

- Where the calico does not form a 90° angle, grasp it firmly with both hands, and pull and stretch it until it returns to its original shape.

Step 3

Now the calico must be pressed. When pressing calico, it is important to handle it gently so that it remains smooth and even. A bit of steam is fine; the calico may also need to be steamed later during the truing-up process and it is preferable to let it shrink before you start draping. If you use too much steam, however, the calico will pucker and become unusable.

Sponge any deep wrinkles in the calico with a damp cloth, rubbing out the creases.

- When pressing, move the iron in vertical and horizontal directions only. If the calico is pressed on the diagonal, or bias, grain, you will pull the threads out of alignment and cause the fabric to stretch.

- After pressing, check the calico again on the grid paper to see if it has torqued; if so, pull and stretch it again until it goes back into right angles at the corners.

Press on straight grain or horizontal grain

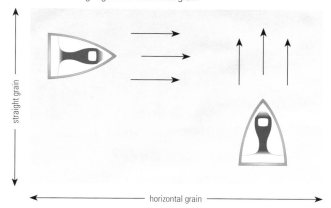

DO NOT press on the bias

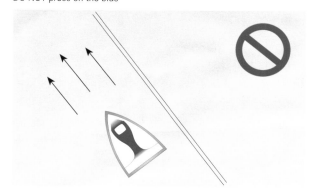

Marking grainlines

There are two methods used in this book to mark grainlines:

- Mark using a medium soft pencil or tailor's chalk and a metre rule and grading ruler to draw the lines on the calico.

  When this method is recommended, you will see a pencil symbol.

- Mark with a 'thread trace'. If you want to reuse the calico pieces, are working with a fabric that will later be sewn into a garment, or prefer working with needle and thread, this method can be used.

  When this method is recommended, you will see the needle-and-thread symbol.

Mark only the lines on the fabric – no measurements or other notes are necessary. Be accurate and precise. After draping, your pattern will be made with these calico pieces.

Neatness is important: when draping, it is essential to be able to concentrate on the shapes you are creating. Superfluous lines and marks will be distracting.

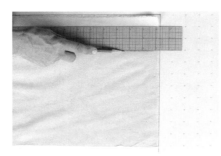

Step 4

Now you are ready to mark the grainlines on the calico. On the first piece, use a soft pencil or tailor's chalk to mark the straight grain, which is parallel to the selvedges. On the second, mark the horizontal grain, which runs across the width of fabric.

- Make two or three small marks on the calico using the given dimensions, measuring in from the left-hand edge.

- Line up the grading ruler or metre rule with the marks, and draw the line needed.

Use this method for the first two pieces.

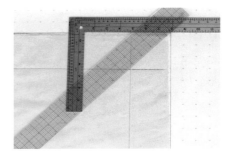

Step 5

On the third piece of calico, draw the bias line. The 'true bias' of the fabric is the 45° angle to the straight and horizontal grains. The bias line is traditionally marked with double parallel lines.

- Find the true bias using a right-angled ruler and a grading ruler. Position the right-angled ruler against one of the edges of the fabric and mark equal distances from the angle point. For example, mark 20 cm (8") from the point, going along the horizontal grain and along the straight grain.

- Line the grading ruler up with the two points and draw in the bias line, a 45° angle.

- For bias lines, two parallel lines are used, 0.5 cm (⅛") apart.

The calico-preparation diagrams on the following pages all contain measurements that will help you position the calico on the mannequin. The pieces are all oriented with the straight grain going up and down, and the horizontal grain going from side to side.

Thread tracing ◉

- First locate the grainline. Measure in from the sides of the calico piece and mark it with a pin line or tailor tacks. Place the pins perpendicular to the sew line, and use the entry point of the pin as your line demarcation.

- Lay the grading ruler or metre rule an even 1.5–2.5 cm (½–1") from the pin or tailor-tack line. Leaving the calico on the table, pull the needle and thread through the fabric, using very large stitches.

- It can help to place weights on the ruler or metre rule to keep the fabric from moving while you stitch it.

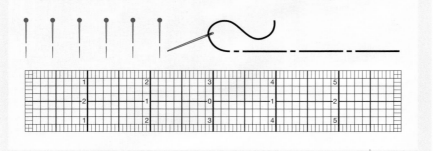

Marking grainlines with pen

Another method is to mark the line with a 'disappearing ink' fabric pen. Test to make sure it works as it should, and also that it lasts long enough for you to finish the drape and transfer it to paper.

Draping the three grains

This exercise will train your eye to see the difference in the three grainlines. Use the three pieces of calico that you prepared for pages 20–22. As you work, try to feel the difference in how the calico drapes, even as you first pin the pieces to the mannequin. If you do not have three mannequins, pin the three prepared pieces of calico to anything you have available so you can study all of them at the same time. ◉

Pinning

Make sure you have a good supply of pins nearby or on a wrist cushion.

The pins are not placed at a 90° angle to the mannequin, but at an angle tilting upwards. This holds the fabric securely in place. If you are supporting a heavier weight of fabric, sometimes instructions are given to 'anchor-pin', or place two pins in a 'V' position, which holds the fabric more securely.

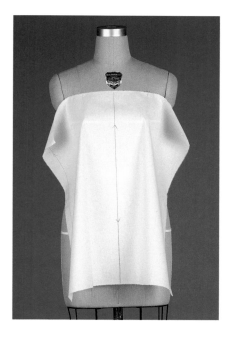

Straight grain

- Holding straight-grain piece of calico in two places at the top, centre grainline by aligning it with centre front line of mannequin.

- Pin calico evenly at two areas above the bust line and smooth out drape with your hands, studying how fabric is falling across mannequin.

Horizontal grain

- Grasp edge of horizontal grain piece of calico with the 2.5 cm (1") straight grain running horizontally and the horizontal grain line falling vertically, and align horizontal grain line with centre front of mannequin.

- Pin areas above bust and observe how fabric is draping.

Bias grain

- Drape the bias piece of calico on the mannequin, with the double bias line lined up along the centre front of the mannequin and hanging vertically.

Analysis

The straight-grain piece forms two strong drapes as it flares out from the bust to the hip, the natural drape of a balanced square. The sides drape with a straight, vertical flow.

The horizontal-grain piece appears slightly wider at the hip and doesn't seem to fall quite as easily. The side areas seem to stand out

more. The stronger straight grain is running horizontally and pushing the fabric out.

The calico cut on the bias grain has the most give and so forms drapes that are softer and less defined than those on the straight or horizontal grain. The fabric gently flares out at the sides, creating a cascade effect.

From the strength of the straight grain to the soft drape of the bias, these different qualities will translate into garments as you drape. Learning to use these grainlines to your advantage will help you achieve specific looks.

Visualizing calico vs fabrics

A fashion designer's skill of visualization comes from familiarity with all types of fabrics and how they drape. When selecting fabrics, a designer will pull, stretch and smooth the fabric; pin it onto a mannequin to see how it falls; and hold a length to the body in the mirror to see how it moves.

Train your eye to see how different fabrics drape, and how they drape differently from calico, with this exercise. Drape several types of fabric onto a mannequin using as inspiration this contemporary dress by Michael Kors. First, drape each fabric over your hand, taking a moment to study its qualities.

- Align CF line of calico with CF of mannequin. Pin at shoulders about midway between neckline and outer shoulder point. Find the spot where, in the photograph, the snakeskin leather piece sits at the shoulder line.

- Now try pinning fabric 2.5–5 cm (1–2") further towards side of calico piece but at the same point of the shoulder, allowing fabric to drape in CF.

- Continue moving fabric towards centre; watch how drape forms as you pin further and further towards sides of fabric.

- Look for the optimum spot where CF neckline drape is low, as in the photograph, but you still have enough fabric left on the sides to create the pretty drape that hangs at the armholes. Pin or tie a twill tape at the hips, if it helps you to find the right drape.

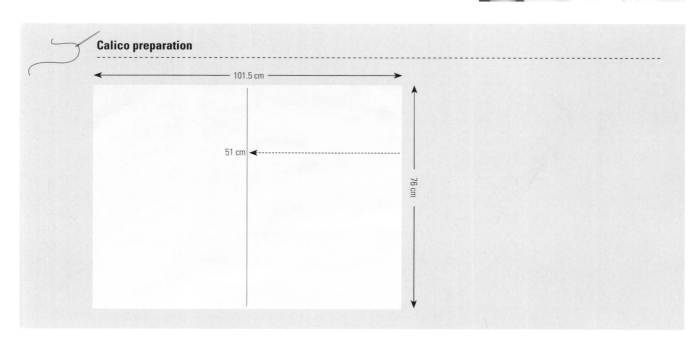

Calico preparation

101.5 cm

51 cm

76 cm

Draping in different fabrics

Using the calico-preparation diagram, prepare these additional fabrics: linen, silk crêpe de chine, chiffon and a knit. If you do not have these easily at hand, use whatever you have – even a silk scarf will do! Do not worry about making the drape look exactly like the garment in the photograph. This is an exercise in observing how different fabrics drape.

Linen

The linen drapes most similarly to the calico. It has a loosely woven grain and so a softer drape than the calico, but still has a lot of body. Both calico and linen tend to 'break' at the centre front, making a sharp bend or crease instead of flowing evenly around the curve of the drape.

Crêpe de chine

The crêpe de chine falls very differently. The centre front drape has a softer look and falls into more folds than the linen or calico. The drapes at the side armhole area tend to flutter rather than just sit.

Why drape with calico?

If calico is stiffer and drapes quite differently from other fabrics, why use it for draping? The answer is that calico has a stable grainline and is easy to work with. Also, its absence of colour creates a neutrality that helps you see the silhouette you are sculpting, providing a blank canvas upon which to create a design. As you experience the qualities of different fabrics, you will begin to instinctively sense how a fabric will behave in comparison to the calico.

Chiffon

The chiffon is even softer than the crêpe de chine, but it has a bouncy quality. Although it hangs beautifully, it is more difficult to handle.

Knit

The knit drapes the closest in look to the Michael Kors dress. Knits tend to hang in a heavier way. The sense of gravity pulling the fabric down creates the sensual look that Kors seems to have intended.

Dance tunic

This tunic – a dance costume for an opera – is based on a Greek chiton. It is made from two rectangles, held together at the shoulders by metal brooches. Traditionally, the tunic would have a belt, but because this is a modern dance costume, the waistline can be drawn in with elastic. The lines are angular and vertical, so both pieces will be cut on the straight grain. The flat sketch indicates the waistline construction, shoulder closures and the proportion of the ornamentation at the neckline.

Visualizing the volume

After the flat sketch is done, the next step is to map out the calico-preparation diagram, deciding the approximate size of each of the pieces.

Try using a muse for this process. Visualize Isadora Duncan dancing in this tunic. Imagine the volume of fabric she needs to give her full freedom of movement, but note that too many gathers at the waist will tend to widen the silhouette and weight her down visually.

Familiarize yourself with the final fabric by draping some of it on the mannequin as shown. The Lycra chiffon used here is light and airy, yet the small percentage of Lycra (a heavy fibre), gives it some weight and definition.

- Pin the fabric to the mannequin at the shoulders and let it drape to the floor.

- Tie a piece of twill tape or elastic around the waist to imitate the construction.

- Study the proportions of the sketch and note down some target length and width measurements for the tunic.

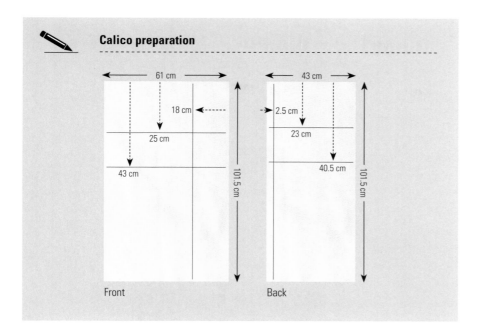

Calico preparation

Front — 61 cm, 101.5 cm, 18 cm, 25 cm, 43 cm

Back — 43 cm, 101.5 cm, 2.5 cm, 23 cm, 40.5 cm

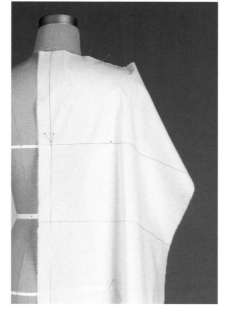

Step 1 ◎

- Pin calico to CF of mannequin, lining up CF pencil line with CF of mannequin, and aligning upper horizontal grain with bust tape and lower horizontal grain with waist tape. Pin to just above waist. Anchor-pin at top CF.

- Pin across shoulder areas about 7.5 cm (3") below neckline.

Step 2

- Pin back piece to back of mannequin, lining up CB pencil line with CB seam of mannequin, and aligning horizontal grains with bust and waist tapes of mannequin. Pin to just above waist (not shown). Anchor-pin at top CB.

- Pin across shoulder about 7–10 cm (3–4") below neckline, keeping horizontal grain lines level.

Step 3

- Tie a narrow length of elastic or twill tape around the waist. The pencilled waist horizontal grain should be right under elastic.

Step 4

- Keeping pencilled horizontal grain parallel to waist, adjust gathers of calico by grasping fabric above and below elastic and pulling.

- Repeat for back.

Step 5

- Add blouson effect by pulling up top front and back waist horizontal grain to about 7–10 cm (3–4") above waist elastic and letting excess fabric fall over waist elastic.

Step 6

- Pin side seams together. Side seam allowances are 2.5 cm (1"), so first gently crease 2.5 cm (1") under on front section and lay it on top of back section, about 2.5 cm (1") in.

- If you need to, lightly chalk the 2.5 cm (1") line to make it easier.

- Start at matching waistline horizontal grains, turning front over back, working down towards hem.

Pinning two pieces of calico together

When pinning two pieces of calico together, try to create the smoothest look possible, by placing the pins perpendicular to the seamline. When studying the shape of the whole garment, you do not want to be distracted by clumsy pinning and wrinkled seams.

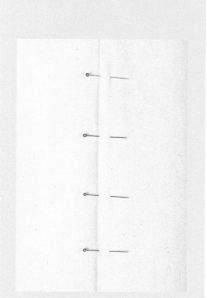

Step 7

- Turn up hem of tunic by levelling it against one of the bars on the cage of the mannequin.

- Place pins perpendicular to edge of hem.

- Check drape against sketch for proportion.

Step 8

- Release CF pins and experiment with how the CF drapes by moving shoulder area towards neck and then towards shoulder. Observe the difference in the way the CF drapes.

- Now compare your toile with the photograph. The calico, of course, is draping much more stiffly, but you should be able to see clearly from the toile whether or not the balance and proportion are correct.

- Finalize the position of the shoulder placement and pin.

Use a mirror to check the drape

At this point, give yourself a 'perspective check'. Look at your drape in the mirror or from a distance, study the silhouette and adjust it until you feel it is correct.

Draping project

This statue is known as Diana of Versailles, a Roman copy of a Greek statue of Artemis, goddess of the hunt. She is an archer, running through the woods with wild animals. Her garment has a comfortable, relaxed, utilitarian feel, its short length giving her freedom of movement for her hunt.

In the photograph, Diana appears to be wearing either a single garment folded up or a top and skirt. Based on research of garments from this era, it would be an ankle-length garment, pulled up to knee length.

The waist has an odd double wrap in the front, which indicates the waist and shoulder sash may have been one piece. However, you can simplify your drape into three basic pieces: tunic, waist wrap and shoulder sash. The hypothetical purpose of the garment is a costume, not an authentic reproduction.

First, draw a sketch of the finished look of the garment to get the proportions right. Then make another set of sketches determining the number of elements: front, back, waist wrap and shoulder sash.

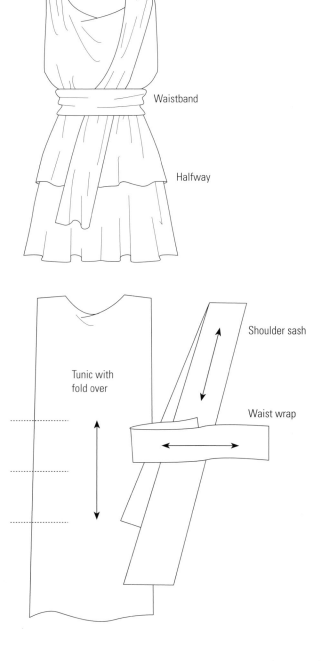

Waistband

Halfway

Shoulder sash

Tunic with fold over

Waist wrap

Visualizing the volume

The actual fabric depicted in the sculpture is either lightweight linen or wool. It has a lot of lines and folds, which means a substantial amount of width in the rectangles. Estimate the maximum amount of fabric you think you will need.

Blocking the calico

Prepare the calico, and don't forget to block and press it as on page 21.

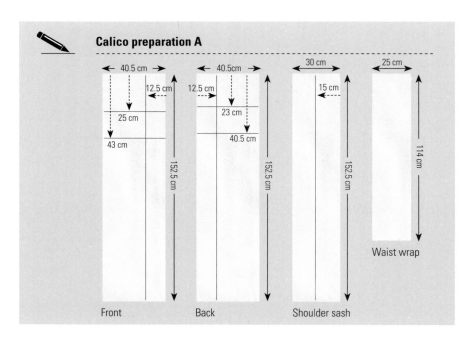

Calico preparation A

40.5 cm · 12.5 cm · 25 cm · 43 cm · 152.5 cm — Front

12.5 cm · 40.5 cm · 23 cm · 40.5 cm · 152.5 cm — Back

30 cm · 15 cm · 152.5 cm — Shoulder sash

25 cm · 114 cm — Waist wrap

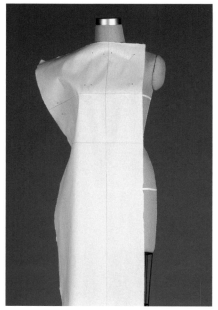

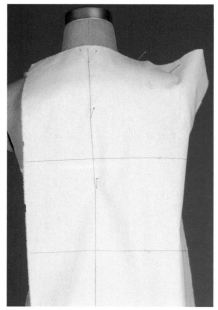

Step 1

- Pin calico to CF of the mannequin, lining up CF pencil line with CF of mannequin, and aligning upper horizontal grain with bust tape and lower horizontal grain with waist tape. Pin to just above waist (not shown). Anchor-pin at top CF.

- Pin across bust area and to side seam below armplate.

- Note that straight grainlines have a strong vertical look. Notice in the photo how the vertical lines of the fabric folds support this strong grainline.

Step 2

- Pin the back piece to the back of the mannequin, lining up the CB pencil line with the CB seam of the mannequin, and aligning the horizontal grains with the bust and waist tapes of the mannequin. Pin to just above the waist. Anchor-pin at top CB.

- Pin across shoulder about 7–10 cm (3–4") below neckline, keeping horizontal grainlines level and wrapping calico over shoulder.

Pinning smoothly

Take the time to pin accurately and smoothly, pins perpendicular to the seams (left) rather than parallel (right). You want your tools to recede so that you can focus on the shape you are creating.

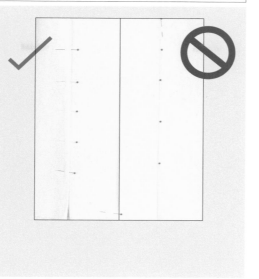

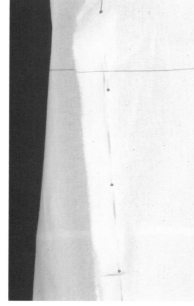

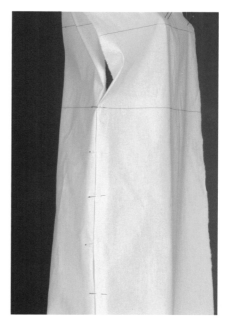

Step 3 ◉

- Pin side seams together wrong sides out from waist horizontal grain to hem.

- To pin front seam allowance over back at the side seam, first pin smoothly (with pins vertical) from waist to hem.

Step 4

- Lightly chalk pin line on both back and front pieces with a broken line.

- Crossmark every 25 cm (10") or so. The crossmark is a horizontal line that is drawn on both front and back pieces to help when realigning two sections after they are separated.

Step 5

- Remove pins a few at a time, turning front over the back at side seam and repinning with pins placed horizontally.

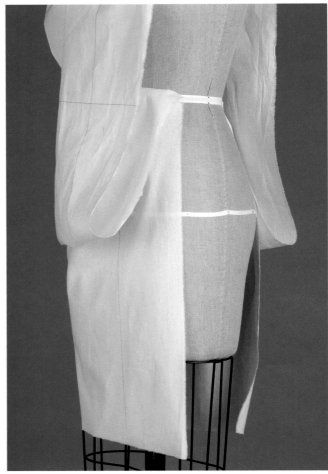

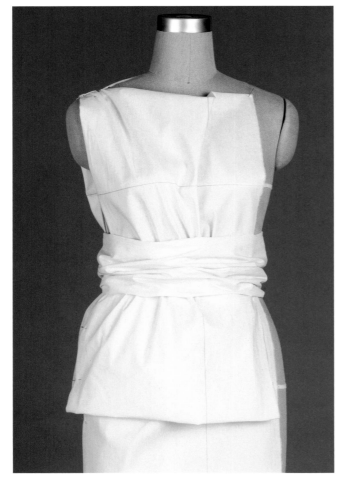

Step 6

- Tie a narrow length of elastic or twill tape around the waist. Pencilled waist horizontal grain should be right under elastic.

Step 7

- Anchor-pin below bust and at side seams to hold firmly in place and remove pins from below waist.

- Pull up to create a blouson effect until desired proportion is reached and hem of garment is parallel to bars on the cage of the mannequin.

Step 8

- Drape waist wrap at waistline, scrunching in folds as in the photograph and wrapping one of the ends over into the waist.

- Drape bodice by unpinning front and bringing side area towards CF. Adjust front and shoulder drape and pin flat to shoulder.

Step 9

- Drape shoulder sash by slipping long rectangle under front and back waist wrap and folding into pleats.

- Now check against the flat sketch on p. 30. Holding the flat, step back to a distance where the lines of the flat match the lines of the drape and check your proportions.

Step 10

- The drape proportions look the same, except perhaps in the width. It is not as full as in the photograph.

- Since there is extra fabric at CF, try shifting this towards the side and note the difference it makes in the front drape and the volume below the waist.

Marking and truing

There are various ways to mark your toile before taking it apart and making the pattern. One is to simply mark with a pencil or chalk all the seams and intersections; another is to 'thread-trace' a line. To thread-trace means to stitch a long running baste (tack) along a fabric area to indicate a line on the toile. The thread trace is done on both sides of a seamline so that when the toile is taken apart, the line is evident on each piece.

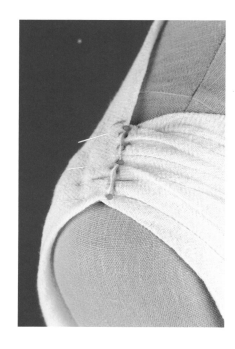

Step 2

- Pencil or chalk-mark lines made by elastic at the waist.

Step 1

- Pencil or chalk-mark pinned areas: shoulders and side seams.

- Crossmark once or twice at shoulder and every 10–12.5 cm (4–5") at side seam.

Step 3

- Thread-trace the sash where it hits the waist front and back.

- Thread-trace the new CF and new CB (not shown).

- Thread-trace the waist wrap along the edge where it folds to the inside.

- Remove the shoulder sash and waist wrap, lift the folded piece and mark the new waistline where it is hitting the elastic.

- Carefully remove the pieces from the mannequin and press gently to flatten out.

  Since this finished piece is the pattern, the only lines that need to be marked are the side seams and the new waistline.

- Side seams will be totally straight with 2.5 cm (1") seam allowance.

- The new waistline will be 55 cm (22") up from the hemline.

- Cut the new calico as indicated in Calico Preparation B.

- Sew side seams from the upper waistline (before the blouson) and the shoulder seams, then re-drape on mannequin, following Steps 1 through 10.

Analysis

Comparing the photograph on page 31 with the drape reveals a fairly accurate match. The proportions are very similar, the lines of the diagonal drapes above the waist have the same angles, and the general volume of fabric is about the same, although it is a little hard to tell from the sculpture because of the movement of the skirt and shoulder sash. It is also difficult to know how much the artist idealized the drape of the fabric; it must have been an extremely thin, fine-quality fabric to drape with such flow.

The waist sash of the drape is not as wide as the statue's, perhaps succumbing to that modern fashion imperative, the desire for a narrow waist. The centre front neck area on the drape is larger than the drape in the statue, and the right bodice of the statue is pulled more tightly. It may be that Diana's quiver strap is pulling the garment towards the back.

The sense of freedom and ease and the look of a utilitarian hunting garment have been achieved. It would be interesting to construct the garment with a very fine silk mesh, to see if that looked closer to the fine folds in the marble statue.

Choosing a fabric to check the pattern

When checking a new, full toile, often a fabric is chosen that is closer than calico to the drape of the intended final fabric. In this case, muslin will be used; it has been washed to imitate more closely the look of the garment in the photograph.

✎ Calico preparation B

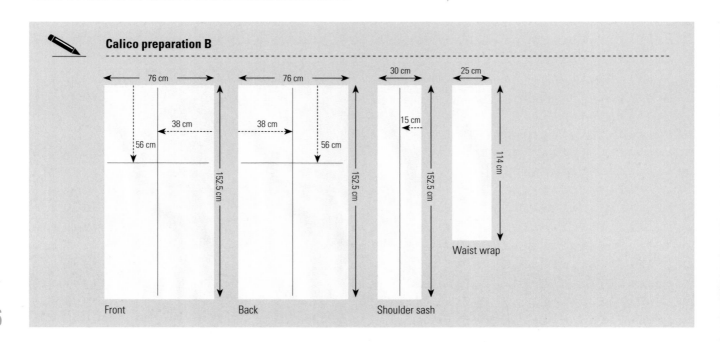

Front   Back   Shoulder sash   Waist wrap

1.2

Dresses

History

The majestic draped panels worn in ancient cultures evolved into more fitted garments for various practical reasons. Clothing that was more fitted offered expanded mobility for activities such as riding horses, getting in and out of carriages, and dancing.

In colder climates, people needed to wrap themselves more tightly for warmth, and also to allow for layering of additional pieces. Northern cultures crafted sleeves and trousers by wrapping and tying fabrics to keep out the cold.

Eventually, woven panels were cut to fit over the head, and one was gathered onto another for fullness. By the time of the Italian Renaissance, the cutting and shaping of fabric was in full swing, as seen in the elaborate, colourful, and close-fitting clothing of that era. The shapes of many of our modern garments evolved through developments in tailoring from the fourteenth century onwards.

For hundreds of years, dresses worn by women in Western cultures consisted of bodices (often tight-fitting for support), full skirts and sleeves either attached or belonging to a separate garment worn under the bodice.

This basic dress structure also existed in Eastern cultures, in garments such as the chuba, which originated in the cold Himalayan mountains of Tibet. In the modern version of the traditional cut shown here, the structure consists of two rectangles for the skirt and two panels lightly shaped into a fitted bodice. As with many historical dresses, the sleeves are part of the undergarment.

Left: Khandro Tseyang's design of a modern traditional Tibetan chuba.

Right: The chuba is constructed from two skirt rectangles and a fitted bodice.

Opposite page:
Left: In this detail from Ghirlandaio's *Birth of the Virgin Mary*, the tight sleeve is opened for a better fit.

Right: Similar in shape to an ancient tunic form, this flapper dress from the 1920s is made of two rectangles with little in the way of fit seams or darting.

The creating of volume and shape with techniques such as darting, seaming and gathering continued to evolve in both men's and women's clothing.

For centuries, women's dresses were constructed around the corset and petticoat. That fashion paradigm finally began to shift in the late nineteenth century, as dress reform movements emerged. The Rational Dress Society, founded in 1881, objected to the tightly laced corset for health reasons and championed looser-fitting clothing.

In the early 1900s, the famous couturier Paul Poiret continued this trend by designing clothing that was roomy and comfortable, with no corsets. His designs were so radically different that seeing women wearing his creations was said to have caused people to faint.

In modern fashion, we have found a balance: existing alongside voluminous shapes, darting and seaming are used to create subtlety in contour and fit. By studying the dress bodices in this chapter, we will see how various types of darts and seams create specific silhouettes.

Exercises
Dart variations

Observe what happens when a perfect square of calico is draped over the female form. The obvious challenge is to work with the curve of the bust and waist. Various types of darts can be used to different effect to fit the bodice. Three are shown here. As you work, train the eye to see subtle differences in silhouette; look closely at how the calico falls and what happens to the grainlines.

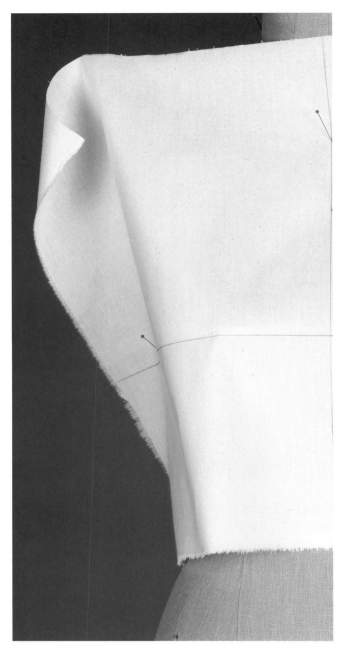

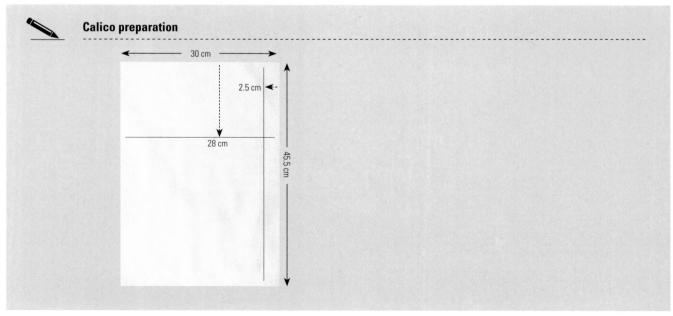

Calico preparation

30 cm

2.5 cm

28 cm

45.5 cm

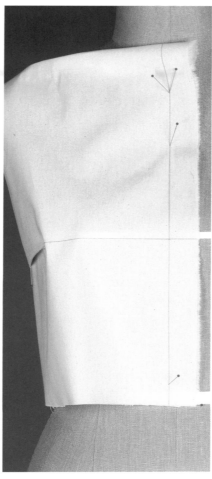
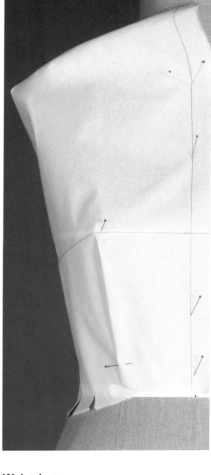

Shoulder dart

- Pin calico down CF and at neckline.

- Keeping horizontal grain level, fold in a dart with excess formed at shoulder area.

- Pin dart and study the silhouette created.

Side bust dart

- Pin calico down CF and at neckline.

- Now smooth calico over the shoulder, letting it fall downwards, and pin side dart by folding excess calico up at side seam.

- Pin dart, ending it just before bust point, and study the silhouette.

Waist dart

- Pin calico down CF and at neckline.

- Now smooth calico over the shoulder, armhole and side seam, allowing excess calico to fall towards front.

- Pin a dart at the princess line, about halfway between side seam and CF.

Creating subtle darts

The deeper the dart, the more exaggerated the point at the end of it will be. Unless this is a style or design decision, darts need to be subtle and as invisible as possible.

Try re-draping all the above darts lessening the intake and observe the difference.

Classic bodice with bust dart

This sleeveless bodice with a side bust dart illustrates the very straight drape this dart creates. Note how the lines of the tartan remain vertical and horizontal with the help of that dart. The sides drop vertically, with only slight shaping out at the bust and in at the waist.

This classic, utilitarian darting is used for blouses and dresses where taking the flare out of the front part of the garment is needed, without fit at the waist.

Notice how the fairly high tie-front neckline and classic armhole shape support the quietly conservative nature of this bodice.

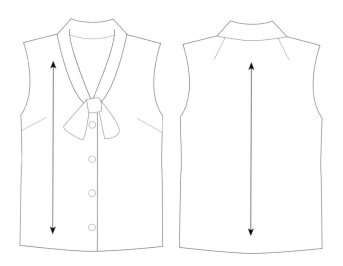

Disappearing darts

Darts are used to create shape, and are not normally featured as style lines. Therefore, the idea is to make them as invisible as possible. When choosing which dart to use for bust shaping, consider not only the silhouette you want to create, but also how that dart will look in the final fabric. Remeber to back the dart off the bust point and keep it as shallow as your style will allow.

Calico preparation

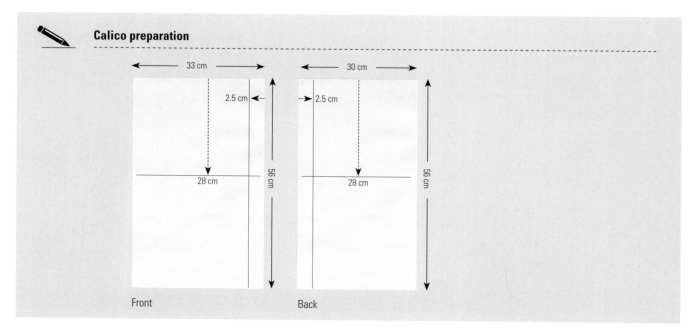

Front   Back

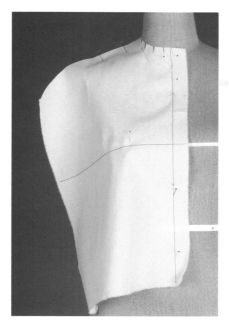

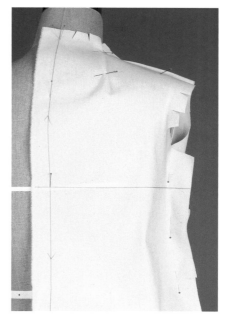

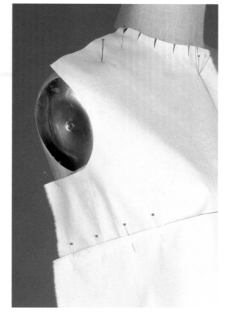

Step 1

- Pin down CF, aligning horizontal grainline with bust line tape. Leave the 1.5 cm (½") or so of ease that is created between bust points and let calico fall free at the curve of the waistline.

- Pin at bust.

- Trim and clip neckline area and shoulder excess until calico lies smoothly.

Step 2

- Form side bust dart by folding lower fabric up. Check the silhouette in the photograph: side seam should be falling quite straight. The dart ends about 1.5 cm (½") before bust point and will be about 2 cm (¾") wide on the double. If the dart is too deep or carries too far towards the centre front, it will create a very pointed look; your goal in this is to let it disappear and create a rounded look without a pucker.

- Pin at side seam to hold in place and check the silhouette again. The horizontal grain should be parallel to the floor, and the look from the front should be smooth and boxy. Note the silhouette in the photograph.

- Trim away armhole excess, leaving approximately 2.5 cm (1") seam allowance.

Step 3

- Pin down CB, leaving space at waistline to hang freely, aligning horizontal grainline with bust tape.

- Create back neckline dart by holding fabric gently at shoulder-blade area and folding excess fabric towards CB. The dart intake should be about 0.5 cm (¼") wide on the double.

- Trim and clip back neckline and shoulder until fabric lies smoothly. Trim armhole area to about 2.5 cm (1") seam allowance.

- Pin wrong sides together at side seam along side seam of mannequin. Trim seam allowance down to about 2.5 cm (1") and clip a few times at waist, which will allow seam allowances to turn more smoothly.

- Turn front over back at side seams and shoulder areas. At the shoulder, pin firmly at either side of seam so fabric does not move, then fold front over back. At side seams, because you are draping away from the mannequin, chalk a pin line lightly, with a crossmark or two along the seam, then fold front over back.

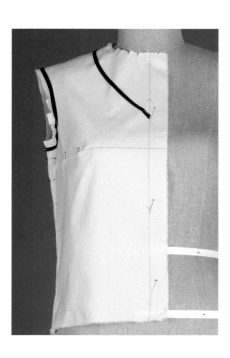

Step 4

- Check the silhouette in the photograph and adjust if necessary by pinning more tightly or loosely until you achieve the look.

- Mark neckline and armhole with twill tape. Note that the neckline you are marking is without the bias collar piece.

Clipping

Clipping takes practice. The idea is to clip enough for the calico to lie smoothly. Where the fabric is restricted, trim and clip, letting the fabric fall where it wants to go.

Bodice with French dart

The French dart is a side bust dart similar to that shown on pages 42–43, but it is angled quite severely from the side waist to the bust. This type of dart, widely used in the 1950s, removes fullness from the front part of the bodice and provides a closer fit to the underbust area. It allows the waist to be pulled in to match the fitted skirt. The neckline is not extremely low or tight. The bodice is form-fitting and feminine, and retains a sense of youthful innocence, personified here by Reese Witherspoon.

Notice how the dart is slightly curved as it moves towards the bust point. The straight grain runs straight down the centre front and centre back. The back bodice does not need a dart as the top edge is below the shoulder blade, the area that normally would need shaping.

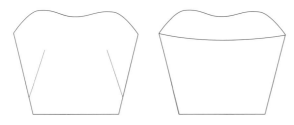

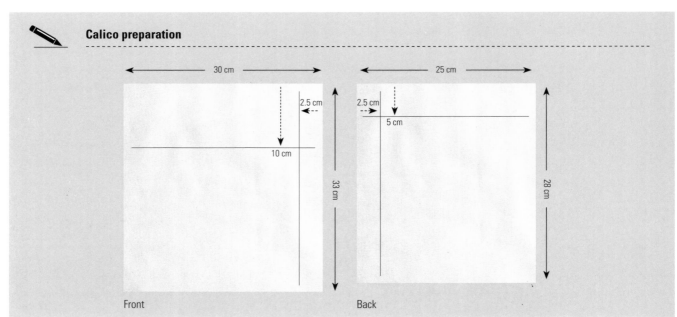

Calico preparation

Front	Back
30 cm	25 cm
2.5 cm	2.5 cm
10 cm	5 cm
33 cm	28 cm

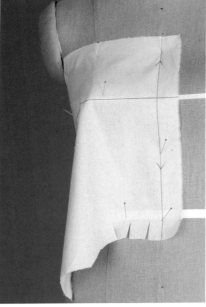

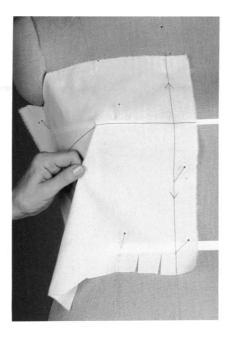

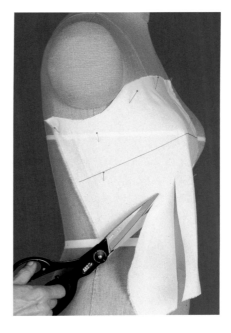

Step 1

- Pin down CF, aligning horizontal grainline with bust line tape. Leave the 1.5 cm (½") or so of ease that is created between bust points and pin at bust and waist.

- Smooth calico over top of bust to side seam, allowing ease to fall towards front.

- Pin down side seam about 5 cm (2").

- Smooth and pin waistline from CF towards princess line, trimming and clipping as needed.

Step 2

- Form French dart by folding fabric from centre upwards towards side seam. The dart should begin at the bust point and end about 2.5 cm (1") above the waist.

- Lightly chalk the lines of the dart.

> **Side bust area**
>
> The upper edge of the side bust is usually kept quite high as it offers more support for that area. The back upper edge should lie along the bra line.

Step 3

- Now re-open dart and, following chalk lines, trim away excess fabric inside dart intake. Leave about 2 cm (¾") seam allowance for the dart. Cutting out the dart will allow you to curve it, thereby achieving a closer fit.

- Folding lower edge over upper, fold in French dart, pulling in as much as possible from underbust area to get a close fit.

- Pin down side seam.

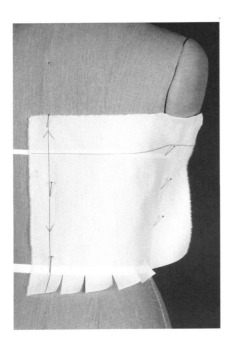

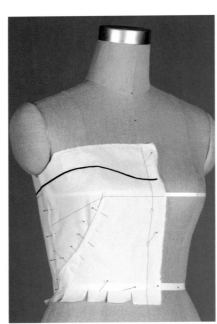

Step 4

- Pin CB lines, aligning horizontal grain with bust tape.

- Smooth calico over back bust area, allowing horizontal grain to float up naturally.

- Pin along waistline from CB towards side seam, trimming and clipping excess as necessary to allow fabric to fall smoothly.

Step 5

- Check photo and create neckline with twill or sticky tape.

Swing dress with no darts

The draping of the 'swing' (or tent/trapeze) dress will illustrate what happens when no darts are formed. All of the ease simply falls to the front over the bust and creates flare in the front.

The mood of the dress is playful and flirty – it can be full and short. It is a day dress so the armholes will be cut in at the back shoulder for a sporty, racerback style.

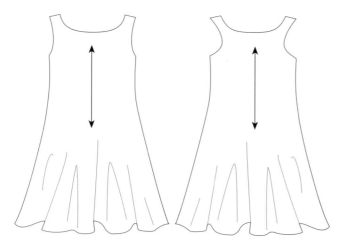

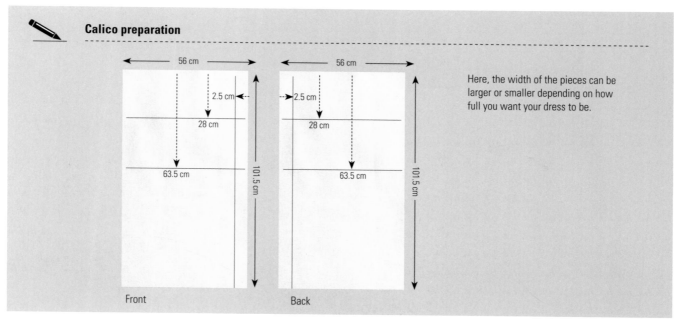

Calico preparation

Here, the width of the pieces can be larger or smaller depending on how full you want your dress to be.

56 cm

2.5 cm

28 cm

63.5 cm

101.5 cm

Front

56 cm

2.5 cm

28 cm

63.5 cm

101.5 cm

Back

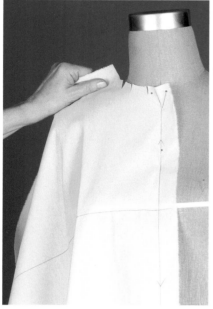

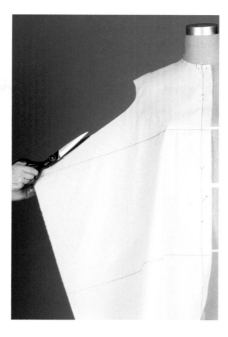

Step 1

- Pin down CF, aligning horizontal grainline with bust line tape and lower horizontal grainline generally at hip line.

- Trim and clip neckline as you smooth ease over shoulder area. Note how the angle of the shoulder seam will control how much front flare is created.

Step 2

- Pin shoulder and upper half of armhole and trim excess to about 2.5 cm (1"), carving out armhole area all the way to bust line/horizontal grainline.

- Repeat from Step 1 for the back.

Step 3

- Pin front over back at shoulder.

- Pin side seam at underarm.

- Hold side seams together and check flare (using a mirror if possible).

- Pin side seams lightly together.

- Trim side seams to about 2.5 cm (1").

Step 4

- Turn front side seam over back (lightly chalk at the pins if necessary).

- Using one of the mannequin's cage bars as a guide, level the hem.

- Twill-tape neckline and armhole shape. The armhole has a slightly cut-in angle in the front and a racerback feel in the back, but will still maintain the classic armhole egg shape, with the narrowest part being 2.5 cm (1") towards the front of the side seam. The armhole will be about 2 cm (¾") below the plate.

Matching grainlines

It is not critical to match the grainlines you have drawn on the calico; they are guidelines to help see if the grainlines are balanced. It is acceptable for the front and back to shift slightly up or down when they are pinned.

Step 5

- Leave neckline high until marked for stability.

- Check hem, armhole and neckline shape for attitude. This dress is young and playful. Look at the balance of the shapes and see if it has the same lighthearted, fun look as in the photograph.

- Try letting down the hem and raising the neckline tape to see how this changes the look of the dress.

Draping project

The famous bateau-neck sheath dress that Audrey Hepburn wore in *Breakfast at Tiffany's* defined an iconic look of the 1950s. Coco Chanel had already popularized the little black dress. Here, Hepburn epitomizes its modernity and elegant glamour.

This dress will be draped in two pieces, front and back, creating the close fit with side bust darts and princess-line vertical darts. The side seams will taper slightly, following the look of the dress in the photograph.

Before beginning the drape, look at the photograph again. Study the silhouette with its sleek lines. It appears to be quite tight-fitting, so drape it with some ease in the fit. The actual dress worn by Hepburn in the film had a waist seam that would have allowed a slightly tighter fit at the waist. The design has been modified here so you can practise the long, vertical darts. The object is to capture the narrow, willowy look of the dress.

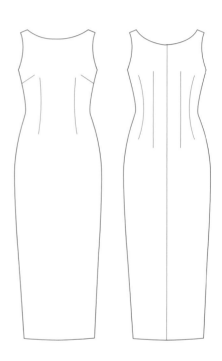

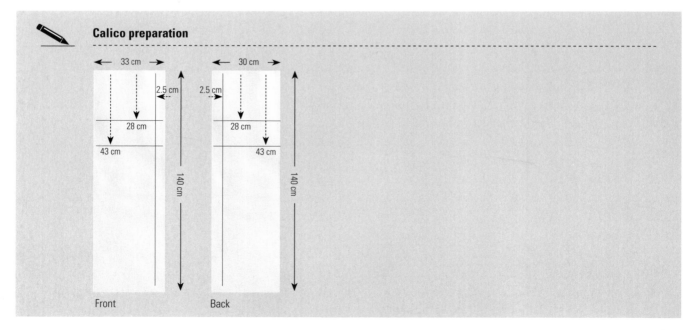

Calico preparation

Front

Back

33 cm • 2.5 cm • 28 cm • 43 cm • 140 cm

30 cm • 2.5 cm • 28 cm • 43 cm • 140 cm

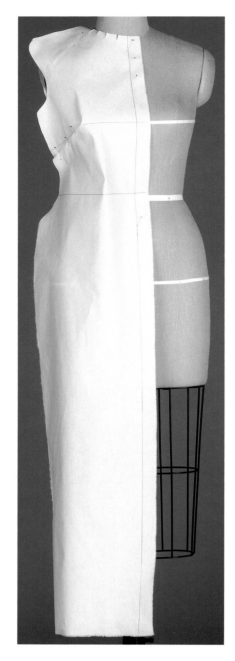

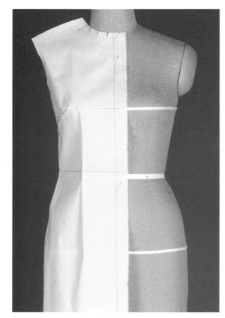

Step 2

- Observe the fullness at the front and how it naturally wants to be folded in.

- Form front vertical dart. Start at waistline, folding fabric towards side (dart will be pressed towards centre), then taper towards bust, ending dart about 1.5 cm (½") before bust point. Taper to hip area, ending dart about 10–12.5 cm (4–5") below the waist.

- Pin calico to side seam of mannequin, leaving ease. The dress will be body skimming, not skin tight. The typical amount of ease is about 1.5 cm (½") at bust, lying away from the mannequin about 1.5 cm (½") at waist and about 2 cm (¾") at hip.

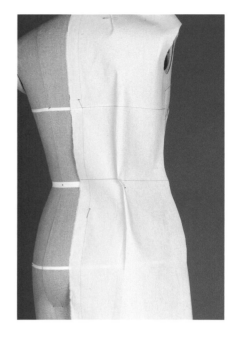

Step 3

- Pin back section down CB and anchor-pin at neckline and hip line.

- Form back neck dart by holding calico at shoulder-blade area (at princess line, about 18 cm [7"] below CB neck point). Then fold calico towards CB with 2 cm (¾") dart intake. Pin dart.

- Trim and clip back neckline and shoulder area.

- Pin front shoulder over back.

- Start back vertical dart by folding in at waist about 2cm (½") on the double. The single back dart will have to be very deep to allow the ease you want in the hip. To shape back more gracefully, split darts and form two instead of one.

Step 1

- Align CF lines and horizontal grainline with bust line. Pin down CF to high hip line leaving the ease between bust point and at waist. Anchor-pin at CF neckline. Pin at bust point.

- Smooth calico over shoulder area, trimming and clipping neckline.

- Form side dart by folding fabric up so waist horizontal grain remains level. This dart is not as severely angled as a French dart, but angled down more than the side dart on pp. 44–45. This allows the calico to fall in at the side.

- Pin side seam from underarm to high hip line and trim away excess at shoulder, armhole and side seam above waist, leaving about 2.5 cm (1") seam allowance.

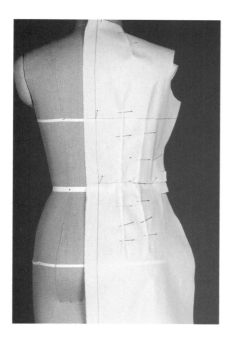

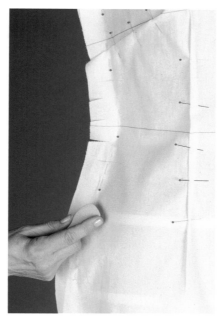

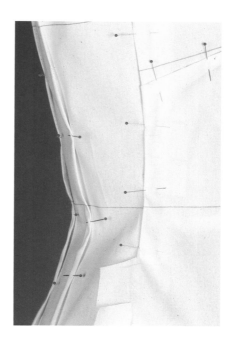

Step 4

- Top end of darts will stop before shoulder-blade area, about 15–18 cm (6–7") above waist. Lower end of darts can go almost to hip line; darts may be longer in back than in front. The dart closest to CB should be a little longer than the one towards the side seam.

- Now pin at sides, wrong sides together, leaving ease the same as the front, and trim away side seam excess, leaving about 2.5 cm (1") seam allowance. Check the sketch to make sure you have the taper towards the hemline.

- Trim seam allowances to about 2.5 cm (1").

Step 5

- Prepare to turn front over back at side seams. Take care not to disturb the drape you have created. Lightly mark every 7.5–10 cm (3–4") with chalk on both front and back of the dress. Chalk in a few crossmarks for reference so the pieces do not shift when you unpin them.

- Clip a few times at the waist to make it easier to fold in.

Step 6

- Unpin side seams, placing pins a few centimetres from the seam to hold the calico in place.

- Starting at waist, turn under front calico to match back calico at side seam of mannequin. Work up towards bust, then down from waist to hem.

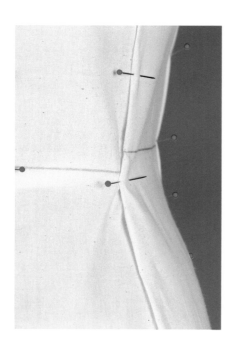

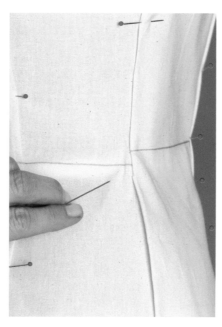

Step 7

- After pinning side seam, check that the seam is lying smoothly. Here at the waistline, one of the pins is pulling the fabric too tightly. Observe the two wrinkles pulling diagonally from the pin.

Step 8

- The solution to this problem is to remove the pin and drape in a little more fabric in that area. Clip more at the curves if it is still pulling.

Step 9

- Notice how here the seam has been smoothed out.

Step 10

- Use a metal right-angled ruler and chalk to mark hemline before turning it up.

Step 11

- Set armhole and neckline style lines using twill or sticky tape. Check the sketch to see where to place the tape.

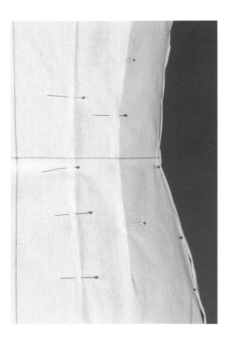

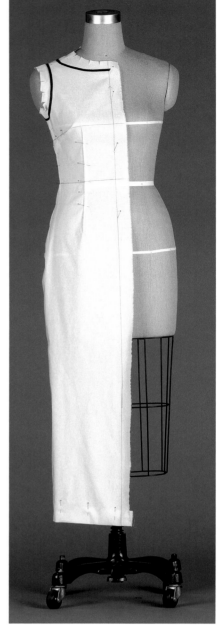

Marking and truing

This is a part of the process that is painstaking at first but will become easier as you learn more about how classic pattern shapes look. It is sometimes difficult to tell whether a mark on the calico is a subtlety of shaping in the drape, or whether it is simply a stray mark. If a great discrepancy appears, you can always re-pin and check that section on the mannequin again.

Cutting the calico

To economize on calico, you can cut another half front and simply seam the two fronts together, with the understanding that the final garment will be cut in one piece.

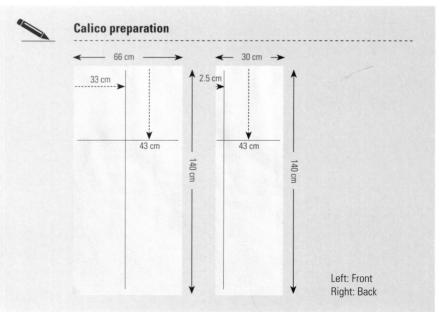

Calico preparation

66 cm

30 cm

33 cm

2.5 cm

43 cm

43 cm

140 cm

140 cm

Left: Front
Right: Back

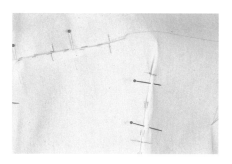

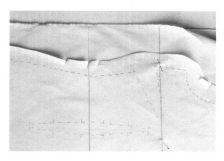

Step 1

- Using a pencil, mark around neckline and armhole on outside edge of twill tape.

- Mark both edges of the darts, mark upper and lower end points, and crossmark every 7.5–10 cm (3–4").

- Mark side seams on both front and back sections; use crossmarks about every 25 cm (10"), making sure to use one at the waistline for easy reference when truing curves.

Step 2

- Unpin the calico and gently press with very little steam so that it does not shrink or twist.

- For this dress, check the full toile. You will, therefore, need to cut a new calico section for the full front and one additional back section for the left back.

- Block new front calico, and draw straight and horizontal grains as shown in the calico-preparation diagram on p. 54.

- Fold new calico in half on CF, pinning at the horizontal grain to ensure it is exactly aligned.

- Now align draped piece onto the folded calico, aligning straight and horizontal grains, and pin into place.

Step 3

- With a clear grading ruler, mark the lines that will be perfectly straight: CF neckline will square exactly with CF line for at least the first 2.5 cm (1"); shoulder seams will be straight; side bust dart legs and hemlines will all be straight.

- Fold in side bust dart to its original draped position and draw a straight line from the waist to the underarm.

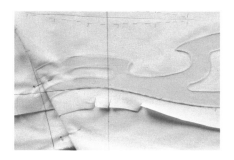

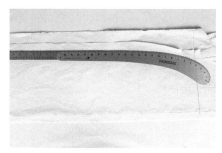

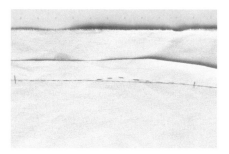

Step 4

- Using a clear hip curve, draw in bateau neckline and armhole.

- Now draw in waist-to-hip curve as it changes from a concave to a convex curve. This tool is especially useful for this area.

Step 5

- Using a long metal hip curve, draw side seam from high hip to hem.

- Use a long metal ruler to finish side seam, which should be very straight from hip to hem.

Step 6

- Sometimes when truing lines there are markings that do not seem to be compatible with others. It is important in these cases to use pattern-drafting training to discern whether the markings are purposeful and adding subtlety to a line, or whether they are stray marks that need to be smoothed out. In this case, the marks are curving in below the hip line, but you know that you want your side seam to fall straight with a little bit of narrowing at the hem. Therefore, ignore those few markings that have strayed beyond that straight lines, and simply draw in a smooth curved line.

Marking the calico

When marking the calico on the mannequin, use a dotted line made with a pencil or chalk. After you have unpinned and are smoothing the curves with the rulers, use a continuous line. That way it will be easier to keep track of which lines you have trued.

- Compare your drape with the photograph. First, look at the overall impression. Is the general shape the same? Have you captured the essence of the design?

- Begin at the top and work down: does the bateau neckline have the right height and curve? Do the armholes have the same cut-in angle?

- Do the side seams taper to the same degree? In the photograph, Hepburn has one leg in front of the other, and the fabric of the dress may have been pulled back. The actual dress cannot be too slim or movement will be restricted.

- Try visualizing the dress in a beautiful black silk crêpe. Does it evoke the modern, glamorous look that Audrey Hepburn personifies?

Step 7

- Using a clear grading ruler, add seam allowances to edges as follows:
  - Neckline and armholes: 1.5 cm (½")
  - Shoulders and side seams: 2 cm (¾")
  - Hem: 5 cm (2")
- Then cut through all layers on the new lines.
- Clip in at crossmarks no more than 0.5 cm (¼").

Step 8

- To mark darts or any interior lines, tracing paper and the tracing wheel are used.
- Slip tracing paper underneath draped calico and draw dart lines with tracing wheel. Since you are working with a double piece, you must also mark the other side by placing tracing paper underneath the folded piece and tracing the line a second time.

Transferring the toile to a paper pattern

Once the toile is marked and trued, you may want to create a paper pattern.

1. Draw straight and horizontal grains on dotted graph paper to correspond to the grainlines on your calico pieces.

2. Align calico piece on the paper, matching the grainlines. If the grainlines have twisted or angled, gently reblock the calico so it aligns with the paper grainlines.

3. Use a tracing wheel to transfer all markings on the calico to the paper. Using carbon paper makes the lines easier to see. For specific points such as the tailor-tacked darts, use an awl to punch through the calico onto the paper.

4. Remove the calico and draw in lines smoothly using the proper rulers for each type of straight or curved line. If this step is done before you re-pin or baste (tack) the toile and do a fitting, make sure you accurately transfer any corrections onto the paper pattern.

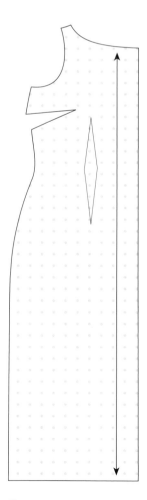

Front

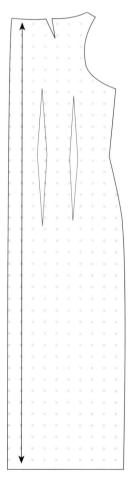

Back

Variations
Setting the princess line into a yoke

In this contemporary design, the fit of the bodice is in the yoke seam above the bust and in the princess line running vertically from that yoke. The basic shape is similar to the Audrey Hepburn dress, but looser. It is a strong, confident, almost aggressive look.

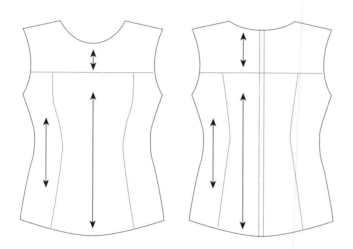

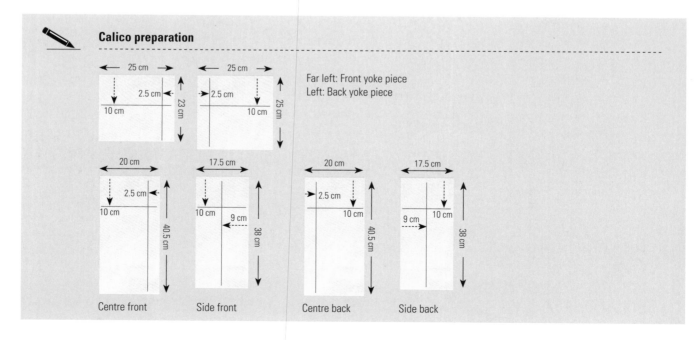

Calico preparation

Far left: Front yoke piece
Left: Back yoke piece

Centre front

Side front

Centre back

Side back

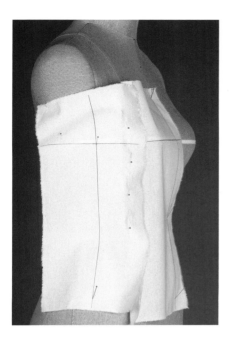

Step 1

- Align CF lines and pin horizontal grain at bust.

- Centre side front section between side seam and princess line, allowing straight grain to fall straight.

- Pin wrong sides together, forming the princess line.

- Check the photo. This is a loose-fitting dress and the princess line is quite wide, at least 2.5 cm (1") wider than the line on the mannequin. The CF shape is fairly boxy.

Any shaping you give to the bodice at this point, therefore, should come from the side front section. The CF princess line should remain almost straight, and the side front section will curve out at the bust and slightly in at the waist. It is difficult to tell from the photo how much shaping has been created at the waist. It will be possible, however, to keep the shape boxy and still have a little shaping at the waist, which will make it more flattering.

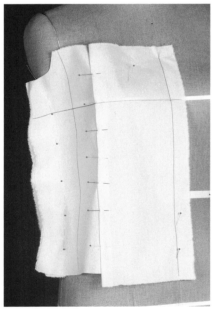

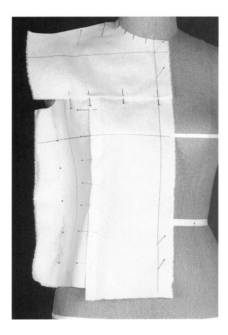

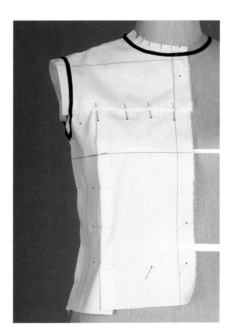

Step 2

- Pin CF section over side front section.

- Slice out seam allowance of armhole leaving about 2.5 cm (1") seam allowance.

Using the yoke line as a dart

The yoke is used here in a similar way to how a dart is used. The joining of the two pieces is straight until the last 7.5 cm (3") or so before the armhole. At that point, each piece is cut in slightly, creating a dart-like shape that takes up excess fabric and allows a closer fit to the body.

Step 3

- Set yoke piece by aligning CF lines and pinning horizontal grain, taking care to keep the grain parallel to the floor.

- Trim and clip neckline until it lies smoothly.

- Turn under yoke line, following style lines of the photograph.

- The yoke line is straight to princess seam and then gently folds up about 1.5 cm (½") more at armhole to take up ease and keep line visually straight.

Step 4

- Repeat from Step 1 for back section. Make back yoke about same width as front.

- Turn front side seam over back side seam.

- Turn front shoulder seam over back shoulder seam.

- Twill tape armhole and neckline. Note that the armhole in this dress is slightly more contemporary than the classic bodice on p. 44. It is cut a little bit lower – a good 2.5 cm (1") below the armplate.

Joining two darts to create the princess line

Princess Alexandra of Denmark popularized the combining of skirt and bodice into one garment, using a long, vertical seam running from the mid-shoulder point over the bust point, down past the hip, centred between the side seam and the centre front. The seam was named after her – the princess line.

The fit is comparable to that you would get from using a shoulder dart (see p. 43) and a long dart as in the Audrey Hepburn dress. If the two darts are joined, you can see how the two pieces will look.

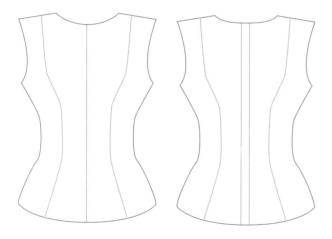

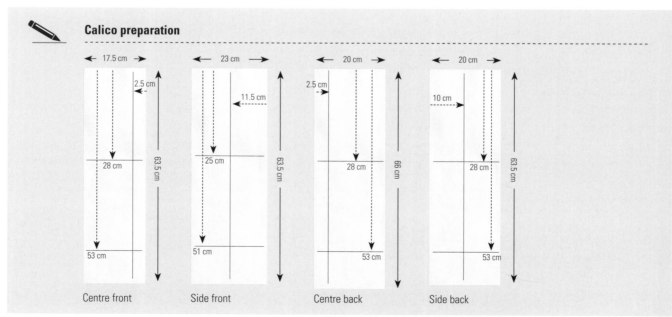

Calico preparation

| Centre front | Side front | Centre back | Side back |

17.5 cm — 2.5 cm — 28 cm — 63.5 cm — 53 cm

23 cm — 11.5 cm — 25 cm — 63.5 cm — 51 cm

20 cm — 2.5 cm — 28 cm — 66 cm — 53 cm

20 cm — 10 cm — 28 cm — 63.5 cm — 53 cm

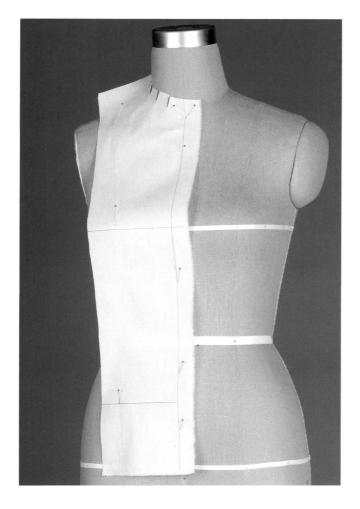

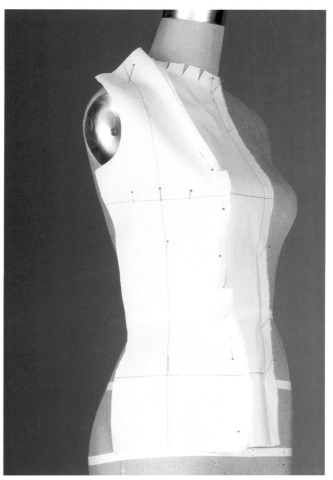

Step 1

- Align CF lines and horizontal grainline with bust line. Pin down CF to high hip line, leaving the ease that forms between bust point and at waist. Anchor-pin at CF neckline to hold firmly. Pin at bust to hold hoizontal grain in place.

- Smooth calico over shoulder area, trimming and clipping neckline as needed.

- Following princess line of mannequin, trim away excess calico, leaving about 2.5 cm (1") seam allowance.

When to shape the neckline

When draping bodices, it is important to leave the calico intact all the way to the neckline so that it does not shift or twist. Once the calico is marked, with twill or sticky tape, you can trim away the excess fabric.

Matching horizontal grainlines

It is not crucial for horizontal grains to match up; they are there only for guidelines on setting the pieces. It is more important, for example, that the side front straight grain is perpendicular to the floor than that the horizontal grains match.

Step 2

- Set side front section by centring straight grainline at approximate centre of side bust area, and align horizontal grainline with bust tape. The straight grainline should remain perpendicular to the floor.

- Pin down straight grainline and across horizontal grainline.

- Leave 0.5 cm (¼") or more ease on armhole area as you drape section across shoulder.

- With wrong sides together, pin side front section to CF section along princess line, starting at bust and pinning up, then pinning down to high hip line.

Clipping or trimming seam allowances

Whenever you are directed to clip or trim a seam allowance to an approximate amount, do not stop and measure, just trim away enough that you can continue draping without obstruction and the fabric lies smoothly. While draping, a general rule of thumb for seam allowances is:

- Necklines: 1.5 cm (½")

- Armholes and side and shoulder seams: 2 cm (¾")

- Hems: 2.5 cm (1") minimum.

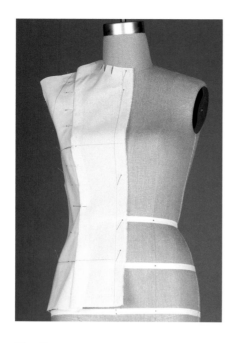

Step 3

- Trim side front seam allowance and clip to pins from underbust to waist.

- Trim seam allowance of armhole and shoulder to about 2.5 cm (1").

- Turn front section over side front section and pin (you can either lightly chalk a few places, or place pins to the side of the seam as you turn).

- Trim side seam to about 2.5 cm (1"), following side seam of mannequin.

- Repeat for back. Align CB lines and horizontal grainline with bust line. Pin down CB to high hip line, allowing fabric to fall in lightly at waist. Anchor-pin at CB neckline to hold firmly. Pin at bust to hold horizontal grain in place.

- Smooth calico over neck and shoulder area, trimming and clipping neckline as needed.

- Following back princess line of mannequin, trim away excess calico, leaving about 2.5 cm (1") seam allowance.

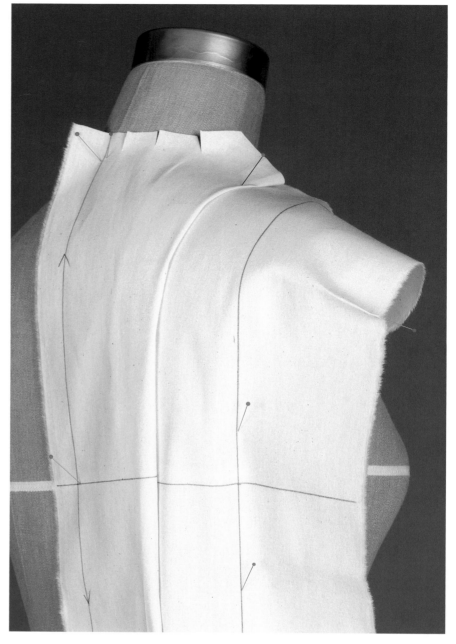

Step 4

- Set side back section by centring straight grainline at approximate centre of side bust area, and align horizontal grainline with bust tape. Straight grainline should remain perpendicular to floor.

- Pin down straight grainline and across horizontal grainline.

- Leave 0.5 cm (¼") or more ease on armhole area as you drape the section across the shoulder.

Avoiding bias at the shoulder

Angle the straight grain towards the outer edge of the shoulder, which will give the ease needed at the armhole and keep the grain from moving towards the bias at the back armhole. It will also keep the grain from shifting to the bias, which will weaken the shoulder line – the area that will support the weight of the garment.

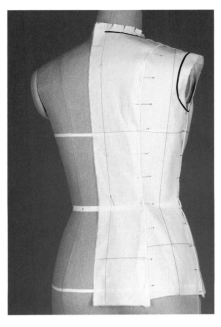

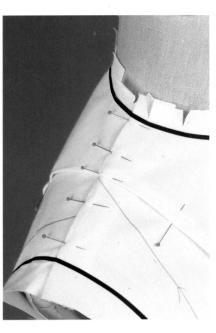

Step 5

- With wrong sides together, pin side back section to CB section along princess line, starting at bust and pinning up, then pinning down to high hip line.
- Pin side seams together, trim seam allowances and clip curves.
- Turn centre section over side section.

Step 6

- Turn front shoulder over back, adjusting princess-line seams to match at shoulder.

Step 7

- Tape armhole and neckline.

Bodice with an armhole princess line

Jacqueline Kennedy Onassis, widow of US President John F. Kennedy, was a style icon in her own right. As one of the youngest (and most beautiful) of the American First Ladies, she set the standard for stylish, fashion-forward dress. She chose as her primary designer Oleg Cassini, but she also wore Dior, Givenchy and Chanel.

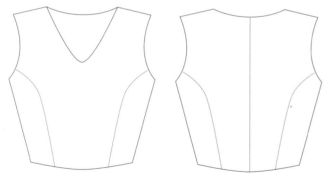

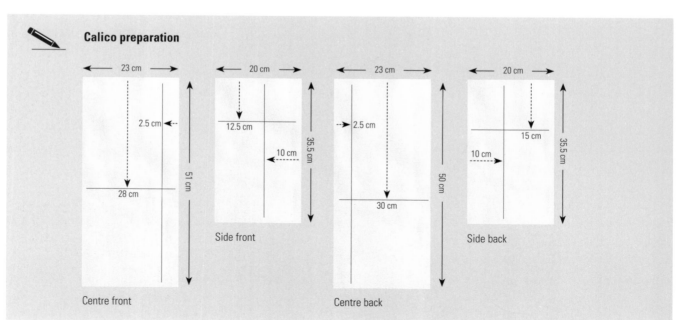

Calico preparation

Centre front

Side front

Centre back

Side back

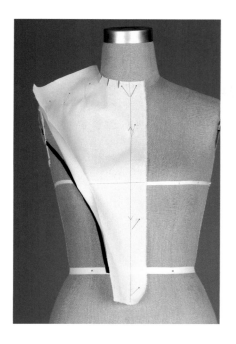

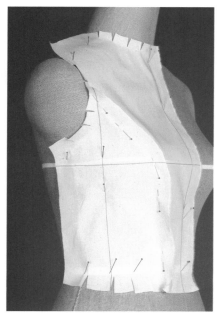

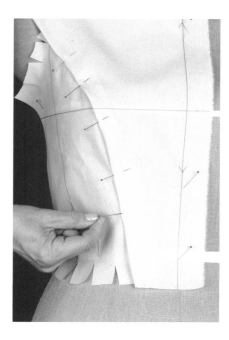

Step 1

- Align CF lines and horizontal grainline with bust line. Pin down CF to waist leaving the ease that forms between bust point and at waist.

- Anchor-pin at CF neckline to hold firmly. Pin at bust to hold horizontal grain in place.

- Smooth calico over shoulder area, trimming and clipping neckline as needed.

- Pin a length of twill tape along armhole princess line, beginning where you feel it will start and ending at waistline. In the photograph, it appears to begin about two-thirds down from shoulder line and end a little towards centre of the princess line.

- Trim away the calico, leaving at least 2.5 cm (1") seam allowance.

Step 2

- Set side front section by centring the straight grainline at approximate centre of side bust area, and align horizontal grainline with bust tape. Straight grainline should remain perpendicular to floor.

- Pin down straight grainline and across horizontal grainline.

- Using the twill tape as a guide, pin the two sections, wrong sides together, beginning at bust point and working up towards armhole, and then down to waist.

- Trim and clip armhole excess, princess-line excess, and at waist to allow calico to lie smoothly over mannequin.

Checking ease

Remember that this is a dress with some ease and should not be tight against the mannequin. Some armhole ease – 1.5 cm (½") or so – and some ease in the underbust area is necessary to allow the fabric to fall smoothly.

Step 3

- Repeat from Step 1 for back sections.

- Pin front shoulder over back and front side seam over back side seam.

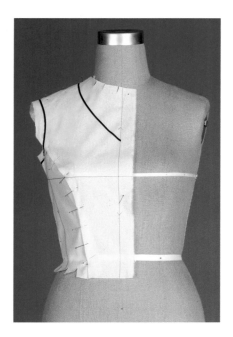

Step 4

- Study the photograph and set the armhole and neckline tapes to catch the attitude of the dress. It is from the early 1960s: armholes were cut very high and small; the neckline is a modest V with a gentle curve, concave from shoulder to CF, lending grace to the style.

1.3
Corsets

History

The plethora of resources for corsets today attest to the enduring appeal of this seemingly restrictive but surprisingly comfortable, timeless garment.

The corset was developed originally to protect, support and shape the female bust. While the basic structure has remained fairly constant, silhouettes changed to accommodate current fashion.

In the Georgian era, corsets had a flattening effect, pushing the upper torso into a tubular form, while the

Victorian corset had a voluptuous, Rubensian look, the seaming and boning sculpting the body into an hourglass shape. In the twentieth century, a popular look of the 1950s was the conical effect of the bust.

Chapter 1.2: Dresses explored how different silhouettes can be shaped through the use of darting

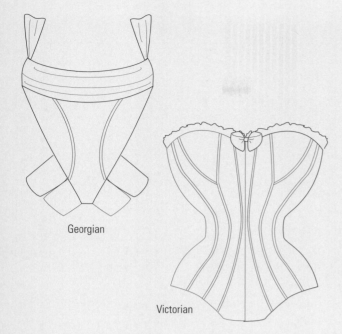

Georgian

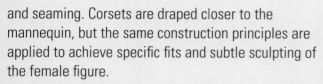

Victorian

and seaming. Corsets are draped closer to the mannequin, but the same construction principles are applied to achieve specific fits and subtle sculpting of the female figure.

Understanding and using grainlines correctly is vital to creating a corset that performs well. The grainlines need to work together with the boning to create support and shape. It is crucial for the straight grain and horizontal grain to balance, otherwise the ring of tension around the body will be broken, the corset will twist and support will be lost. It is useful to think of the grainlines as an architectural blueprint. As the steel structure of an architectural form creates the stable foundation of the building, the strength of the grainlines and positioning of the boning enable the corset to give support and shape.

Jean Paul Gaultier created this cone-shaped corset for Madonna's 1990 Blond Ambition tour. While the costume was designed to be sexually provocative, it offered a throwback to the bras of the 1950s and explored the concept of underwear as outerwear.

Opposite page: In this still from *Gone with the Wind*, Scarlett O'Hara (played by Vivien Leigh) is being laced into her corset by her maid, in an attempt to achieve the highly prized tiny waist in vogue at the time. This corset probably consisted of more than a dozen lengths of boning placed vertically along the straight grain of the fabric, and was laced in the back to allow for tight fit.

Above left: Corsets have been shaped to create different silhouettes throughout history to match the aesthetic of the time. Here the flatter Georgian silhouette is contrasted with the rounder shape of the Victorian era.

Above right: This Issey Miyake sculpture shows the complex curves of the female figure.

Exercises
Preparing the mannequin for draping the corset

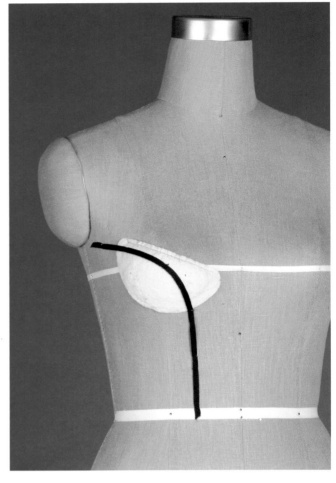

Study the measurements of your mannequin. If you are draping the corset to fit a specific person, compare the two sets of measurements. Many mannequins do not have much bust definition. Usually the upper bust measurement – about 7–10 cm (3–4") above the bust point – of an average female will be smaller than the mannequin's. The measurement of the underbust, a few centimetres below the bust point, where the lower bra line would fall, is also quite a bit smaller on a real person than on a mannequin.

Determine what shape and size of corset you are going to create. If desired, you can add a bra or bust pad to the mannequin to give more definition.

Step 1

- Depending on the volume needed, cut one to three layers per side of felt or fibrefill, following the pattern.

- Stitch them together along the top edge and pull the thread slightly to ease it in until it forms a curve.

- Steam over a ham until desired shape is reached.

Step 2

- Set the pad slightly under the bust and to the side, and pin it into place. The human bust line will be fuller than the mannequin's under the bust point.

- Check the silhouette that you intend to create and determine the best way to achieve it with the seaming. Remember that the closer your seams are to the bust point, the smoother your fabric will lie.

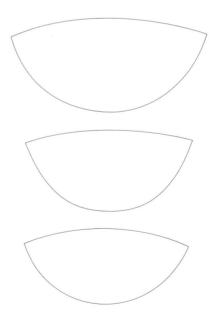

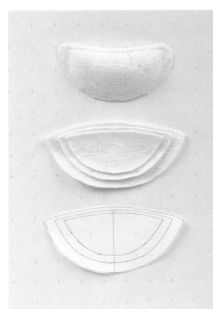

Preparing the mannequin

Draping corsets is best done with the shoulders of the mannequin pushed into the armplates, creating a smaller, softer shape that more closely resembles a woman's body from the underarm to bust point.

Preparing the fabric and materials for the corset

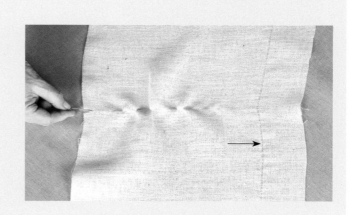

For garments where grainline accuracy is particularly critical, like the corset, a thread is pulled to mark the line where the fabric can be cut instead of torn, or to locate the line where the grainline of the piece can be marked with pencil.

- Mark the dimensions of the piece, clip in 1.5 cm (½"), find a thread and pull gently until you see it moving through the fabric.

- If the thread comes all the way out, you will have a clear path on which to cut the fabric. If not, cut along the pulled line. If the thread breaks before you are at the end of the piece, you can simply take a pin, pick out another thread and keep going.

- To mark the grainline with pencil, simply draw along the 'run' in the fabric where the thread is missing.

Fabrics Contemporary corsets are made with a variety of fabrics, even knits or stretch panels containing Lycra. Fortunately for the modern woman, this allows some flexibility in fit and breathing room even when tightly fitted. However, for full control and support, and a more precise fit, using strictly woven fabrics, is preferable.

Corsets are commonly used as foundations for gowns. They are ideally made of a flat-weave fabric in which the straight and horizontal grains have equal strength, such as a damask or fine cotton. Chiffon, light voile and even silk tulle can also be used. They are delicate and beautiful, but will only work if the grainlines are balanced and sufficient boning is used to keep the fabric taut.

Interlining The calico or finished fabric will often be fused or backed to create a firm panel.

Boning A careful decision is needed as to where the boning will go. It will play a large part in determining the silhouette and look of the corset. It is usually placed in areas where most support is needed, like the side front. This will hold the bust towards the centre front. Traditionally, it is also placed in the centre front and the side back. Boning placed in the sides is often uncomfortable.

Boning comes in various forms; sometimes it can be stitched directly onto the lining, or it may come in a casing which can be stitched on before the boning is reinserted. Metal spiral boning will need a bias casing made for it or a tunnel constructed between layers of fabric.

Petersham ribbon It is useful to construct the corset with a length of ribbon stitched at the waistline. Petersham ribbon is strong, yet can be steamed into a curve. This element serves a dual purpose. First, anchoring the corset firmly at the waist with the ribbon makes it easier to know exactly the distance from bust point to waist, which is helpful when fitting the more difficult bust area. Second, when putting on a corset, if the waist ribbon is done first, it is then easier to fasten the other closures, which can sometimes be awkward to do without help.

Closures Corsets can be fastened in a variety of ways: zips, buttons, hooks and eyes, or a busk. Buttons will gap unless the corset is not too tight or it has an underlayer with a more secure fastening. Zips are efficient, but be careful in a fashion show or costuming situation because they sometimes break at a critical moment. Hook-and-eye tape or a busk is a common solution.

Fabric A hemp/silk blend is used here for the corsets because it is so easy to see the grainlines. The corsets are draped very tightly to the mannequin, and if you are able to see the grainlines clearly, you can tell right away when the pieces are twisting or pulling.

Princess-line corset

The lace-front princess-line corset shown here is a soft, lingerie garment as opposed to a heavily structured foundation. The princess line gives the shaping over the bust. In this case, the lace overlay makes it easy to see the style line. The corset does not have a very tight fit, so the buttons on the front closure do not pull. As with the dress on pages 64–65, this is an armhole princess-line seam. The fitting seam begins at the armscye area, then extends over the bust point and down towards the waist.

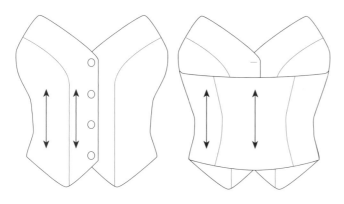

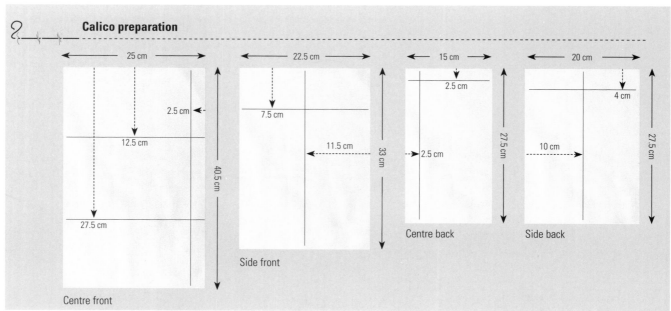

Calico preparation

Centre front

25 cm
2.5 cm
12.5 cm
27.5 cm
40.5 cm

Side front

22.5 cm
7.5 cm
11.5 cm
33 cm

Centre back

15 cm
2.5 cm
2.5 cm
27.5 cm

Side back

20 cm
4 cm
10 cm
27.5 cm

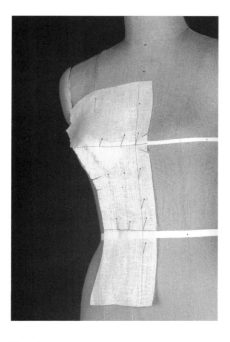

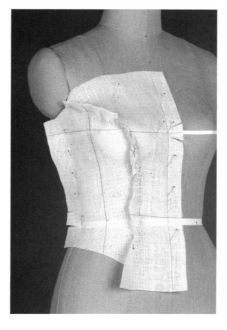

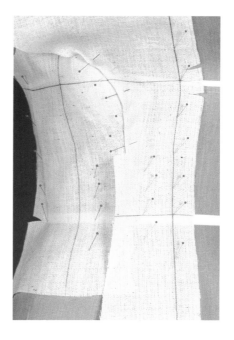

Step 1

- Align horizontal grain with bust line and pin CF straight grain along CF of mannequin, clipping at bust line to allow fabric to lie smoothly.

- Following the style line you have created for the princess line, trim away excess calico leaving about 2.5 cm (1") seam allowance.

- Clip at underbust and waistline to style line to allow fabric to fit snugly against the shape of the mannequin.

Step 2

- Set side front section by aligning horizontal grain with bust tape and centring straight grain between princess line and side seam, keeping grainline perpendicular to floor.

- Pin along grainlines and side seams.

- With wrong sides together, pin side front at the princess line to CF section.

- Trim seam allowance to about 2 cm (¾") and clip every 2.5 cm (1") or so to pin line.

- The calico should be now fitting quite snugly and grainlines should be stable and holding their vertical and horizontal lines. Check pencil lines carefully: if any are wavy, twisting or pulling, carefully remove pins one at a time to determine how to correct them.

Step 3

- Turn front over side front section and pin, removing pins a few centimetres at a time and placing them to the side of the seam to keep them from moving.

Pinning

When draping a very fitted garment, remember that you will need to place the pins more closely as you drape more tightly.

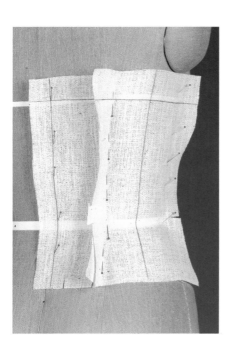

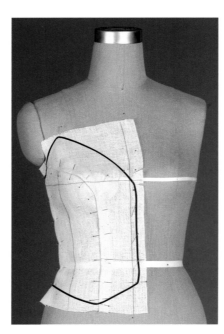

Step 4

- Set CB section, aligning straight grain with CB and horizontal grain with bust tape.

- Pin down back princess line, angling slightly in towards the waist.

- Trim seams to about 2.5 cm (1") and clip waist area.

- Set side back section as side front, keeping grainline vertical.

Step 5

- Pin front over back at sides and CB over side back.

- Tape hemline and neckline.

Corset with Georgian shape

Contrast the mood of this corset with the one on page 72. This Versace corset has a tougher, edgier quality. The metal zip and heavy topstitching add to the armour-like quality.

The grainline placement creates a Georgian silhouette. The centre front lines are vertical, and the side panel grainlines slant towards the centre front, causing the energy to focus towards the waistline with the bust line receding.

The multi-seam front divides the fit of the bust into three panels instead of the two used in the princess-line corset. The bust shape will be softer and flatter than the more defined silhouette achieved with the single seam.

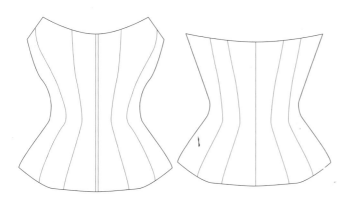

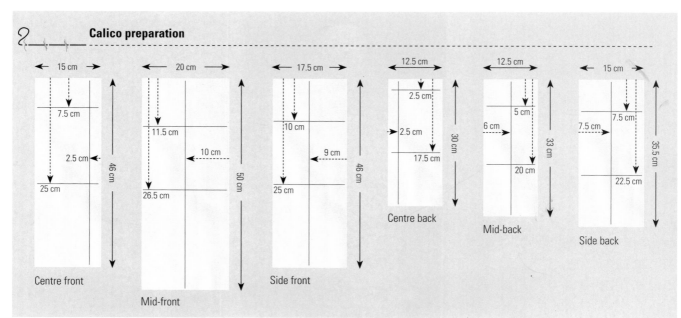

Calico preparation

Centre front
- 15 cm
- 7.5 cm
- 2.5 cm
- 25 cm
- 46 cm

Mid-front
- 20 cm
- 11.5 cm
- 10 cm
- 26.5 cm
- 50 cm

Side front
- 17.5 cm
- 10 cm
- 9 cm
- 25 cm
- 46 cm

Centre back
- 12.5 cm
- 2.5 cm
- 2.5 cm
- 17.5 cm
- 30 cm

Mid-back
- 12.5 cm
- 5 cm
- 6 cm
- 20 cm
- 33 cm

Side back
- 15 cm
- 7.5 cm
- 7.5 cm
- 22.5 cm
- 35.5 cm

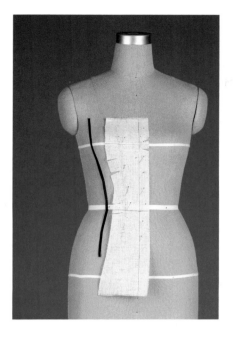 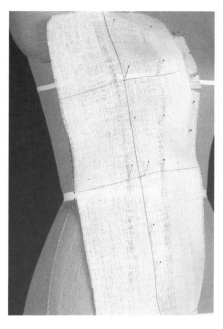 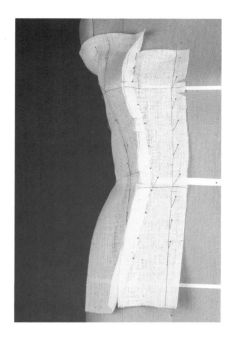

Step 1

- Create two style lines on mannequin with black twill tape in front and to side of princess line from armhole to waist.

- Align horizontal grain with bust line and pin CF straight grain along CF of mannequin, clipping at bust line to allow fabric to lie smoothly.

- Following the style line you have created, trim away excess calico leaving about 2.5 cm (1") seam allowance.

- Clip at underbust and waistline to style line to allow fabric to fit snugly against shape of mannequin.

- Pin across bust line, underbust and waist.

Step 2

- Set mid-front section by aligning horizontal grain with bust tape and waist horizontal grain with waist tape on the mannequin.

- The straight grain here is angling towards CF, allowing the strength of the grain to run alongside the bust. This gives support where it is needed on the side bust.

- Pin down straight grain and across bust and waistlines.

Step 3

- Pin mid-front and CF sections together, wrong sides out. They should fit the mannequin quite tightly.

- Trim seam allowances to about 2 cm (¾").

- Clip at waist and underbust. Trim away seam allowance on the edge towards the side to about 2 cm (¾").

Using bias for stretch

Note how the grainline becomes bias below the waist, allowing some give where it is needed for the shape of the high hip.

Aligning horizontal grains

Remember that the horizontal grains do not have to match exactly when you join two pieces of calico. They are guides for the proper placement of individual sections. The horizontal grains in the corset should generally be along the same meridians, but it is not a goal to have them match at the seams. Often they will not.

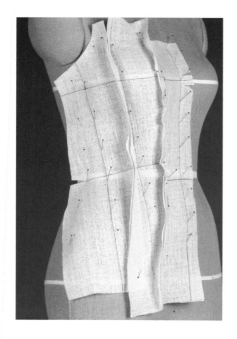
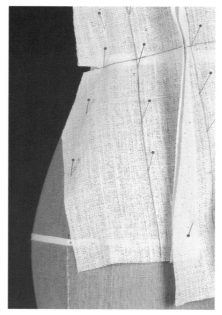
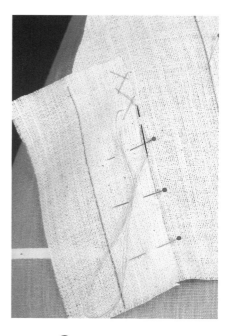

Step 4

- Set side front section by aligning bust horizontal grains with bust tape and waist horizontal grains with waist tape.

- Straight grain will angle forwards and run parallel to grainline of mid-front section.

- Pin down grainlines.

Step 5

- Pin side front section to mid-front section and trim away seam allowances to about 2 cm (¾").

- Clip where needed.

- Observe how, at the side seam, the fabric has run short. A small piece must be added.

Step 6

- Cut a small piece that will allow draping to continue. Align grainlines and herringbone-stitch it in place.

- Continue to drape side panel by pinning down side seam of mannequin and trimming away excess seam allowances.

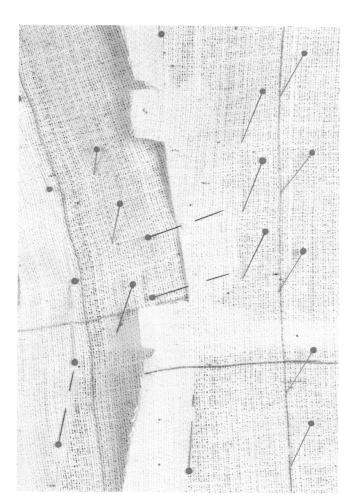

Adding sections of fabric

When draping, you can simply add on a piece of fabric if the initial calico has run short. It is, however, critical that the piece added is of the same grainline as the main piece.

Turning the seams of a fitted garment

The best method for this tight-fitting garment is to make a line of pins on either side of the seam that is being turned. Then, a few at a time, unpin and re-pin, folding front over back, allowing the pins on the sides to hold the fabric firmly in place.

Step 7

- Turn seams front over back.

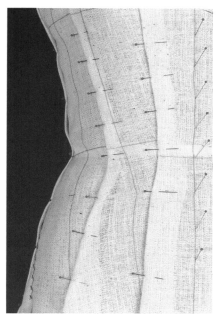

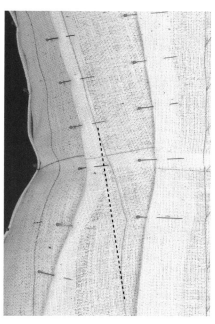

Step 8

- Stand back, hold up your flat sketch and check the style lines. You can shift them at this point if necessary.

- Check for twisting and pulling by studying the grainlines. They should be running smoothly in straight lines down the pieces. Note how, on the mid-front section, the pencil line is curved in below the waist. That means it is 'off grain' and needs to be corrected.

- Release any pulls in the grainlines and re-pin to straighten lines.

- Repeat from Step 1 for back.

Step 9

- Mark top and lower edges with twill or sticky tape.

- Keep the top edge high at the front underarm area to give additional support to the bust.

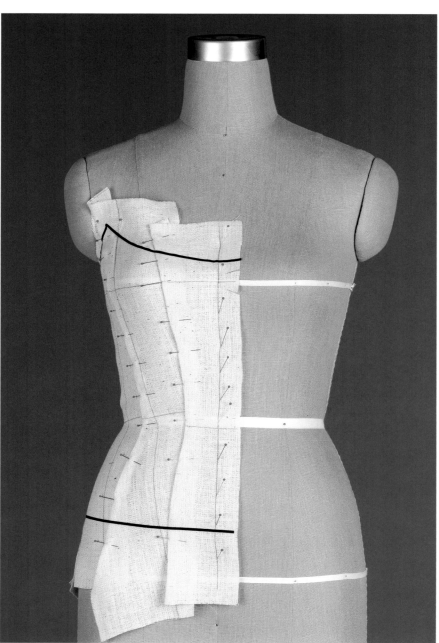

Draping project

This corset from Christian Lacroix's Autumn/Winter 1997 collection is a play of contrasts: the soft and sensual flowers and S-curve seaming with the hard structure and tight fit. The forwards motion of the overflowing flowers is held back by the vertical lines that restrain and hold the body erect.

The low and sexy top edge is covered by ornamentation. The accompanying skirt supports this theme, with soft folds spilling out from beneath a hard leather belt, which cuts across the front of the skirt, holding it in. The tension of these two aspects creates energy – a perfect balance of the magnetic and dynamic.

This is a Victorian silhouette, evident in the bust definition and small waist. The upright quality of the corset – the sense that it holds the wearer erect – indicates that the grainlines should be vertical, although the seaming is curved.

The princess-line seam will give the bust definition. The two seams of the mid-section, as in the Georgian-style corset on pages 74–77, give additional fit to the bust and waist.

The two boned seams curving forwards help to hold the waistline in. The side-piece grainline becomes bias as it extends towards the front, giving stretch and, therefore, more shape to the front high hip area.

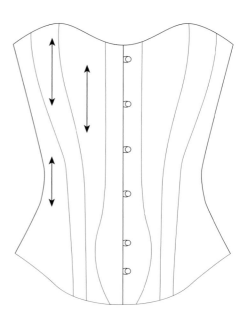

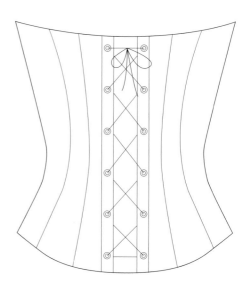

Visualizing the volume

Before preparing the calico, visualize the volume: the pieces angle towards the front, so they will need enough width to keep the grainlines vertical from top edge to hem.

The photograph shows the proportions of a model's body. The mannequin is realistically proportioned, so note that your style lines will look slightly foreshortened.

As you drape, try to strike that balance between soft sensuality and a 'held-in' quality. Imagine how the woman in this corset feels: the boning is holding her upright. The restraint is not negative; she feels supported and dignified.

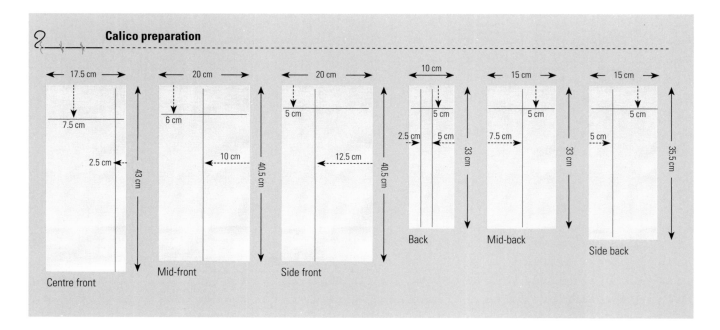

Calico preparation

17.5 cm · 7.5 cm · 2.5 cm · 43 cm · Centre front

20 cm · 6 cm · 10 cm · 40.5 cm · Mid-front

20 cm · 5 cm · 12.5 cm · 40.5 cm · Side front

10 cm · 5 cm · 2.5 cm · 5 cm · 33 cm · Back

15 cm · 5 cm · 7.5 cm · 33 cm · Mid-back

15 cm · 5 cm · 5 cm · 35.5 cm · Side back

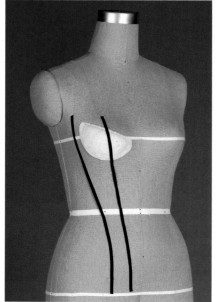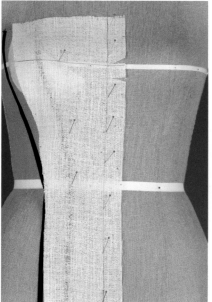

Step 1

- Following the flat sketch on p. 78, set two pieces of twill tape on the mannequin.

- Set bust pad in place at underbust area, or put a bra on the mannequin.

- Using twill tape, create the two front seamlines. Do not relate to curved vertical line next to CF line yet. That line is simply an overlay and not a construction seam.

Step 2

- Set CF section by aligning straight and horizontal grains with CF and bust tape; pin.

- Clip at CF bust to allow fabric to lie smoothly.

- Trim excess along twill tape line, leaving about 2.5 cm (1") seam allowance.

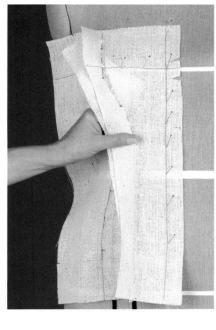

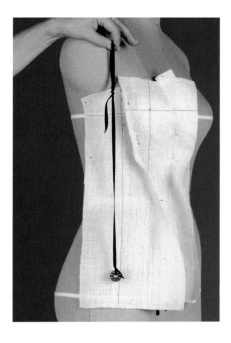

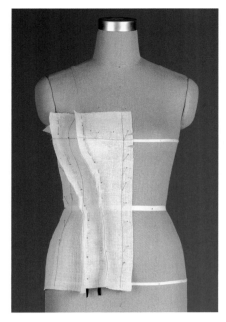

Step 3

- To set mid-front piece, align horizontal grain with bust tape and centre straight grain between the pre-determined style lines.
- Pin the mid-front and CF sections wrong sides together, placing pins quite close together to get a snug fit. Do not forget to accentuate the underbust area.
- Trim together to 2 cm (¾"); clip waist and underbust curves.

Step 4

- Pin along next twill tape style line. Trim seam allowances to about 2.5 cm (1").
- Set side front section by aligning horizontal grain with bust tape and letting straight grain fall vertically. If it becomes confusing to find the right line, hang a plumb-line weight to correct your line.
- Pin mid-front piece to side piece, wrong sides together.
- Trim side seam allowance to about 2.5 cm (1"), following side seam of mannequin.

Step 5

- Now check style lines of three front sections and compare with the sketch.
- It may help to lay some twill tapes on the pinned seams and see if they have the same beautiful flow that the Lacroix does.

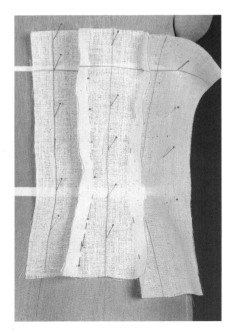

Step 6

- Set CB section by aligning straight grain with CB and horizontal grain with bust tape.
- Set mid-back section by aligning straight grain with back princess line and horizontal grain with bust tape.
- Form a dart in centre of mid-back section to fit back waist very tightly.
- Pin back section to mid-back, wrong sides together.
- Set side back section as for mid-back, forming a dart at waist.

Fitting

Because the corset is very fitted, an exaggerated back curve will help keep the corset in place.

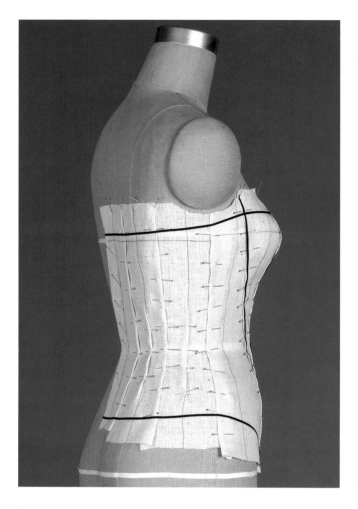

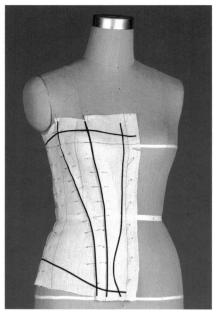

Step 8

- Tape CF overlay piece, which will be an important part of the look.

- Tape top edge and hemline.

- Check style lines of the photograph again for accuracy. It may help to highlight seamlines with black tape, so that when you step back and analyse the drape you can see if the look is achieved.

- Correct your lines accordingly.

Step 7

- Pin all seams to inside, folding seam allowances towards CF and CB.

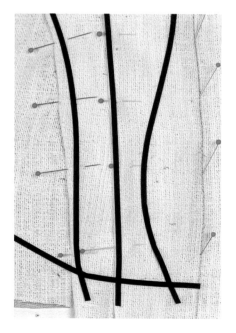

Step 9

- The side front line will be moved slightly towards the front to achieve a more dramatic hip emphasis.

- Check line again from a distance and re-pin seam accordingly.

- Mark all seams with crossmarks, which will help you re-match the pieces after you take them apart. Use your pattern-cutting skills to double-notch or crossmark back pieces and notch or crossmark front pieces at different levels. Mark waistline on all pieces for an easy reference point.

Marking and truing

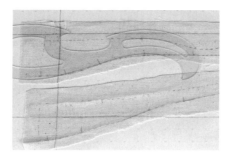

Step 1

- True up CF piece. Use a clear French curve to smooth the lines that move from convex to concave curves from bust and waist to high hip areas.

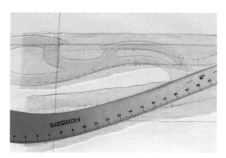

Step 2

- True the lines on mid-front section using the long metal hip curve to draw in longer, straighter areas.

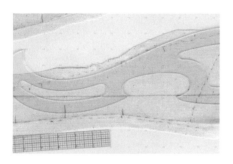

Step 3

- Use a small grading ruler to true the straight lines and to add seam allowances. Use a 1.5 cm (½") seam allowance to join body pieces, and 4 cm (1½") at CF and CB.

Step 4

- True mid-front to side front at crossmarks.
- For this corset, sew the full toile. You will, therefore, need to cut the mirror-image second sections for all pieces.

- First, block the new calico pieces, and draw straight and horizontal grains as shown in the calico-preparation diagram on p. 78.
- Now align draped piece onto folded calico, align straight and horizontal grains and pin into place.
- Cut the two pieces together along the lines you have trued.

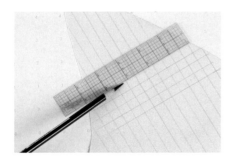

Step 5

- Now coordinate all the details of the piece. The quilted sections will have to be prepared before the garment is sewn. Using a pencil, determine the proportion you feel is right and draw the lines using a grading ruler.

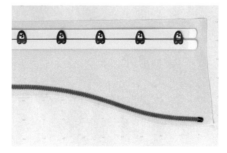

Step 6

- For the closure, use a 'busk': two metal strips containing a knob and loop piece. You could also use hook-and-eye tape.
- For the boning, use metal spiral boning, which, unlike its plastic counterpart, curves with the seaming. This is important, as the two main front seams follow S-curves.

Step 7

- Sew seams and then sew an additional line close to raw edges of the seam allowance, forming a casing into which boning can be inserted.
- In the photograph, it appears that the boning and seaming may be topstitched differently, but this will suffice.

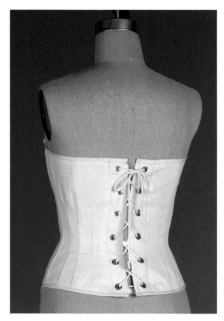

Step 8

- Cut and twist some muslin roughly to give an idea of the form and shape of the flowers you want for the ornamentation. A design assistant can use these mock-ups as a guide when choosing silk flowers for your final piece.

- Attach flower pieces by tacking them onto the top edge or tucking them inside.

Step 9

- The CB will be constructed with a lace-up treatment. This will allow the wearer to adjust the corset and help it further settle into the subtleties of the fit.

- Two boning pieces are placed at the tunnel created by the CB fold. Grommets are attached just to the inside of those tunnels, which helps CB stay straight.

Analysis

- Look carefully at the original Lacroix photograph and your drape. On your toile, the Victorian silhouette has been achieved with the use of two front seams. But the Lacroix has slightly more of an S-curve as it travels from the top edge to the waist. Also, there seems to be less distance in the Lacroix from the top edge to the waist. It appears to be cut slightly lower than the toile, which would account for that.

- The model's waist may be smaller than the mannequin's, but in any case, the waist of the Lacroix looks a little narrower. Notice how the first front seam of the toile is slightly wider at the waist. If the two seams had been brought in a little closer there, this may have given the illusion of a smaller waist.

- Using the designer's skill of visualization, imagine how this would look in the final fabric with the delicate silk flowers. That balance of the push/pull or magnetic/dynamic energy feels present.

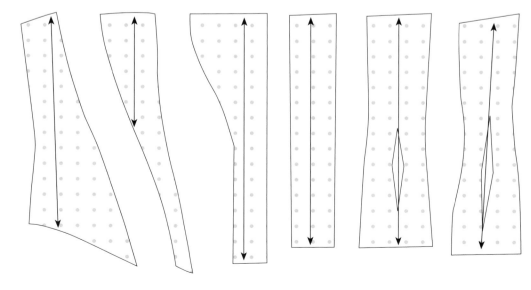

Side front   Mid-front   Centre front   Centre back   Mid-back   Side back

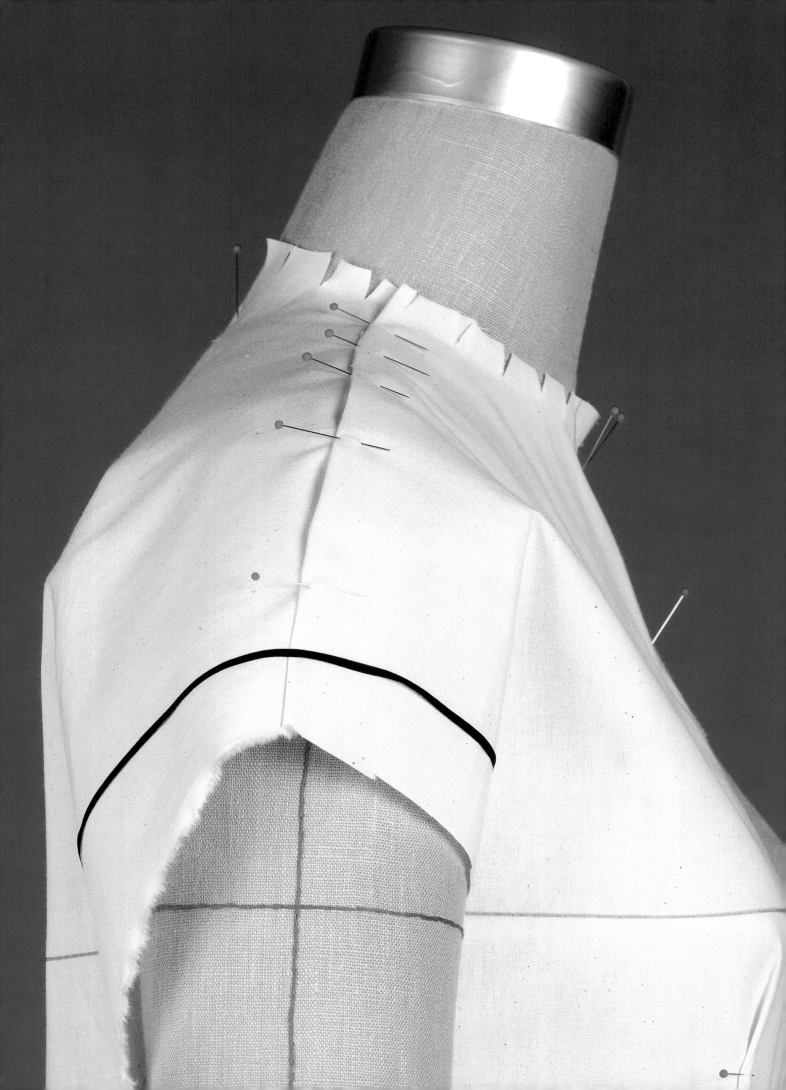

2 Intermediate Draping

2.1 Skirts
2.2 Blouses
2.3 Trousers
2.4 Knits

In this section, your aim is to find the balance of an individual garment or ensemble. The multiple elements in garments such as blouses or jackets are more complex to coordinate than the simpler shapes explored in Part 1. The trained eye begins to recognize a well-proportioned fit, a balanced line, an interesting focal point or a new silhouette.

Now that you have some experience with draping, practice will help you gain precision and dexterity, and basic skills will become second nature. Knowing how to create volume with tucks, pleats and gathers and being able to handle complex curves that work together will allow you to more easily control the silhouette you are creating.

As you gain confidence you will develop a 'good eye'. By maintaining a vision of the finished creation, you will learn to recognize it as the toile takes shape, and your individual style will begin to emerge.

2.1
Skirts

History

In 2004, Prada opened an exhibition called 'Waist Down', featuring skirt designs from 1988 to the present. The variety of shapes was seemingly endless. Pleated, darted, tucked, gored, gathered and ingeniously seamed, each silhouette was unique.

One of the features of the exhibition was an array of spinning skirts suspended by wires from the ceiling. The different shapes they created underscored an important quality of the skirt: the beauty of fabric in motion.

The fitted bodices featured in Chapter 1.2 were created through different methods of darting and seaming. These same techniques, and those listed above, are used to

Left: Visible in the sarongs worn by these two women are the long straight lines that form typically from a simple rectangle tied at the waist. In the garment on the right, the draping effect is created by wrapping and tying at the top edge.

Above: The flat sketch of this Burmese sarong clearly shows the simple shape of the fabric.

engineer movement and flow in skirts. The various effects of these methods result in the myriad of skirt styles worn throughout history.

The earliest skirts were made from simple woven panels worn by both men and women. From culture to culture, differences lay only in the way the panels were wrapped or tied. The Africans of Tanzania had the kanga, pre-Islamic tribes of the Arabian peninsula had the izaar. The sarong, a Malay garment also worn widely in Southeast Asia and the Pacific Islands, continues to appear in modern fashion as a swimsuit wrap or resort skirt.

The way that the fabric panels were fastened to the body defined the silhouette. In Western Europe, peasants used a simple rope-like belt drawn through a folded edge at the top of the skirt to gather in the fullness. Traditional Indian skirts, or ghagras, were made from a very thin silk, with the fabric simply folded repeatedly until it fit the waistline.

Over time, as womens' bodices became more fitted and shaped, skirt panels began also to be cut and more specifically fit. While skirts generally remained long, modestly covering the ankle — at least for non-working women — they fluctuated in width and silhouette,

ranging from the rectangular shape, supported by panniers, of the 1750s, through the narrow silhouette of the Empire line of the 1800s, to the rounder silhouette of the 1850s, formed over the crinoline that required many yards of fabric. Skirts then began to be pulled back by bustles; they continued to shorten until, by 1915, hemlines were finally above the floor.

Skirts held out by petticoats were not really seen again in daywear until Christian Dior's 'New Look' was revealed in 1947. As a reaction to the constraints of the war years, Dior introduced extravagant full skirts with small waists that became the silhouette of the following decade and re-established Paris as a fashion capital.

Hemlines continue to go up and down, bubble skirts go in and out. A fashionable modern skirt today often uses these same timeless techniques of darting, tucking and gathering to sculpt skirt silhouettes that seem fresh yet familiar.

Multiple pleated folds falling open from the waist create the fullness of the traditional Rajasthan ghagra skirt.

Exercises
Kilt

The kilt, a traditional Scottish garment worn by men and women, is a rectangular length of woollen tartan, constructed to lie flat in the front and then pleat symmetrically around the body. The pleats are stitched vertically in place and released at the high hip line, creating the freedom of movement. Compare the silhouette of the Rajasthan ghagra on page 91, also constructed of multiple vertical pleats, with the kilt.

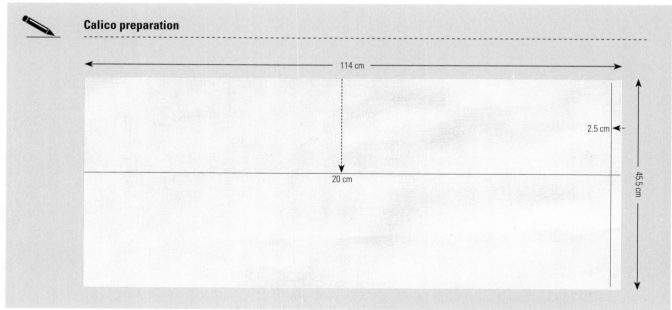

Calico preparation

114 cm

2.5 cm

20 cm

45.5 cm

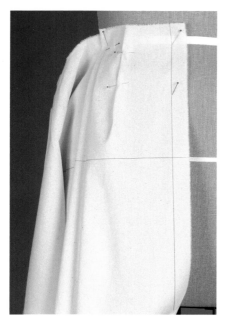

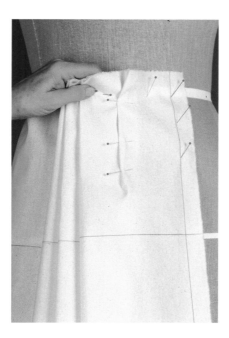

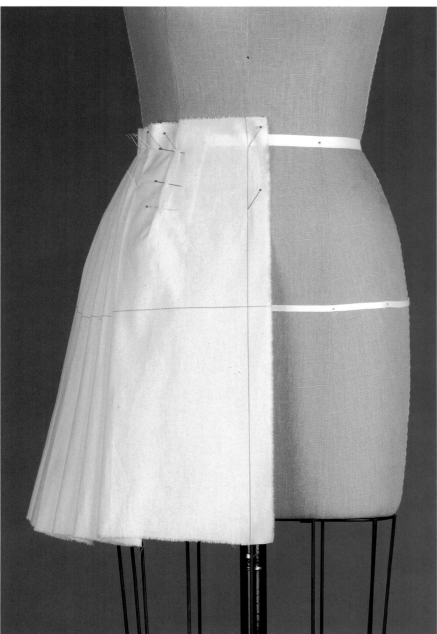

Step 1

- Pin CF line, aligning horizontal grain with hip tape.

- Form a small dart at the princess line to help fit the waist and to keep the horizontal grain level as it travels around the curve of the hip.

Step 2

- Pleat in about 10 cm (4") on each of the pleats until the end of the fabric.

Step 3

- Observe the silhouette created by the pleating. Traditionally, all pleats were sewn down about 10 cm (4") and then released. This treatment creates a silhouette that follows the line of the hip and then flares outwards in an angular way.

Skirt silhouettes

Dirndls and ballet skirts, as with the kilt, are constructed of basic rectangular panels of fabric held in at the waist, as worn for centuries in many cultures. Pleating provides the fullness for the kilt; in dirndl and ballet skirts, the volume is created by simply gathering the fabric at the waist.

In this exercise, you can see how, even when both skirts are made of calico, the lengths of the skirts and the amount of gathers result in very different silhouettes.

Dirndls and ballet skirts

Dirndl: A dirndl is a European folkloric-style skirt worn by peasants for hundreds of years in various cultures. It is made from simple woven panels held at the waist by a band or drawstring.

Ballet skirt: A ballet skirt, obviously inspired by the dance, is generally understood to be any skirt constructed of large volumes of fabric of any length, usually very lightweight, gathered in at the waist.

✏ Calico preparation

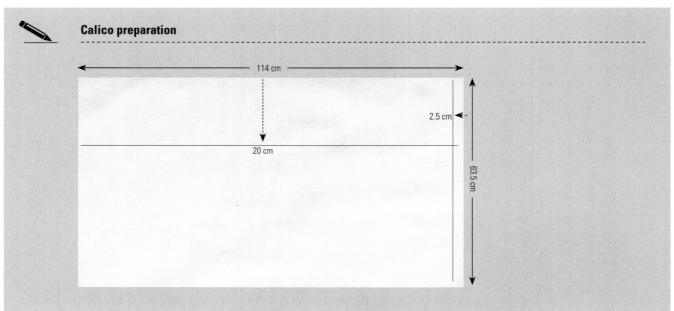

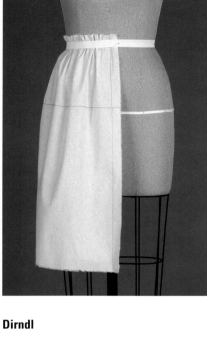

Dirndl

- Prepare for the drape by tying a length of elastic around waist of mannequin.

- Pin calico at CF. Slip top edge under elastic.

- Now adjust the calico, gathering it evenly towards the back, keeping horizontal grain level at hip line.

- Observe the silhouette created: the gathering at the waist causes the fabric to puff out slightly before falling in a straight line.

Ballet skirt

- Measure down 45.5 cm (18") from top edge of dirndl skirt. Tear bottom part of skirt off.

- Adjust gathers towards the front so that what was the centre back line is now even with the side seam.

- Observe the silhouette created by the shorter length and additional fabric. The volume of the gathered fabric pushes the hemline out.

Three simple skirts

Study the three silhouettes carefully so that you begin to train your eye to see the subtle but distinct differences created by the construction techniques.

Note that these pleating, tucking and gathering techniques will create the same types of looks when translated into a sleeve or neckline.

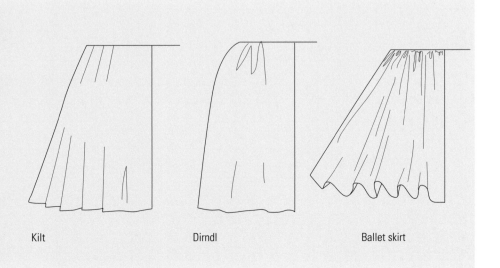

Kilt   Dirndl   Ballet skirt

Straight skirt

The straight skirt can be seen as a modern version of the dirndl as it also is constructed of simple woven rectangles wrapped around the body. However, where the dirndl is gathered at the waist, the straight skirt uses darts to eliminate the fullness, thus creating a smoother line. Often this type of skirt will have a pleat or slit opening from the hem in the centre back for ease of movement.

Sometimes called a 'pencil' skirt, this slim-fitting garment was popularized during World War II when a struggling economy dictated cutting down on fabric usage. What began as a working woman's practical, basic skirt has evolved into a timeless fashion staple.

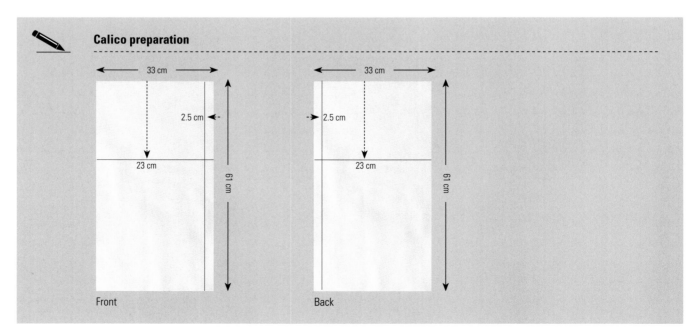

Calico preparation

33 cm

2.5 cm

23 cm

61 cm

Front

33 cm

2.5 cm

23 cm

61 cm

Back

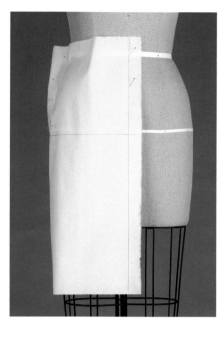
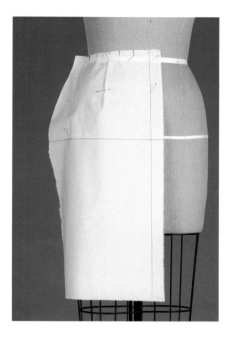
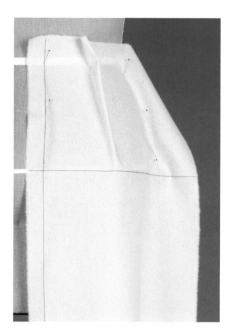

Step 1

- Align CF grainline with CF of mannequin and pin down about 15 cm (6").

- Allowing about 2.5 cm (1") ease, pin at hip line, keeping horizontal grain level.

- Smooth calico from hip line up to waist. Observe excess formed at front.

Step 2

- Fold in princess-line dart with an intake of about 2.5 cm (1") in total.

- Pin from waist to about 10 cm (4") down. Dart should angle slightly out towards the side to shape fullness of front hip area.

- Trim and clip at waistline until calico lies smoothly.

Step 3

- For the back, repeat Step 1.

- As you pin up the side seam, observe that there is even more excess fabric here than in the front due to the rounder shape of the back hip area.

- Experiment with folding darts. A single dart creates a prominent end point and will need to be quite long.

- Try separating ease into two darts. Now darts can be shorter and, because they are not as deep, create a much smoother back area.

Matching horizontal grains

It is not important that the horizontal grains meet. They are there as a guide to keep the grains of the individual pieces of calico balanced. It is not a goal to make them match.

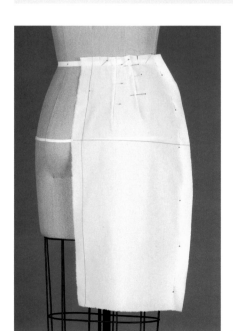

Step 4

- Pin side seams wrong sides together; trim to about 2.5 cm (1").

- Turn front side seam over back side seam, making sure ease is equal in front and back.

Step 5

- Place a tape around the waist to make it easier to mark.

- Turn hem up, levelling it against one of the bars on the cage of the mannequin.

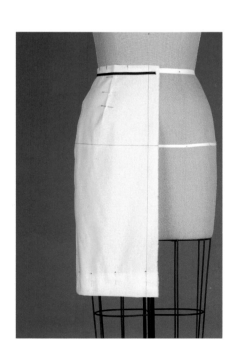

A-line skirt

The flared or 'A-line' skirt generally refers to a style that is closely fitted at the waist or hip and becomes fuller at the hem. The silhouette of this drape will depend on the final fabric being used. A thin silk in a longer length would create a softer, more flowing look at the hemline.

As the skirt is draped over the high hip, the extra fabric will fall towards the front, allowing for a much smaller dart than in the straight skirt.

Do not forget the closure; determine whether you want a side or back zip.

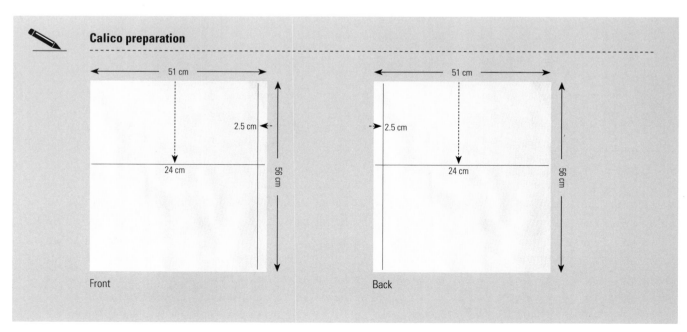

Calico preparation

Front

Back

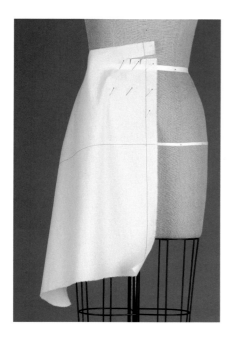

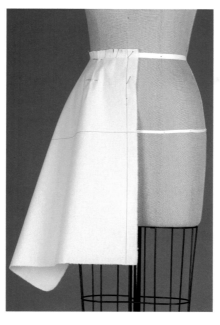

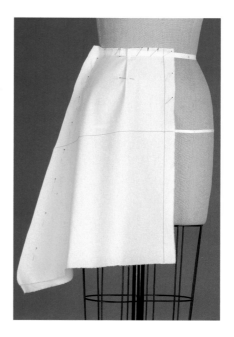

Step 1

- Align CF grainline with CF of mannequin and pin down about 15 cm (6").

- Pin high hip line about 7.5 cm (3") across from CF.

- Start pinning across waistline, trimming and clipping as you go, allowing fabric to fall forwards, starting the flare.

Step 2

- Smooth calico over waist and high hip line, continuing to clip at waistline.

- Form a small dart at princess line to keep flare from becoming too exaggerated.

- Check the photograph. The skirt is fairly flat in the front and the small dart will allow the flare to be controlled towards the side, giving a more balanced look.

Step 3

- Trim away side seam allowance to about 2.5 cm (1"), following side seam of mannequin.

- For the back, repeat from Step 1.

- Pin side seams wrong sides together. Pin line will follow mannequin for about the first 10 cm (4") and then become a straight line, angling out towards hem to create flare.

- Check flare from the side. For this skirt, the flare should be of equal fullness. Note that, classically, skirts are flared slightly more in the back than front for a more graceful flow when in movement.

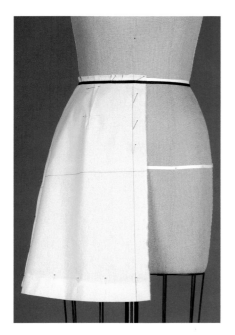

Step 4

- Turn front side seam over back. First, lightly chalk hip line on both sides and draw a crossmark so pieces can be realigned when re-pinning. Remove pins and fold front over back.

- Be accurate with the balance. If the front side seam shifts up in relation to the back, or vice versa, it will change the way the flare drapes. Be careful not to lose the style of drape you have created.

- Twill-tape waist to hold firmly.

- Using a long ruler or right-angled metal ruler, mark hem and turn up.

Side seam

Note that as the front or back waistline shifts up or down, the side seam angle will change as well. The side seam should follow the side seam of the mannequin.

Bias circle skirt

In the bias circle skirt, no darting or seaming is used and the fabric is simply smoothed over the waist and high hip line and allowed to fall freely into flares at the hemline. The straight grains fall at the centre front and back, the horizontal grains at the side seams and the true bias at the princess lines. The generous amount of fabric at the hemline and the use of the bias areas create a wonderful, swirling flow when in motion.

With its upbeat attitude, this skirt became a signature look of the optimistic 1950s. It is seen here on Audrey Hepburn in *Roman Holiday*.

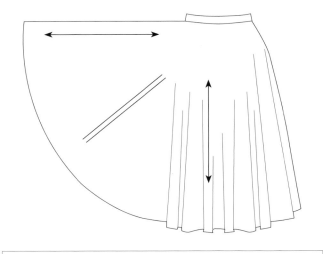

Bias lines

Bias lines are marked as a double line 0.5 cm (⅛") apart.

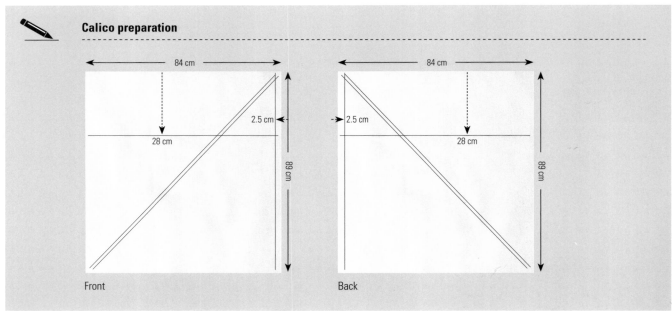

Calico preparation

Front

Back

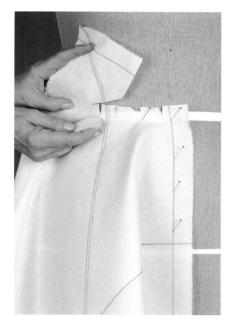

Step 1

- Align CF grainline with CF of mannequin and horizontal grain with hip line. The top edge of the fabric will reach almost to the bust line.

- Pin down the CF about 12.5 cm (5") and across 2.5 cm (1") (latter not shown).

- Slash horizontally about 2.5 cm (1") above the waist and clip to the waist about 2.5 cm (1") towards side seam.

Step 2

- Since you are using entire quarter-circle for half the front, drape top edge downwards so that horizontal grain is now running parallel to side seam of mannequin and bias line is vertical. Bias lines should be at about the princess seam.

- Lightly mark waist with chalk for reference.

Step 3

- Begin trimming and clipping at waist, every 1.5 cm (½"), keeping flare falling evenly.

- Repeat from Step 1 for back.

- Pin front over back at sides.

Clipping and pinning

Remember to be as precise as possible when clipping and pinning. Even a 0.5 cm (¼") difference in the placement of your pin will change the way the flares drape.

Step 4

- Level hem using a right-angled ruler or one of the bars of the mannequin cage. Start at side seam where skirt will be shortest.

- Note how flare can be adjusted by further clipping at waist.

- Finalize waist pins and tie twill tape around waist for an easy waistline marker.

Draping project

This Bill Blass skirt has a basic cut similar to that of the straight skirt on page 96. However, subtle differences in the shape give it a more dynamic attitude. The side seam follows the contours of the body and the hemline 'pegs in', or narrows at the knee. The high waist and close fit accentuate the classic, curvy feminine hourglass shape.

Catwalk models are typically very tall. When planning your calico pieces for the drape, consider any difference in proportion between what you see in the photograph and the eventual size you are working towards. Before starting the drape, decide on the length of your skirt. This will make it easier to establish the rest of the proportions. You also will need to decide how much 'ease', or extra fabric, will be built into the fit of the skirt. It appears to be very fitted on the model, but practically speaking, it needs to have at least 2.5–5 cm (1–2") ease at the hip.

As you begin the drape, visualize the wearer, the shape of the skirt and the strong, sexy look.

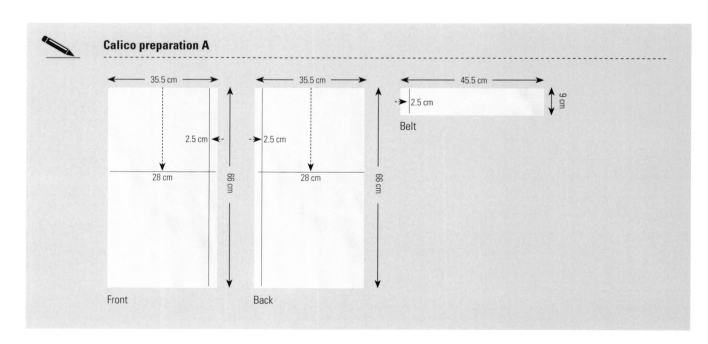

Calico preparation A

35.5 cm

2.5 cm

28 cm

66 cm

Front

35.5 cm

2.5 cm

28 cm

66 cm

Back

45.5 cm

2.5 cm

9 cm

Belt

Step 1

- Align CF grainline with CF of mannequin and horizontal grain with hip line. Pin down about 15 cm (6").

- Calculate how much ease you will have at the hip/side seam area and pin from hip line to waist.

- To place the dart, study the photograph and note that the high hip area has a broad feeling to it. This is partially because of the horizontal stripes, but also because the dart is towards the side of the princess line and angles slightly outwards. Pin the dart from the waist to the lower end.

- Because the dart is angled towards the side at the lower end, as it runs up past the waist it naturally continues that angle, which becomes unflattering. You will need to clip the dart to angle it towards the side above the waist.

Step 2

- Unpin CF and clip dart in centre near waistline.

Step 3

- Pin dart again, with its top end angling towards side seam. This will accentuate the waist-conscious look.

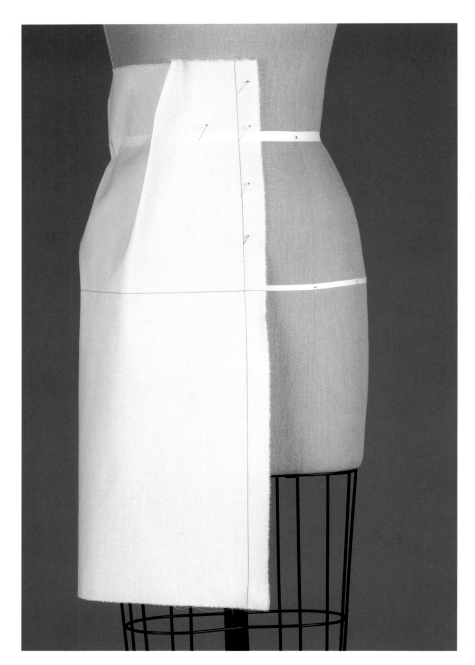

Precision pinning

The more accurate your drape, the easier it will be to transfer it to a paper pattern. Practise pinning very carefully, placing pins horizontal to the seams as shown. Crease the folds of the fabric as evenly as possible. If you are experiencing puckers, try re-pinning one pin at a time to figure out where the problem lies.

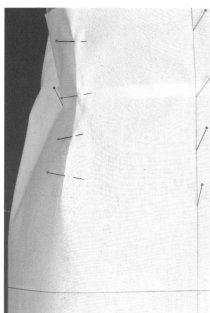

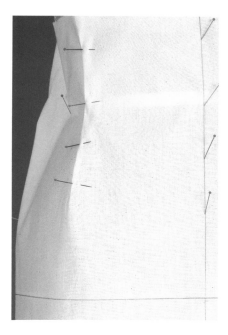

Step 4

- Determine side seam by looking at the photograph and determining angle of peg. Keep horizontal grain level.

- Check seam in the mirror and against the sketch.

- Pin side seam to mannequin, leaving some ease.

- Trim seam allowance to about 1" (2.5 cm).

- Clip at waistline.

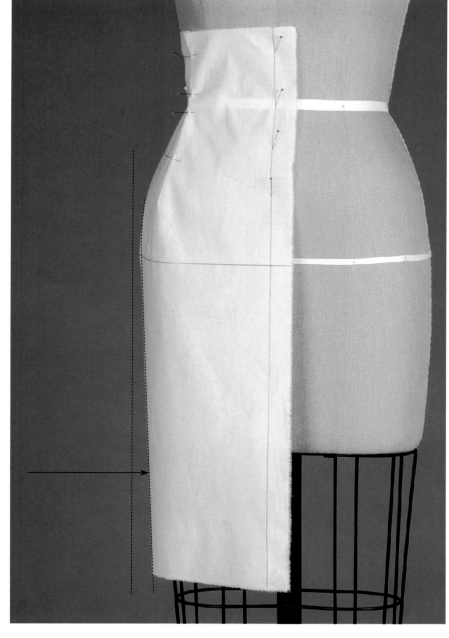

Step 5

- Align CB straight grain with CB of mannequin, aligning hip horizontal grain with hip tape.

- Fold in double darts at back waist, clipping as with front.

- Pin side seam to mannequin, from hip line up. Trim to 2.5 cm (1").

Step 6

- Pin side seam to front from hip line down.

- Check peg in the mirror and against the sketch.

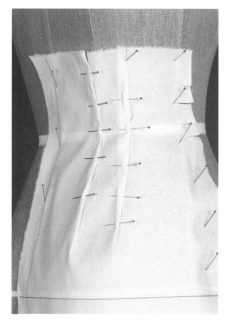

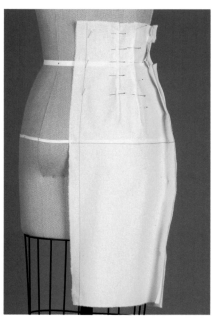

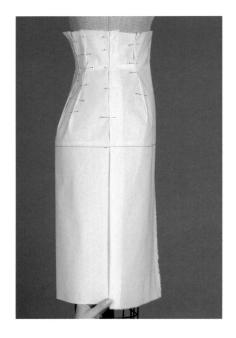
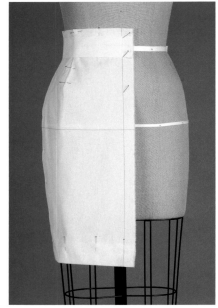
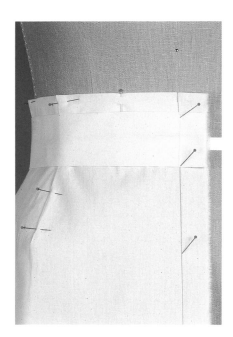

Step 7

- Pin front over back at side seams. Start at hip line and pin up.

- Now hold at hem and fold the two pieces in, holding calico taut so that it falls into place smoothly.

- Check the silhouette from 360°. Is there the right angle of the pegged side seam from waist to knee? Does it have the hourglass curve?

Step 8

- To drape the belt, first check the sketch. The belt is as much as 5 cm (2") wide.

- Chalk-mark the lines and press under both raw edges to create a 5 cm (2") piece.

- Drape around waist, about two-thirds above the waist and one-third below.

- Turn under top edge of skirt and the hem.

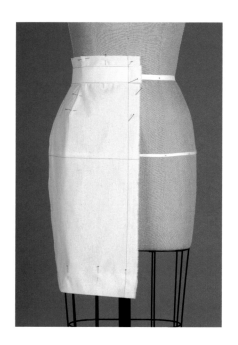

Step 9

- If the belt seems too wide, try a smaller proportion. On these narrow pieces, even 0.5 cm (¼") makes a big difference.

- Mark all seams and darts.

Checking proportions

Details such as the belt width are very important to setting the proportions. Study how the two different widths change the look of the skirt from slightly clunky and awkward with the wider belt to more refined with the narrower belt.

Marking and truing

It is not always the case that the front and back curves will match; some specific styles will call for a differently shaped seam. In this case, however, the front and back have similar shapes. You will even them out to be assured of a smooth side seam.

When the hem is a concave curve such as this one, either the hem must be small enough to be able to turn back comfortably, perhaps 2.5–4 cm (1–1½"), or it must be finished with a facing.

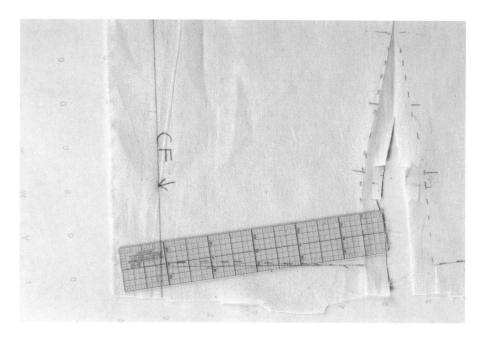

Step 1

- Draw dart lines and cut seam allowance to 1.5 cm (½").

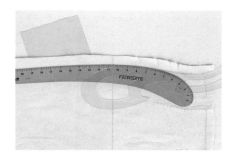

Step 2

- Draw side seam line of front and back.
- Pin front and back together, matching waistlines and at hem.
- Slide a piece of carbon paper underneath the back; using a tracing wheel, mark the curve of the front side seam onto the back side seam.

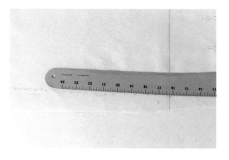

Step 3

- Compare the two side seam lines – they should balance. If one is much larger than the other, take the measurement. Add a little to the smaller one and subtract from the larger to balance them out.

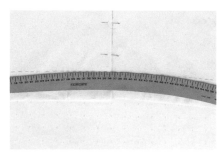

Step 4

- Use a hem curve to draw the hemline; it will be slightly concave because of the peg of the skirt. From your pattern-cutting knowledge, you know that side seams will have to be drawn at a right angle to the hemline. Therefore, the hemline will naturally slant up towards the skirt. After drawing in the right angles, the line will straighten out in the centres of the front and back hemlines.
- Using a clear grading ruler, add seam allowances to edges as follows:
  - Side seams: 2 cm (¾")
  - Top edge: 1.5 cm (½")
  - Hem: 2.5 cm (1").

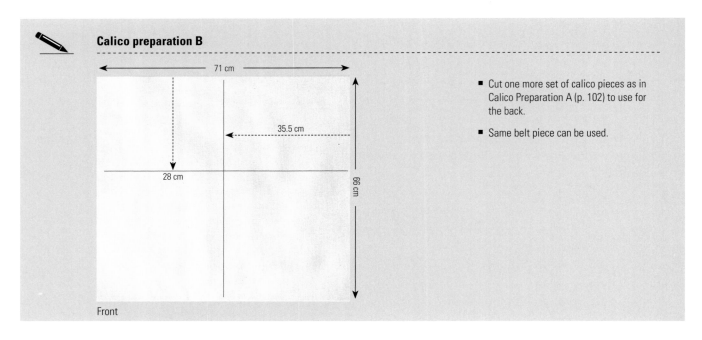

71 cm

35.5 cm

28 cm

66 cm

Front

- Cut one more set of calico pieces as in Calico Preparation A (p. 102) to use for the back.

- Same belt piece can be used.

For this skirt, sew the full toile. You will, therefore, need to cut the mirror-image front and back sections.

- First, block the new calico pieces, and draw straight and horizontal grains as shown in calico-preparation diagram.

- For the front, use centre straight grain as a foldline and align CF line of draped piece onto fold of new calico. Align horizontal grains and pin into place.

- Cut the two pieces together along the lines you have trued and to which you have added seam allowance.

- For the back pieces, align straight and horizontal grains, pin into place and again cut along trued lines to which you have added seam allowance.

- Clip in at crossmarks, no more than 0.5 cm (¼").

- Use tracing paper and a tracing wheel to mark darts or any interior lines. Slip tracing paper underneath the calico and draw the dart lines with the tracing wheel. Since you are working with a double piece, you must also mark the other side by placing tracing paper underneath the folded piece and drawing the line a second time.

Analysis

- To analyse your skirt drape, have the photograph on hand and get a little distance from the mannequin. How well has the shape worked? Does it have the right amount of fit to be comfortable yet have the body-conscious attitude of the photo?

- Study the side seam. Looking at the negative space, try to see if your drape has the same angle from the waist to hem as the photograph.

- The belt is an accessory, but here it plays an important part in assessing the proportions. After adjusting it during draping, it seems to be the right look.

- It can be challenging to visualize the toile in the black stripe fabric, but it is a good exercise to try to see it.

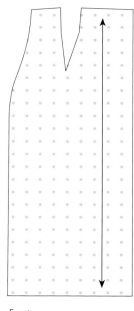

Front

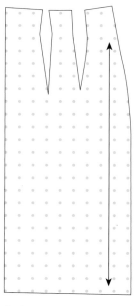

Back

Belt

Variations
Yoked skirt with gathers and flare

The fitted panel, or yoke, of this skirt provides a base that supports the gathered and flared lower section. Because the yoke ends at the high hip line, no darts are necessary. The top edge will curve, creating the fit. Note how the hem falls in rolling flares, similar to the bias circle skirt. Because the skirt section is not rectangular but curved, the side areas begin to incorporate some bias grain, which gives the skirt a lovely swing as it moves.

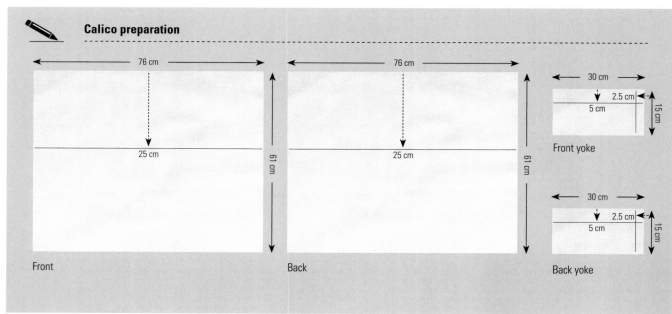

Calico preparation

Front — 76 cm · 25 cm · 61 cm

Back — 76 cm · 25 cm · 61 cm

Front yoke — 30 cm · 2.5 cm · 5 cm · 15 cm

Back yoke — 30 cm · 2.5 cm · 5 cm · 15 cm

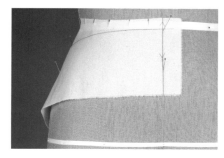

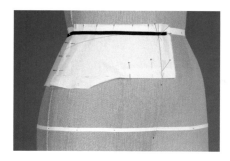

Step 1

- To set front yoke piece, align CF grainline with CF of mannequin and horizontal grain with waist tape.

- Pin downwards and flat across waistline for the first 2.5 cm (1").

- Then trim and clip, smoothing yoke towards side seam.

- Repeat for back yoke.

Step 2

- Pin yoke wrong sides together at side seam. Since weight of the skirt will hang from the yoke, it can be draped quite close to the mannequin with no ease.

- Turn front over back and pin.

- Twill-tape waist and anchor-pin firmly at CF and CB.

- Determine necessary width of yoke to create desired proportion; measure and lightly chalk the line.

- Turn up yoke edge along marked line.

Step 3

- To drape the skirt front, you will create flare and gathers. As in the dance tunic exercise on pp. 26–29, set a piece of elastic to help you adjust fabric evenly.

- Lift yoke pieces up gently and pin a piece of elastic about 2.5 cm (1") above yoke line, keeping elastic horizontal to floor.

- Slip skirt front under elastic, aligning CF grainlines. Pull it up evenly to 10–15 cm (4–6") above elastic.

- Note the silhouette is now the same as that of the dirndl on pp. 94–95. Since you want some flare in the skirt, the rectangle will need to become a curved piece.

Step 5

- Pin side seams together.

- Trim top edge just above elastic piece.

- Finalize gathering. Note how, in the photograph, sides are fairly flat to give a more flattering silhouette and gathering is concentrated towards CF and CB.

- Fold yoke back down and pin to skirt along folded edge.

- Turn up hem using bar of mannequin cage to level.

Step 4

- Reference the drape of the bias circle skirt on pp. 100–101 and note how the fabric drops to the side as you clip and create the curve. Starting at the side seam, grasp the fabric at the hem and pull downwards, adjusting the gathers as you go, and note how the flare is being created. Continue until the desired flare is reached.

- Note that the horizontal grain is no longer horizontal, but drops down towards side seam. The side seam will now be angled and large triangle at top edge can be cut away.

- Repeat from Step 3 for back section.

2.2
Blouses

History

Early clothing often consisted of variations and layers of tunics – woven panels wrapped and tied in ways particular to a certain region or tribe. In Western culture, these simple shapes evolved into the 'peasant' smock, which made use of gathers and combinations of square-cut panels.

By the late fourteenth century, panels were being cut and shaped into more elaborate forms for men's 'shirts'.

For women, however, the 'blouse' didn't make an appearance in the fashionable wardrobe until the 1860s, when Empress Eugénie of France popularized the red Garibaldi shirt, named for the Italian revolutionary. The garment echoed a man's shirt and was cut from a series of squares and rectangles fashioned from a single piece of cloth with no wastage.

When the concept of the yoke was introduced, along with shaped armholes and sleeve heads, this shaped shirt offered a much more comfortable fit and became the precursor to the woman's blouse. By the 1890s, the 'shirtwaist' was developed in response to the needs of a rising number of women entering employment who required a new, practical look.

In modern fashion, women's blouses are among the most complex cuts of garments and are often beautifully detailed and embellished, as were the peasant smocks of centuries past.

This detail from a 1494 painting by Carpaccio shows men wearing very fitted, complex garments, made from cut and shaped woven panels.

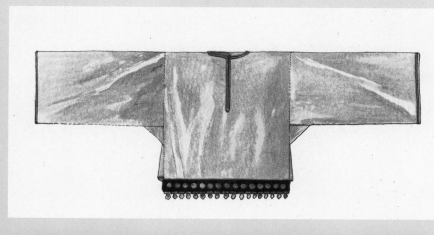

This shirt of a Tartar woman from Nucha illustrates the simplicity with which the early 'blouse' was traditionally constructed. The ribbon trim, gold plaques and coins at the hem exemplify the elaborate ornamentation used in many cultures.

This cotton shirt from about 1866–90 shows a similar construction to the peasant blouse: front and back rectangular panels with an underarm gusset.

Fold →

This modern version of a peasant blouse is the same cut as the historical one in the illustration of the Tartar woman's shirt (above). Note how the triangular piece at the underarm is a folded square, creating a gusset that allows for more movement of the arms.

Exercises
Draping the blouse

Techniques such as pleating, tucking and gathering that bring volume and movement to skirts are similarly used in blouses to create the shapes needed to fit the curves of a woman's shoulders, bust and waistline.

Proportion is of utmost importance in blouses, as there are multiple elements to coordinate. The height of the neckline, shape of the sleeve and cut of the side seams must flow together. The sizing of collars, cuffs and buttons must be coordinated to keep the whole in balance.

Blouses are usually lightly fitted for comfort. Draping construction elements such as gathering or tucking must be done with practical sensitivity to the shapes they are accommodating. Areas that need ease, such as the bust, top of the arm and shoulder blades, require working away from the mannequin as opposed to fitting to it. This takes practice and skill.

The fitted sleeve and curved armhole of the modern blouse were a later development in clothing. Compared to the elegant, elemental forms created by square/rectangular woven panels, modern sleeves and armholes are far trickier to engineer. The combination of curves that comprise a graceful and well-fitting sleeve is complex but very important to master. A sleeve often tends to be a focal point, and frames the upper torso. If an armhole is awkward, the untrained eye may not know why the garment does not look right but will be instinctively aware that something is askew.

Sleeves and armholes: An infinite variety of curves

The armhole and sleeve fit together in a complex combination of curves. Slight differences in these curves result in a drastically different look and fit to a sleeve.

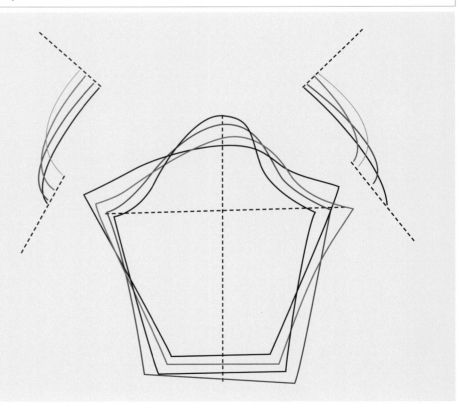

Since sleeves are relatively difficult to drape, it will help to understand some basics of how sleeve patterns work before beginning the draping exercises. Shown here are three sleeves and armholes that create very different effects. Study the differences in the curves of the sleeve patterns and the resulting underarm fit to understand how carving out more in the lower curve functions like a dart to remove fullness from that area.

Traditional African daishiki

The sleeves and body of this traditional tunic are cut geometrically as squares/rectangles. The fit is full and graceful. Note the many folds of fabric that result as the sleeve falls to the side, but also that full freedom of movement is possible.

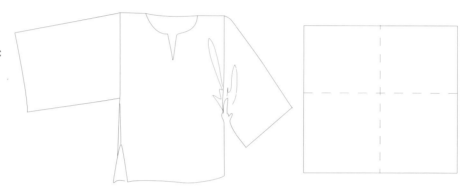

Classic shirt

On this classic shirt, the yoke absorbs some of the bust and armhole ease. There are no darts; it is loose fitting. Note how the curve at the sleeve crown has allowed a wedge of fabric to be cut away. There are still folds and fullness at the underarm area, though not as much as with the daishiki. The arm can still be lifted fairly high.

Women's tuxedo shirt

This slim-fitting women's tuxedo shirt has a front panel at the princess line that absorbs bust ease, taking the place of a dart. The crown of this sleeve is quite high, which allows the underarm area to be closely fitted. Note the additional fabric that has been removed from the sleeve pattern lower curve, and with that, the folds at the underarm. However, here the lift of the arm is more limited.

Peasant blouse

In this peasant blouse, based on a jumpsuit from the Moschino Spring/Summer 2008 collection, the front, back and sleeves are cut from rectangles that are gathered around the neckline. The uniqueness of this garment is in the play of its proportions. The elongated front and back is accented by the wide epaulettes, cuffs and placket.

Adapting existing styles

Quite often in fashion, designers will adapt existing styles or classic cuts to suit their own purposes. Here, a one-piece garment has been cut off just below the high hip line and made into a blouse.

Calico preparation

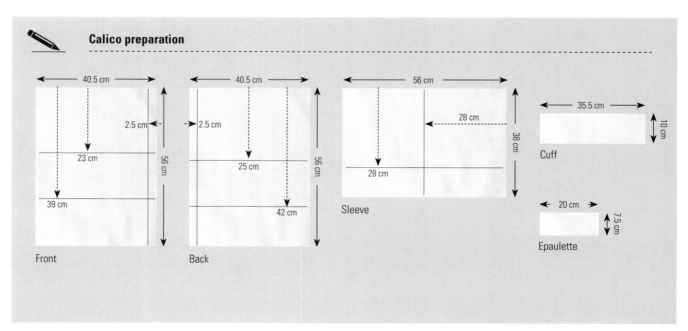

Front — 40.5 cm, 2.5 cm, 23 cm, 39 cm, 56 cm

Back — 40.5 cm, 2.5 cm, 25 cm, 42 cm, 56 cm

Sleeve — 56 cm, 28 cm, 28 cm, 38 cm

Cuff — 35.5 cm, 10 cm

Epaulette — 20 cm, 7.5 cm

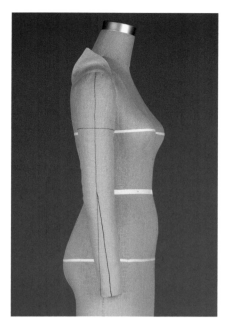

Step 1

- Attach stuffed arm to mannequin by pinning triangular piece onto shoulder area from the point and at the two edges. The arm seam should line up with the edge of the mannequin's shoulder. Do not let it hang over the edge; pin it firmly.

- Note that the arm should angle slightly towards the front with a similar hang to the natural position of the arm.

Step 2

- Pin CF straight grain down CF of mannequin, aligning first horizontal grain with bust tape and second with waistline.

- Check photo and determine amount of fullness to the front of the blouse, then pin at side seam area (not shown), keeping bust horizontal grain level.

- Hold in top area of calico to check amount of gathers, then pin in place.

Step 3

- Pin a piece of twill tape over gathers to help keep them evenly distributed.

- Repeat from Step 1 for back section. Coordinate the gathers with the front, creating an equal amount at the back.

- Pin front and back side seams together wrong sides out, flaring slightly at hem.

Step 4

- Place sleeve piece on stuffed arm, aligning straight grain with centre line on arm.

- Clip to seam allowance at underarm to allow you to turn front over back and pin down side seam (not shown).

Basic construction of the blouse

What you have now are two squares similar to those in the blouse illustrations on p. 115. The basic construction of the blouse is similar. Seeing this will help you to visualize how the sleeves may be attached to the body pieces.

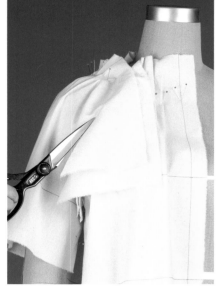

Step 5

- Drape sleeve by aligning straight grain of calico with shoulder line and outside line of stuffed arm, and horizontal grain of musin with underarm line of stuffed arm.

- Hold in fullness at shoulder area and pin in place.

- Lift arm and check photograph to determine volume of sleeve.

- Pin underarm seam wrong sides together, matching horizontal grains.

- Clip to seam allowance about 7 cm (2–3") above underarm line, to allow you to turn and pin underarm area front over back.

Step 6

- Trim away excess triangles of fabric formed at the front and back of the top of the sleeve.

- Now trim away the similar triangles formed at the front and back of the blouse sections.

Step 7

- Tie a length of twill tape or elastic around cuff area to start getting an idea of the volume of the sleeve.

- Pin sleeve section over front and back sections, starting in the middle and then working upwards to neckline and downwards towards underarm.

- Study carefully how look of sleeve changes as you shift sleeve seam back and forth, taking more or less fabric into armhole. Now shift sleeve seam up and down and observe again the change in shape. Check the photograph and try to place sleeve seam at the same angle.

Pinning the underarm area

The underarm area is difficult to pin. It takes practice, but it is an important part of the silhouette you are creating. Try twisting the arm a bit towards the back and using the stuffed arm to press against while you pin. About the last 7 cm (2–3") of the underarm seam and of the side seam can also be left unpinned and then finished up on the table after you remove the drape from the mannequin.

Step 8

- When working with the final proportions, it helps to have the photograph right next to the drape so you can continually check on the details you are draping.

- Drape sleeve band around sleeve hem and adjust gathers to determine length and volume.

- Twill-tape neckline and hemline following style lines in the photograph. To visualize the look, it may help to cut the excess from hem and neckline.

Step 9

- Use finishing details such as the epaulette, buttons and placket to help you achieve the right proportions.

Balancing the proportions of the details

The success of your blouse drape will depend on the way the proportions of the details are balanced. The size of the cuffs and epaulettes, for example, must relate to each other and complement the volume of the blouse – not too large and not too small.

Experiment with your widths and observe how minor changes shift the look.

Gibson Girl blouse

The 'ideal' American woman of the 1900s was created by artist Charles Dana Gibson. The Gibson Girl had an upright posture, luxurious hair and a tiny waist. The classic version of her blouse was a yoke style, with buttons down the back, puff sleeves and a stand collar. It was sold in more than a hundred variations at the height of its popularity.

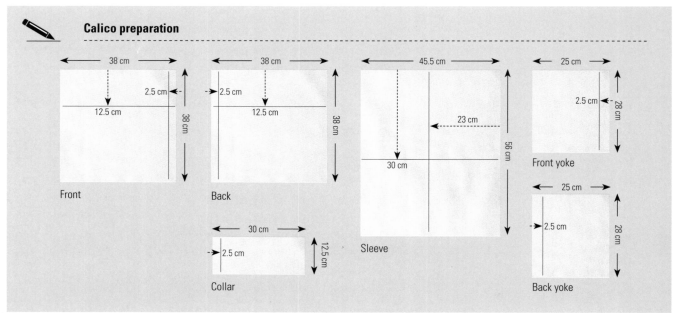

Calico preparation

Front — 38 cm, 2.5 cm, 12.5 cm, 38 cm

Back — 38 cm, 2.5 cm, 12.5 cm, 38 cm

Sleeve — 45.5 cm, 23 cm, 30 cm, 56 cm

Front yoke — 25 cm, 2.5 cm, 28 cm

Collar — 30 cm, 2.5 cm, 12.5 cm

Back yoke — 25 cm, 2.5 cm, 28 cm

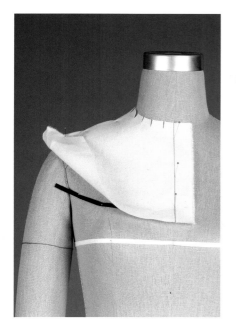

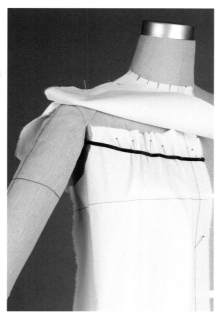

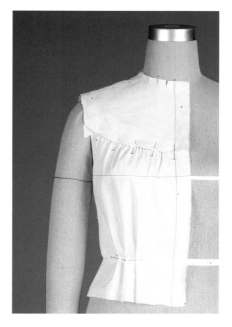

Step 1

- Tape position of yoke line on mannequin.

- Pin front yoke section to mannequin, aligning CF grainline with CF of mannequin, trimming and clipping neckline until it lies smoothly.

- Trim yoke line following twill tape, leaving at least 2.5 cm (1") seam allowance.

- Pin back yoke section to mannequin, aligning CB grainline with CB of mannequin, trimming and clipping neckline as front (not shown).

- Trim shoulder excess and pin front over back.

Step 2

- Flip up yoke to get it out of the way, then set front section by aligning CF with CF of mannequin and horizontal grain with bust tape.

- Study the photograph and try to determine volume of the front piece. Set a pin at the side seam.

- Place twill tape across yoke line and pull the fabric underneath it. This will help you adjust the gathers. Arrange more fullness over the bust where it is needed and less gathering towards the side, where it will create unwanted volume.

- Cut away the armhole section to allow side seam to lie smoothly up into underarm area.

Step 3

- Fold in a few tucks under bust at waistline to help control shape of bodice.

- Check the photograph and make sure you have the rounded look at the bust.

- Repeat from Step 2 for back section.

- Pin side seams together and turn front over back. (Pin wrong sides together first if you need to, then mark, unpin and turn.)

- Turn yokes back down. Shape curve and pin to the bodice front, continuing to adjust gathers evenly.

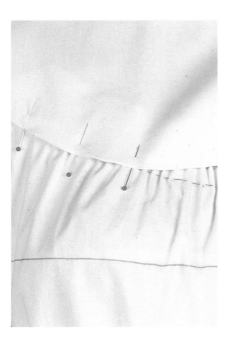

Step 4

- If gathers do not look even, you can use a running baste (tack) along the seam line.

- Mark armhole with tape or twill. The armhole will be the classic shape: the front lower curve carved out slightly more than the straighter curve of the back. Because a sleeve is being attached, the armhole will be slightly lower than on a sleeveless bodice.

- Mark neckline with tape. At CF, it should be about 1.5 cm (½") below mannequin neckline, and at neckline seam of mannequin at CB.

- Check your taped lines against the photograph and mark them lightly with chalk. Remove tape before beginning sleeve drape.

Easy sleeve draft

The next step is to drape the sleeve. You can either drape it from scratch (see p. 126, Step 5), or you can use the easy sleeve draft method shown here as a starting point.

There are many methods to draft sleeves using precise measurements rather than draping. With draping, however, you have the advantage of being able to see the shape you are creating as it develops, and the flexibility to further refine its subtleties.

This particular method is intended to help you drape the sleeve. Having some measurements and a basic shape to follow is useful when starting the drape. It is not, however, intended to be a final pattern, but rather a time-saving device to set the general parameters of the sleeve's volume.

This draft can be done on paper and then transferred to a calico piece, or it can be drawn directly onto the calico.

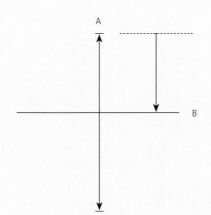

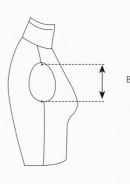

Step 1

- Determine length of sleeve, A, by measuring from edge of armhole at the shoulder to wrist or to the place on the arm where sleeve will finish.

- Draw a vertical line and label it 'A'. This also signifies straight grain of fabric.

  Gibson Girl blouse: A = 51 cm (20"); three-quarter-length sleeve

Step 2

- Next determine crown height, B. This is the length from sleeve crown to underarm line. There are three ways to arrive at this measurement:

  1. Divide armhole measurement by three (crown height is one-third of armhole measurement).

  2. Measure drop of underarm from edge of shoulder to where armhole ends below underarm.

  3. Estimate underarm length. Decide on optimum lift of arm and measure from the wrist to bottom of armhole. In this way, you arrive at the horizontal line on the pattern by measuring from the wrist up rather than from the top edge down.

- Using one or more of these methods, or perhaps an average of the three, measure down from top of vertical line and draw a horizontal line centred on the vertical line, labelling it 'B'. This is the underarm line and also signifies the horizontal grain.

  Gibson Girl blouse: B = 23 cm (9")

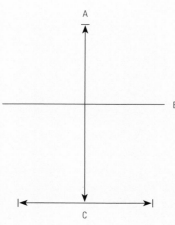

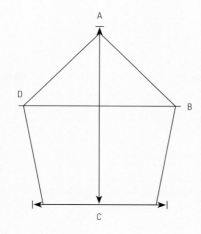

Step 3

- Estimate hem circumference, C. Approximate amount of fullness at hem edge and draw a horizontal line centred at the bottom of the vertical straight grainline A. Label this horizontal line 'C'.

  Gibson Girl blouse: C = 35.5 cm (14")

Step 4

- Determine underarm circumference, D. To do this, set points on line B to create angle of crown height to underarm line. The traditional method is to calculate half of the armhole measurement and draw the diagonal line of that length between the top of line A to the point where it meets line B to the left and right. Label these new points 'D'.

- An alternative method is to simply approximate the volume of the sleeve you want at the height of the underarm line, which is the underarm line for a higher armhole, or 2.5 cm (1") or so below that for a lower armhole. Centre this measurement on line A and mark points to the left and right on line B. Draw diagonal lines to the left and right from the top of line A to meet the points on line B.

- Draw lines from both points D to each end of line C.

  Gibson Girl blouse: D = 28 cm (11")

Step 5

- Now create S-curve of sleeve crown.

- Mark front and back of sleeve. Front is usually on right and back on left.

- Divide the lines from A to D into thirds.

- On the front, mark a point 2 cm (¾") out from the mark signifying the top third.

- On the back, mark a point 1.5 cm (½") out from the mark signifying the top third.

- Draw a line from the above points through the lower third point. This intersection at the lower third point is called the 'pivot point'. It is the place where the sleeve goes from following the top of the armhole with a convex curve to falling towards the lower armhole in a concave curve.

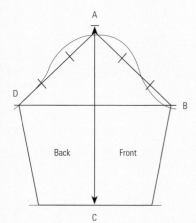

Step 6

- Draw S-curve from top of line A through pivot point to underarm line B.

- Study the shape of the sleeve. It helps to be able to visualize the eventual shape of your pattern piece when you are draping, even if it is only a starting point for the sleeve.

The shape of the sleeve crown

The upper third of the front part of the sleeve is larger than the back of the sleeve to accommodate the bony part of the shoulder about 2.5–5 cm (1–2") below the top of the shoulder. The slope at the back of the sleeve is softer and wider to create extra room for the arm to move forwards.

Measuring the crown height

- Observe what happens when a simple square shape is used to wrap the arm. When matched at the underarm side seam, the obvious missing shape is the triangle needed to fill in the space up to the shoulder. This is called the crown of the sleeve.

- Measure the distance from the edge of the shoulder seam to the top edge of the fabric as it matches up with the lower edge of the armhole. This will be your 'crown height'.

- Sleeves are easier to drape if you begin with some target measurements such as this one.

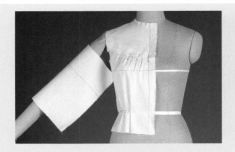

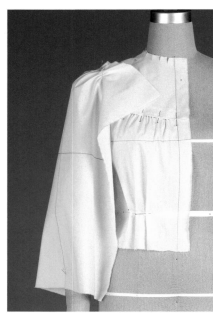

Step 5

- If you have used the Easy Sleeve Draft, lightly mark the lines on the calico to use as reference. If you have draped from scratch, take crown height measurement (see box above) and mark it on the calico for reference.

- Align straight grain with outer line of stuffed arm. Pin at underarm line and again towards wrist area.

- Allow sleeve to angle slightly forwards following natural hang of arm, indicated by the blue line on the stuffed arm.

- As the triangle of excess fabric folds back, you can see the shape of the sleeve starting to emerge.

Step 6

- Set crown volume by pinning in gathers until the look of the photograph is achieved.

Step 7

- Starting at the wrist, determine volume of lower edge. It looks in the photograph as if it may be slightly flared.

- Pin wrong sides together about halfway up to elbow area.

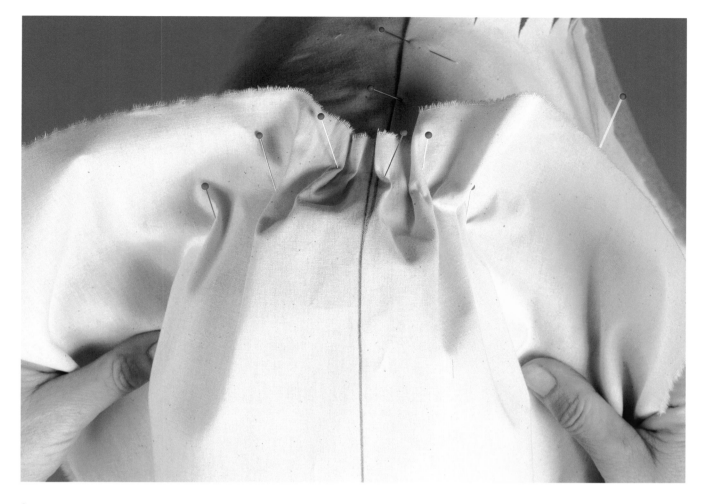

Step 8

- Set the notch points. Start by looking at the sleeve from the side and determine the volume around the arm at about the underarm level. Check sleeve through 360° and adjust volume until you feel it has the look of the photo. The notch point, or 'pivot point', is the point where the sleeve head begins to fall to the underside of the arm. Experiment with moving notch point of sleeve piece up and down the armhole 2.5 cm (1") or so, and notice how this changes the balance of the sleeve drape. Find the position that feels the most balanced and graceful.

- Pin firmly at front and back to about halfway down depth of armhole.

- Clip to the pin, and trim off excess triangle above it (not shown).

Pinning the underarm

Pinning the underarm is an awkward process that takes some practice. Try using the stuffed arm to support the seam as you pin.

Step 9

- Turn underarm seam of sleeve front over back from wrist to elbow, checking that horizontal grains are matching up.

- Once it is turned, tie a piece of twill tape or elastic at lower edge and begin to adjust gathers.

- Check drape from the side and make back slightly longer than front to allow room for elbow. Trim the excess, leaving about 1.5 cm (½") seam allowance (not shown).

Step 10

- Finish crown adjustment by checking the balance again and turning it under along armhole line.

- Turn triangles of excess fabric below notch to the inside and allow them to fall along armhole line.

- Pin along lower curve, raising and lowering stuffed arm and studying the way the sleeve 'breaks'. Ideally, armhole seam should be covered by drape of sleeve.

- Alternately, pin down underarm seam on sleeve and up underarm seam to armhole.

- The last 7 cm or so (2–3") will be difficult to finesse; after you have finished the collar drape, it is acceptable to remove the blouse from the mannequin and finish pinning this area last (see Step 13).

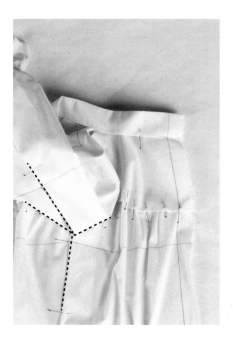

Collars

Collars can be draped from front to back or from back to front. This simple band collar will start from the front. The closure will be at the back.

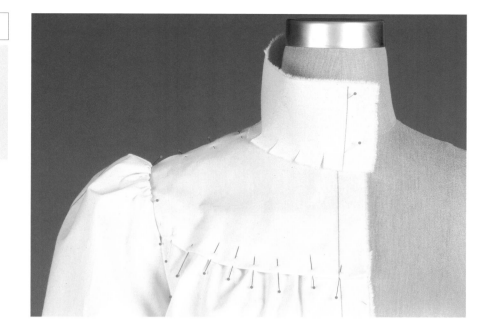

Step 11

- Start the collar at CF by aligning straight grains. Pin firmly and begin clipping to neckline as you wrap band collar around to back.

Step 12

- Turn upper edge over to desired width.
- Turn lower edge under and pin to neckline.

Step 13

- Mark sleeve and remove calico from mannequin. You can continue pinning the underarm seam on the table (see Step 10).
- Study shape of sleeve and height of your crown. The underarm point of front and back should be on the same horizontal grain, and the shape should look similar to the flat sketch below.

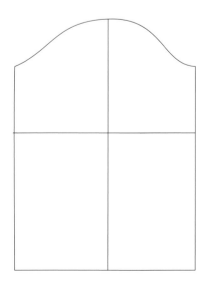

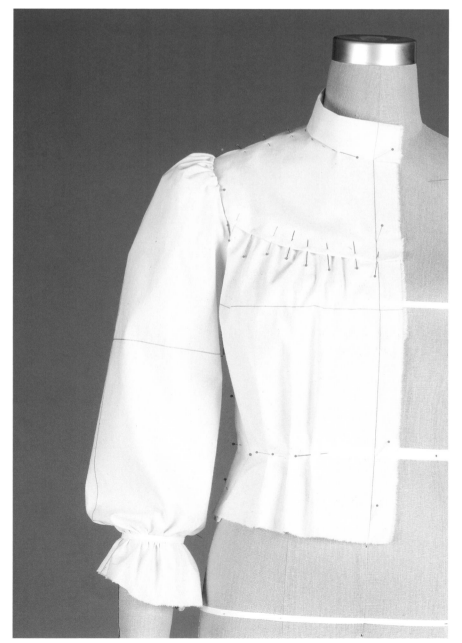

Draping project

A modern version of the Gibson Girl blouse can be seen in this design from Bill Blass.

Both blouses strike a balance between the masculine and the feminine. The tailored elements, the collar and cuffs, reference the feel of a strong, independent, working woman's blouse, while the shapes have a soft femininity. The convertible collar frames the face and the sleeves frame the torso; achieving the right proportions of these is key.

In making construction decisions for the bust fit, the ribbon trim will work well to hide a princess-line seam.

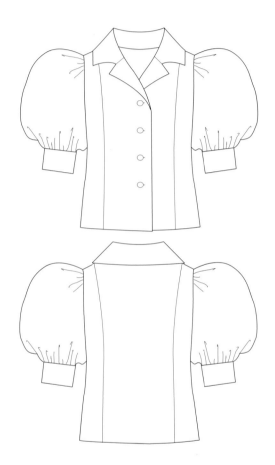

Visualizing the volume

The focal point of the blouse is the exaggerated sleeve. Because the fabric is a sheer organza, the sleeve can be large without seeming too overwhelming. Visualize the wearer and try to set a proportion for the sleeve. Use a tape measure to determine an approximate circumference.

As you begin to drape the blouse, try to feel what it would be like to wear it. How much ease is there in the torso? How much puff does the sleeve need to be a focal point without being out of proportion?

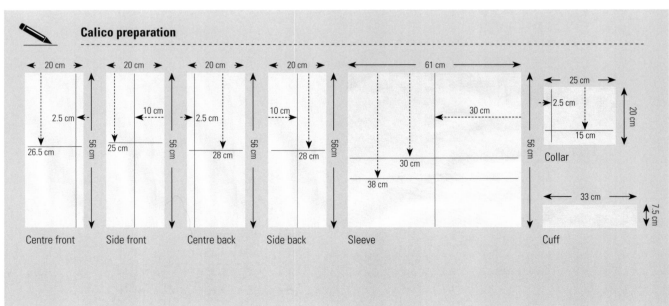

Calico preparation

Centre front — 20 cm / 56 cm / 2.5 cm / 26.5 cm

Side front — 20 cm / 56 cm / 10 cm / 25 cm

Centre back — 20 cm / 56 cm / 2.5 cm / 28 cm

Side back — 20 cm / 56cm / 10 cm / 28 cm

Sleeve — 61 cm / 56 cm / 30 cm / 30 cm / 38 cm

Collar — 25 cm / 2.5 cm / 15 cm / 20 cm

Cuff — 33 cm / 7.5 cm

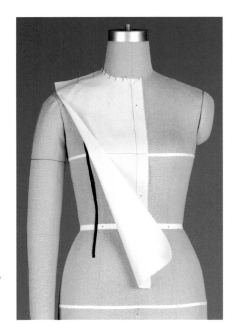 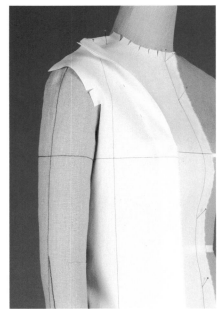 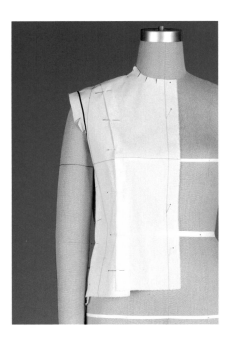

Draping the bodice

Step 1

- Twill-tape style line of the pink ribbon.

- Set CF section by aligning CFs, trimming and clipping neckline and smoothing calico over shoulder area. Trim shoulder angle, leaving 2.5 cm (1") seam allowance.

- Trim CF section along twill-tape line, leaving about 2.5 cm (1") seam allowance.

Step 2

- Set side front section by aligning horizontal grain with bust tape, keeping straight grain vertical.

- Slice out armhole area to allow arm to hang freely, but leave as much seam allowance as possible. Clip at notch points, allowing calico for underarm area to fall towards side seam.

- Pin at side seam, trying to approximate the volume of the blouse.

- Pin along princess line. The line on this design is actually farther to the side seam than the actual princess line; here you need to keep the CF section as straight as possible. The fabric required to fit the shape of the bust will be added to the side front piece.

- Pin shoulder area.

- This is not a fitted bodice like that on pp. 60–63; it is a looser-fitting blouse, so keep grainline as vertical as possible and leave about 2.5 cm (1") ease in armhole.

- Repeat from Step 1 for back.

Step 3

- Pin front over back at shoulders, matching princess lines.

- Pin sides, first wrong sides together, then trim and clip and turn front over back.

- Pin at hem, as if blouse were tucked into a skirt, and check the silhouette. It should have about the same amount of fullness at the lower edge (not shown).

- Tape armhole as a classic shape. It should be about 2 cm (¾") below armhole plate to accommodate the full sleeve (not shown).

- When you feel you have the right curves, lightly pencil in the line and remove tape.

- Trim seam allowance to about 2 cm (¾").

Embellishing the princess line

Classic princess lines are curved; however, as you are going to embellish the princess lines here with ribbon, they need to be straight so the ribbon will fall vertically. Ribbon will not sew well on a curve.

When draping the front princess-line seam, keep the CF section as straight as possible so the ribbon trim will fall vertically, as in the photograph. To create the bust fit, the fabric will be shaped, or curved out, in the side front section.

Marking and truing the bodice

Before beginning the sleeve, true up the bodice shape to ensure the armhole is smoothly drawn.

Step 1

- Unpin all pieces and gently press them flat.

- Look at CF piece and side front section: note how the CF is almost a straight line and the shape of the side front section is quite curved. The same happens with the CB and side back sections.

- Smooth out curves and check crossmarks.

Step 2

- Re-assemble toile by pinning front to side front and back to side back, turning under the excess or seam allowance on the line drawn. Pin first the princess seams and then the sides and shoulder seams.

Step 3

- Mark armhole with tape.

- Pin waist as if blouse were tucked in to check silhouette and volume.

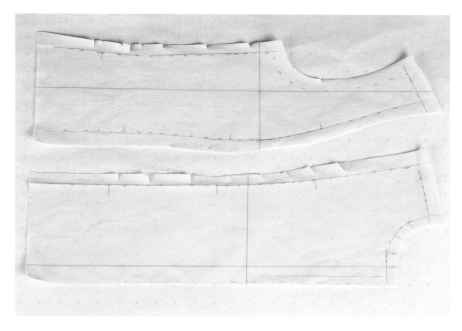

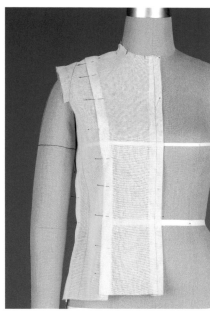

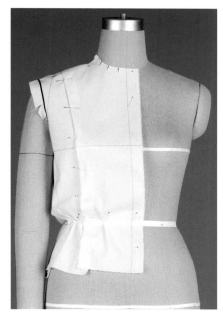

Draping the sleeve

Review the Sleeve Draping Order before beginning to drape the sleeve.

Sleeve draping order

This draping order works on many different styles of sleeve. Work alternately from the crown area to the wrist and back, working down the armhole and up the underarm seam, ending at the underarm point.

1. Set correct angle of sleeve, with straight grain slightly towards front.

2. Pin crown at shoulder.

3. Set wrist and pin circumference. Match horizontal grains.

4. Set pivot/notch points.

5. Work underarm seam from wrist to elbow.

6. Trim excess and refine upper half of sleeve crown.

7. Move up the underarm seam, turning excess to the inside and finalizing sleeve width in bicep area.

8. Work lower sleeve curves from pivot points to underarm point.

9. Finish underarm seam, joining it with underarm point of sleeve.

Step 4

- Review the Sleeve Draping Order (p. 133).

- Begin the sleeve drape by aligning straight grain of sleeve section with outer line of stuffed arm.

- Allow sleeve piece to angle slightly forwards, following the blue line on the stuffed arm.

- Lift straight grain up towards the elbow and pin again, starting to visualize the fullness of the sleeve taking shape.

The natural hang of the arm

When beginning a sleeve drape, first make sure your stuffed arm is pinned securely to the shoulder with the arm seam just meeting the edge of the mannequin. It is crucial that it angles slightly forwards, like the natural hang of the arm. This means that the red 'straight grain' of the stuffed arm will be aligning with the side seam of the mannequin.

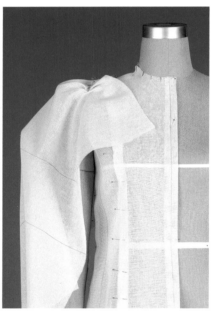

Step 5

- Set crown volume by gathering in the upper edge at shoulder area.

- Observe proportion of neck to shoulder seam. Set your sleeve with the same proportion.

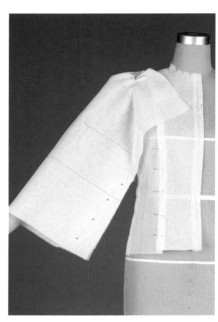

Step 6

- Starting at the wrist, determine volume of lower sleeve edge. It looks like it may be slightly narrower at the elbow than at the top, so bring in the seam at a slight angle.

- Remember that horizontal grains must match up at underarm. As you pin this area, match up the lower horizontal grains.

- Pin wrong sides together from wrist up to elbow area.

Step 7

- Pin gathers at crown with the distribution that you see in the photo.

- Check height of fabric above shoulder line: is it as high as you would like it to be?

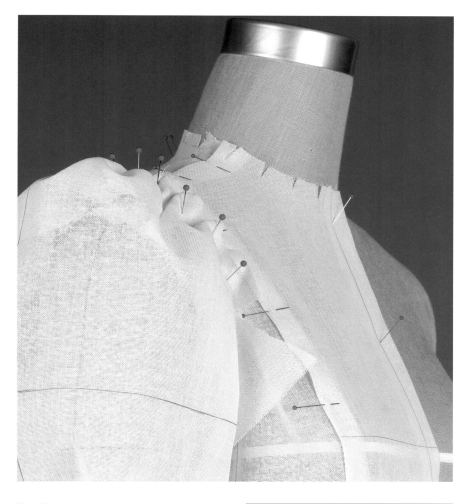

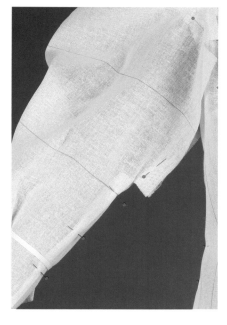

Step 8

- Set notch points. Looking at sleeve from the side, determine volume around the arm. This step is made easier by the sheerness of the fabric in the blouse. You can see that the sleeve width is about double the width of the arm.

- Check the sleeve through 360° and adjust until you are sure it is balanced and has the look of the photo.

- Pin firmly to about halfway down depth of armhole.

- Clip to the pin, and trim off excess triangle of fabric above it.

- Repeat for back.

Fabric vs calico

When setting a sleeve, it is important to consider the fabric. A skilled designer knows how the actual blouse fabric will react differently from the calico. In this case, when the blouse is sewn in organza, it will have slightly more height than the calico, as organza is a lighter and crisper fabric.

Practise visualizing this by gathering a length of organza as for a sleeve crown and pin or hold it next to your calico sleeve to study the different silhouettes.

Step 9

- Clip to your pins on the underarm seam.

- Turn underarm seam front over back from wrist to elbow, checking that horizontal grains are matching up.

- Once seam is turned, tie a piece of twill tape or elastic at lower edge and begin to adjust gathers.

- Check the photograph: raise the arm of your drape to the same height and see if the volume looks the same.

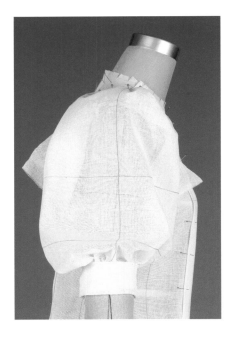
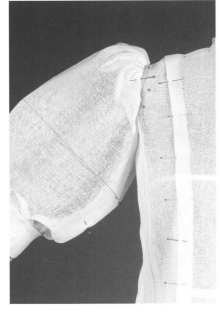
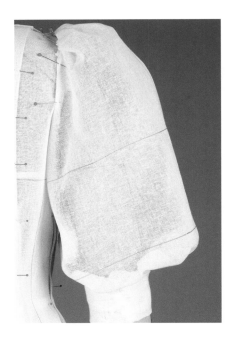

Step 10

- Check drape from the side; make back slightly longer than front to allow room for the elbow.
- Trim the excess, leaving about 1.5 cm (½") seam allowance.
- When you feel you have achieved the look, drape a rectangular sleeve band piece.

Step 11

- Finish crown adjustment by checking the balance of the line again and turning it under along armhole line.
- Continue pinning front over back up underarm seam, finalizing width of bicep area.
- Turn triangles below notch to the inside and allow them to fall along armhole line.
- Pin along lower curve, raising and lowering the stuffed arm and studying the way the sleeve 'breaks'. Ideally, armhole seam should be covered by drape of sleeve.

Step 12

- Pin down the underarm seam on sleeve, alternately pinning up the underarm seam to armhole.
- The last 7 cm or so (2–3") will be difficult to finesse; after you have finished the drape, it is acceptable to remove blouse from mannequin and finish pinning this area last.

Finessing the sleeve drape

In Step 12, note how the back of the sleeve is caving in along the armhole. This means that more needs to be taken from the curve of the sleeve. See the dotted line in this diagram for amount to remove.

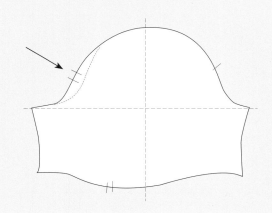
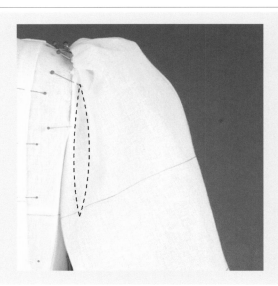

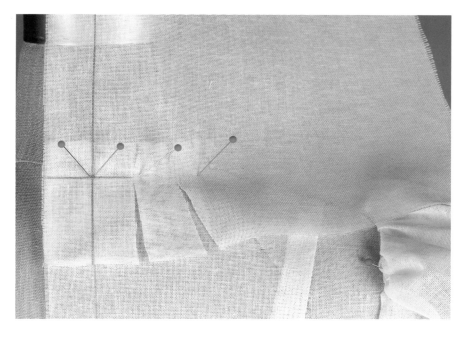

Step 13

- Lightly chalk neckline so that you have a guide for your collar drape.

- Begin collar drape by placing calico piece at CB neckline and pinning perpendicular to the CB for the 2.5 cm (1") or so.

Step 14

- Continue clipping as needed and pinning to the neckline as you pull collar section around to about 2.5 cm (1") in front of shoulder line.

- Now determine the stand of the collar. Keep CB of collar aligned to CB of mannequin all the way up collar piece. At a point 2.5 cm (1") in front of the shoulder line, keep collar calico about a finger's width from neck of mannequin and experiment with moving lower edge of collar up and down on neckline. Note that if the lower edge is almost a straight line, as in a band or mandarin collar, the stand is very high at the back.

- You will have to flip hem of collar up to allow it to lie smoothly.

Step 15

- Turn collar down and check that there is space between neck of mannequin and collar for ease.

- Turn under outer edge, following style line in the photograph.

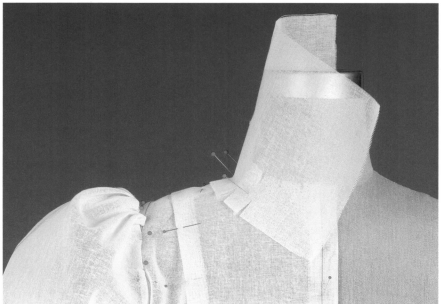

Step 16

- Turn collar back up and make sure it is lying smoothly all the way around.

- Look at the photograph and note area by shoulder where fabric is caving in. This indicates that it needs to be clipped in further.

Step 17

- Clip collar edge a little bit at a time until it is standing smoothly from CB to CF.

Step 18

- The collar should now be lying smoothly all the way around.

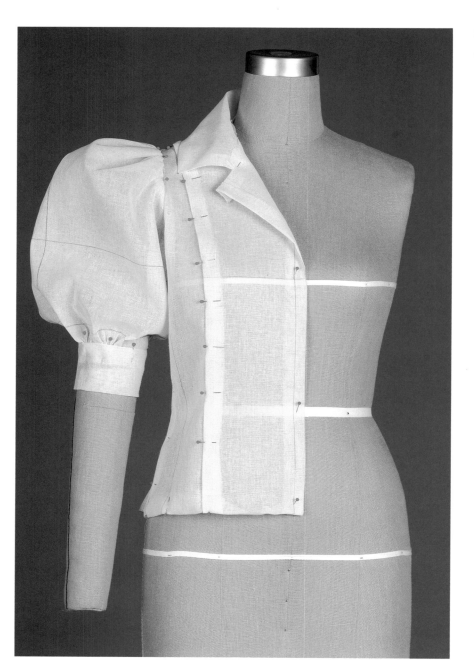

Step 19

- Finish the blouse by determining the 'break point' where the first button will hold the fold of the blouse between front and collar.

Marking and truing the sleeve and collar

Step 1

- Mark all seams with pencil or chalk and crossmark where needed.

- With a convertible collar, it will help to have the collar line and the neckline marked on both sides. Using carbon paper and a tracing wheel, mark along the neckline so that the line is recorded accurately on the underside as well.

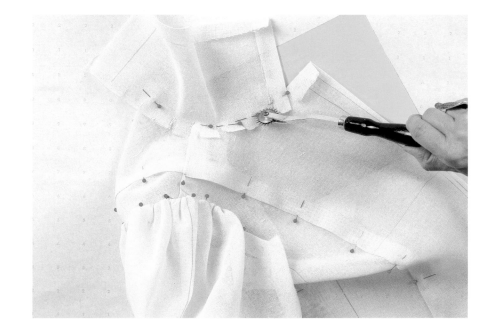

Step 2

- True up collar, first using a clear grading ruler to make sure that CB straight grain is square with CB neckline for the first 2.5 cm (1") or so.

- Then use a French curve to draw the neckline curve as it goes up slightly towards front area.

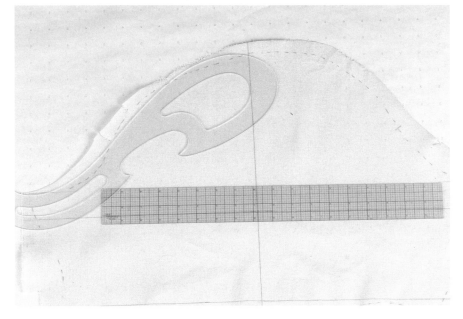

Step 3

- Smooth out lines on sleeve. The back sleeve curve should be flatter and broader; the front will be deeper. Compare the curve to the classic sleeve shape.

- Make sure underarm points of each side are on the same horizontal grain.

- On the lower sleeve edge, the back will be longer and the front shorter, as the back sleeve needs more length as it travels over the elbow.

- Using a clear grading ruler, add seam allowances to the edges. The following are suggested seam allowances. If you are going to be fitting the blouse on someone larger, it is fine to add more; just keep track of what you are adding by notching the measurement at the pattern edge.

- Side seams and shoulder seams: 2 cm (¾")
- Front and back princess seams: 1.5 cm (½")
- Neckline and collar: 1.5 cm (½")
- Hem: 2.5 cm (1")

Step 4

- Because of the gathering of the sleeves, it will be difficult to analyse your final result by pinning or hand basting, so make up a full toile of the blouse. You will therefore need to cut the mirror image of all the pieces. Refer to the calico-preparation diagram on p. 130.

- Block new calico pieces. Draw straight and horizontal grains as shown on the diagram.

- Align straight and horizontal grains of draped piece onto the lines of the new calico pieces and pin or secure with weights.

- Cut the two pieces together along the lines you have trued and to which you have added seam allowances.

- Clip in at crossmarks, no more than 0.5 cm (¼").

- For the presentation, the ribbon seen in the photograph will be basted (tacked) onto the seams in the same places and buttons will be attached.

Analysis

- First, look at the overall feeling of the blouse. The calico, of course, looks heavier, but use your designer's eye to visualize how the shape would look in crisp, sheer organza.

- Begin at the top of the piece and compare the elements. The collar and lapel are slightly wider on the drape and the shoulders slightly narrower. The princess-line ribbons are closer together on the drape than on the Bill Blass blouse.

- If the blouse were styled on a model as on p. 131, with the collar up, buttons opened further down and sleeves pushed up a bit higher, that attitude of feminine chic would be more apparent.

Analysis of the ensemble

This blouse is paired with the Bill Blass skirt you draped in Chapter 2.1: Skirts (see p. 102).

- The model in the photograph is probably around 180 cm (6') tall, so your first impression when comparing the total look will be that your toile looks wider. This illustrates another visualization challenge a designer faces: garments almost always look better on catwalk models due to their elongated shapes, narrow waists and broad shoulders. As a designer, you must train your eye to visualize how the work will look on an average woman.

- Study the proportions of the blouse and skirt together: they are synchronized. The wide belt seems to balance out the width of the collar and cuffs. The soft, full, rounded sleeves and the sharp, curvy silhouette of the skirt create the balanced contrast of femininity and strength.

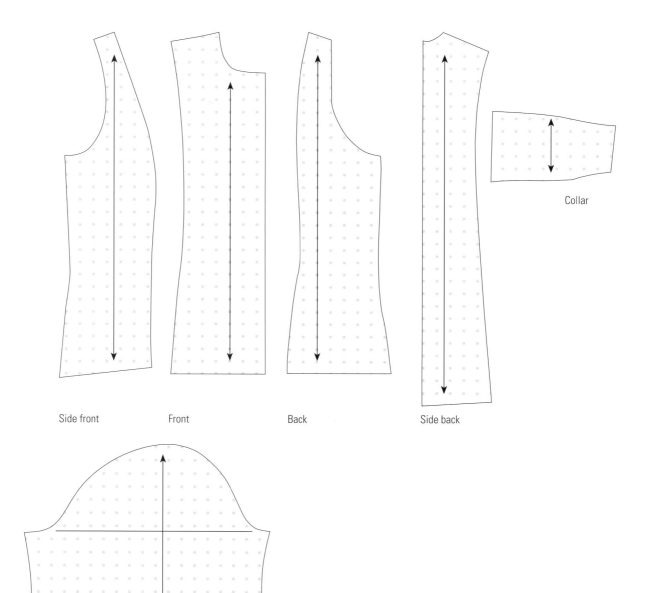

Side front   Front   Back   Side back   Collar

Sleeve

Cuff

Variations
Tunic with bell sleeve

This contemporary design is reminiscent of the elemental tunic, combined here with a bell sleeve. While ancient tunics were often loose fitting, this modern version is fitted in the torso with darts. The bell sleeve is slim fitting from shoulder to elbow and then gently flares to the wrist in a bell shape.

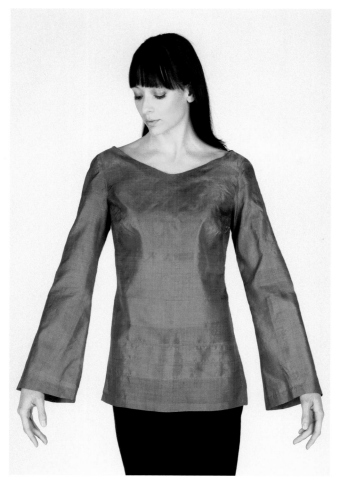

Using negative space to refine shape

When draping, train your eye to see the negative space around the shape instead of focusing only on the toile. For example, with this bell sleeve, you can easily see the space between the sleeve and the side of the blouse. Referring to this will help you achieve the right curve in the side seam and refine the subtle shape of the sleeve: narrow at the underarm level and widening towards the wrist.

Calico preparation

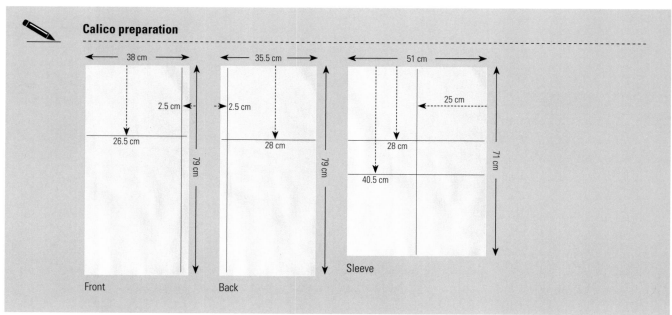

Front   Back   Sleeve

38 cm · 2.5 cm · 26.5 cm · 79 cm

35.5 cm · 2.5 cm · 28 cm · 79 cm

51 cm · 25 cm · 28 cm · 40.5 cm · 71 cm

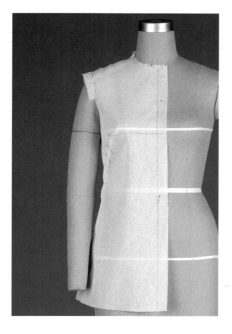  

Step 1

- This sleeve will be draped on a tunic with a classic armhole. First create a bodice with a side bust dart in the front and a single vertical dart in the back.

- Tape, then mark, a classic egg-shaped armhole with a drop of about 2.5 cm (1") below the armplate (not shown).

Step 2

- Align straight grain with outer line of stuffed arm and pin at underarm line (not shown).

- Allow sleeve to angle slightly forwards, following the blue line on the stuffed arm.

- Set crown volume by holding upper edge in slightly at shoulder area. There will not be any gathering, but there will be slight easing in of the calico. If it helps you, pin out 1.5 cm (½") on front and back crown.

Step 3

- Starting at the wrist, determine volume of lower edge. It is narrower at the elbow than at the wrist, so bring in the seam at an angle.

- As you pin, remember that the horizontal grains must match up at underarm.

- Pin wrong sides together from wrist to elbow area; clip to your pins.

Sleeve-crown notches

Classic sleeve patterns are marked with a single notch where the sleeve matches the shoulder seam. A double notch indicates the back of the sleeve, a single notch indicates the front. Accustom yourself to this widely used system.

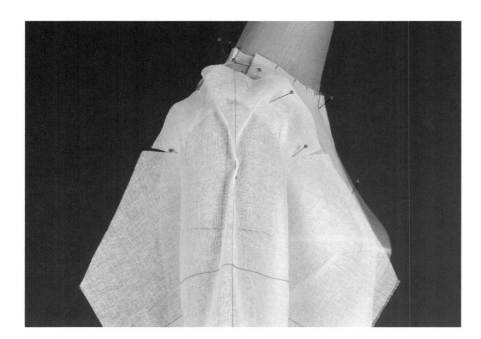

Step 4

- Set notch points. Looking at sleeve from the side, determine volume around arm.

- If you have not already done so in Step 2, pin out 1.5 cm (½") or so ease on outside of arm. Even though the sleeve has a very slim fit, it will still need some ease.

- Check the sleeve through 360° and adjust until you are sure it is balanced and has the look of the photo.

- Pin firmly to about halfway down depth of armhole.

- Clip to the pin, and trim off triangle of excess fabric above it.

- Repeat for back.

Step 5

- Turn underarm seam front over back from wrist to elbow, checking to see that horizontal grains are matching up.

- Turn up hem.

- Finish crown area by adjusting the ease and then turning it under along armhole line.

Step 6

- Trim away excess on lower sleeve in a curve that approximates the curve of the lower armhole.

Step 7

- Allow lower sleeve to turn to the inside. Note where it falls against armhole line.

- Pin the front lower curve.

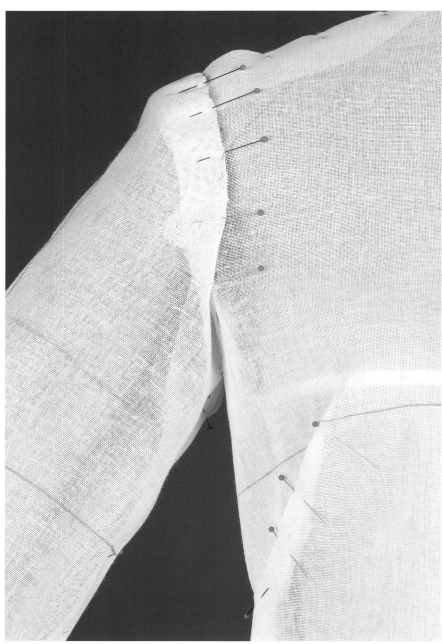

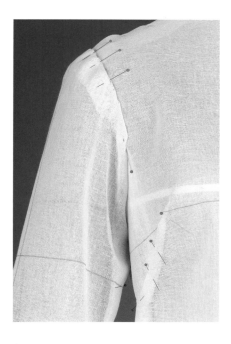

Step 8

- Observe how fabric is draping at the underarm. It has too many folds, which means more fabric needs to be taken out of the sleeve at the underarm curve.

- Pin along lower curve, raising and lowering the stuffed arm and studying the way the sleeve breaks.

- Find the balance between being able to lift the arm freely, yet resulting in lots of folds at the underarm, and having a smooth fit with no lift.

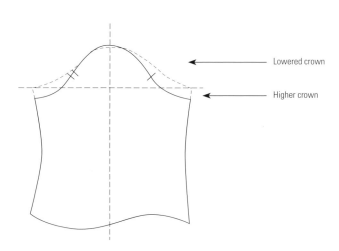

Lowered crown

Higher crown

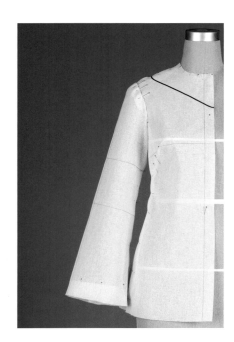

Step 9

- Pin down the underarm seam on sleeve, alternately pinning up the underarm seam to armhole.

- The last 7 cm or so (2–3") will be difficult to finesse; after you have finished the drape, it is acceptable to remove blouse from mannequin and finish pinning this area last.

- Tape neckline.

Maintaining a stable neckline

Note that the neckline is kept high and not cut away. Unless it is crucial to observing the silhouette, leave this area in place to help maintain the stability of your drape. A cut-out neckline is usually bias, which is prone to stretching. This is especially important with a lower neckline such as this one.

Mandarin collar

The mandarin collar in Western clothing probably dates from the 1930s, when there was a vogue for the Chinese cheongsam, a one-piece form-fitting dress that is still prominent in Asian fashion. The style originated with the mandarins (civil servants) of Imperial China. The collar, usually 1.5–5 cm (½–2") in height, frames the face as it follows the neckline around to the centre front.

Calculating ease for blouses

Blouses are looser fitting than corsets and often looser even than the dress bodices in Chapter 1.2. The amount of ease on blouses varies, but the minimum average ease around the bust for a comfortable fit is about 7.5 cm (3") total.

✏️ **Calico preparation**

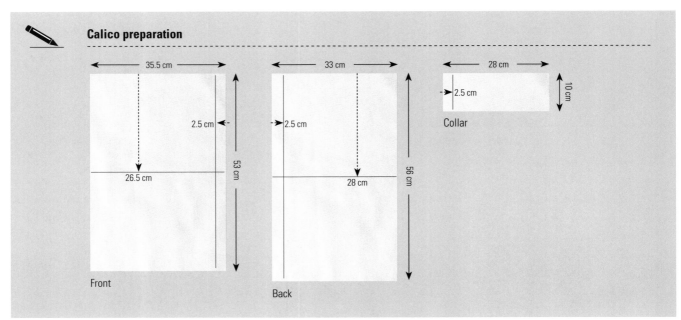

Front — 35.5 cm · 2.5 cm · 26.5 cm · 53 cm

Back — 33 cm · 2.5 cm · 28 cm · 56 cm

Collar — 28 cm · 2.5 cm · 10 cm

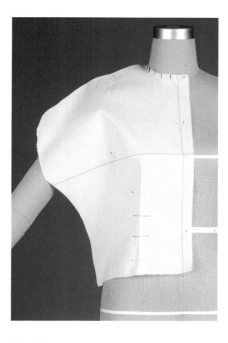

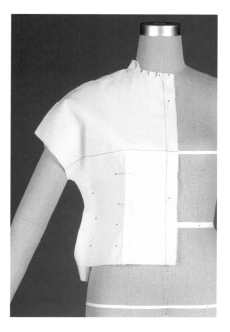

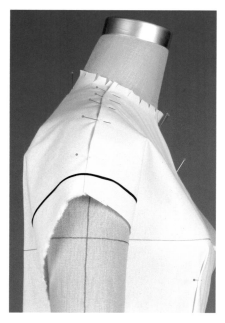

Step 1

- Set front section by aligning CFs, pinning across bust line and shoulder. Clip and trim neckline until it lies smoothly against mannequin.

- Smooth excess ease towards waist and pin dart near princess line with about 2.5 cm (1") dart intake. As dart continues below waist, it should become smaller to accommodate high hip area. Note how the calico shapes in at the waist and back out again over the high hip.

- Trim shoulder excess to approximate cap sleeve line.

- Trim side seam excess allowing for the shaping of the waist curve.

Step 2

- Set back section by aligning CBs, pinning across bust line and shoulder.

- Pin dart as for front section in Step 1.

- Pin shoulder seams front over back and allow them to extend over the stuffed arm to create the cap sleeve.

- Pin side seams together, wrong sides together first, then turn front over back, shaping in slightly at waist (not shown).

Step 3

- Check side view of cap sleeve area. The 'break' (where the calico is folding) should be larger and lower in the back and higher and smaller in the front.

- Tape armhole. On a cap sleeve, the front area is carved out to allow the arm to move freely. The back armhole will be fuller, to cover the underarm area.

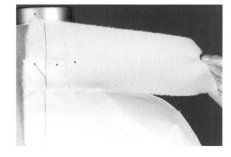

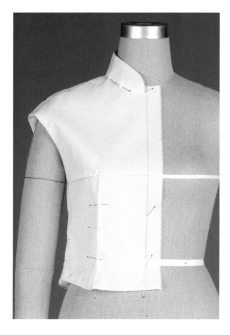

Step 4

- Begin collar drape by placing calico piece at CB neckline and pinning perpendicular to the CB for the first 2.5 cm (1") or so.

Step 5

- Continue clipping as needed and pinning to the neckline as you pull collar section around to CF. At shoulder point, collar piece should be about a finger's width from neck of mannequin to allow for ease.

Step 6

- Turn under neckline edge of collar, then top edge of collar.

- Turn under hem of sleeve.

Peter Pan collar

The Peter Pan collar made its appearance under that name in the mid-1900s, named after the costume worn by Maude Adams in the production of *Peter Pan*. Similar collars were named for Little Lord Fauntleroy and Buster Brown. The flat, round-cornered collar has remained popular primarily in children's clothing, but periodically in contemporary fashion as well.

In this blouse from Louis Vuitton's Autumn/Winter 2012 collection, a classic Peter Pan collar contrasts with a tight and tough leather bodice.

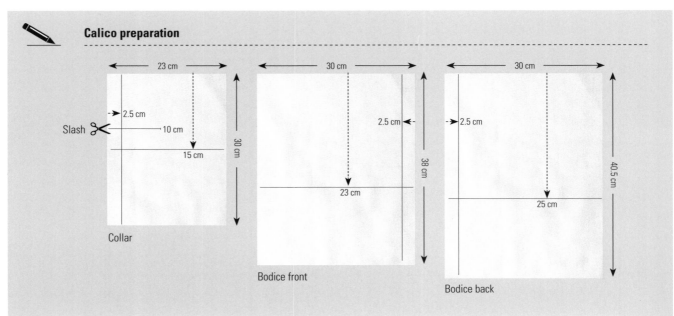

Calico preparation

Collar

Bodice front

Bodice back

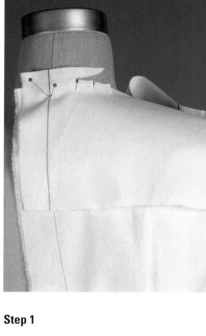

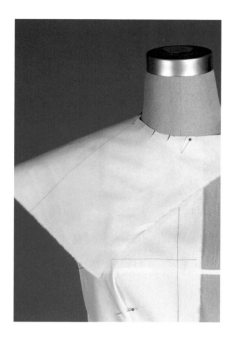

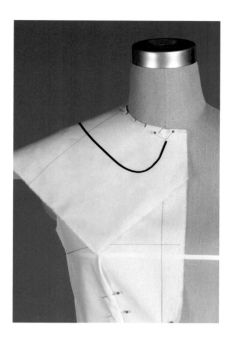

Step 1

- Prepare a classic bust dart bodice (see p. 44), but smooth bust ease into a dart at underbust area. Keep neckline high and neatly clipped and trimmed. Mark it lightly 1.5 cm (½") down from CB seam on mannequin, 1.5 cm (½") out from seam at shoulder point, and 2 cm (¾") down at CF.

- Align CB of collar calico piece with CB of bodice neckline, allowing slashed area to lie at shoulder line.

- Trim and clip neckline to match neckline of bodice.

Step 2

- Continue clipping and trimming as you bring fabric around to front. Allow it to lie smoothly on bodice front.

Step 3

- Tape the shape of the collar.

Line and proportion corrections

Pay close attention to the front collar curve in the photograph. To find the correct shape, it can be helpful to check the negative space. Here, for example, the negative space between the two collar curves at the centre front forms an inverted V. Duplicate the look by focusing on that shape rather than the shape of the calico collar.

It can also help to connect reference points. Here, draw an imaginary line from the front collar curve to the bust point. Do the same for the photograph and compare the angles of those two lines.

Step 4

- Turn under outer edge of collar and neck edge, matching neck edge of bodice.

- To help you check proportions, add finishing details such as the buttons and armhole line.

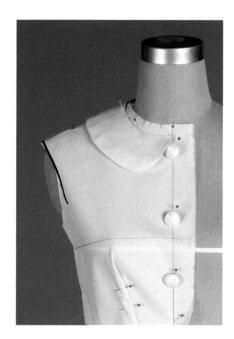

Blouse with peplum and classic bishop sleeve

The elegant and sensual look of this wrap-front blouse is created by the full volume of the sleeve, the softly flared peplum and the focal point, a bias-cut silk georgette neckline that finishes in a bow closure at the waist. The blouse is made of silk crêpe georgette, a lightweight, semi-sheer fabric that has a beautiful, swingy, fluid drape.

The fit is achieved by released tucks at the waistline and side seams that angle in at the waist. A light shoulder pad supports the weight of the full 'bishop' sleeve. The peplum skirt section is the same basic cut as the bias circle skirt on pages 100–101.

A trained eye comes with practice

The fluid drape of the silk georgette that makes the blouse so pretty also makes it difficult to drape with. Draping it in calico makes it easier to achieve a balanced pattern. Before you begin the drape, take time to study the 'hand' of the georgette (the way it moves and falls) so you can visualize it while you work and take into consideration how it differs from the calico.

Calico preparation

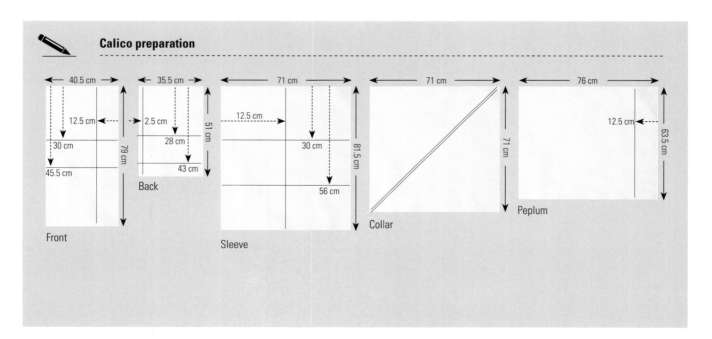

Front — 40.5 cm, 12.5 cm, 30 cm, 45.5 cm, 79 cm

Back — 35.5 cm, 2.5 cm, 28 cm, 43 cm, 51 cm

Sleeve — 71 cm, 12.5 cm, 30 cm, 56 cm, 81.5 cm

Collar — 71 cm, 71 cm

Peplum — 76 cm, 12.5 cm, 63.5 cm

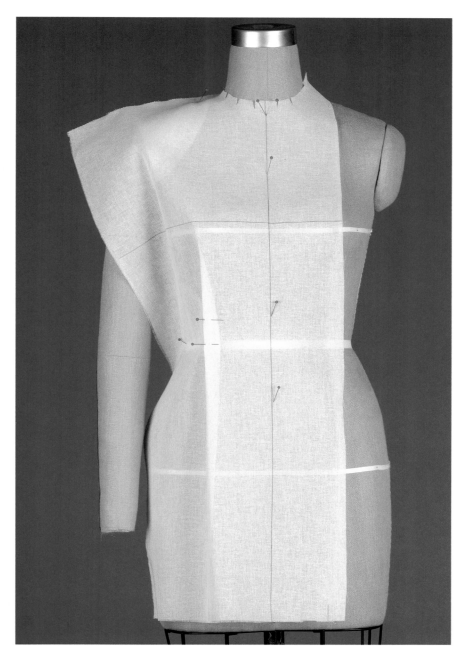

Step 1

- Prepare mannequin by setting a small shoulder pad to give the square shape to the shoulder edge.

- Pin front section to mannequin, aligning CF straight grain with CF of mannequin.

- Pin across bust and trim and clip until neckline lies smoothly.

- Allow excess bust ease to drape to the waistline and pin a tuck at about the princess line. Keep it angled towards the bust, where the extra fullness is needed.

Angled tucks

The angles of the front and back tucks are important in determining the fit and the look of the silhouette. If they are angled too far to the side, they will add width to the body and make the wearer look bigger. They need to angle towards the areas that need more space: the bust in front and the shoulder blade in back.

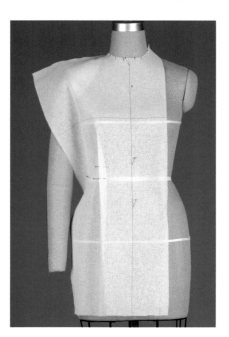

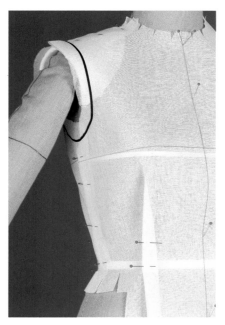

Step 2

- Repeat for back bodice, allowing ease to fall to the waist; slightly angle tuck towards shoulder blade.

Step 3

- Pin shoulder and side seams front over back.

- Tape armhole as the classic shape, about 2.5 cm (1") below the armplate.

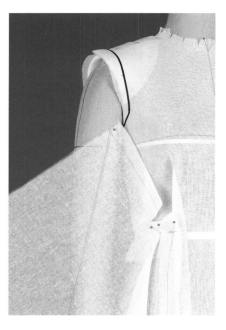

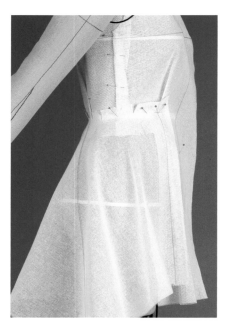

Step 4

- Begin drape of bias peplum piece by aligning straight grain with straight grain of front section at the princess line. Start 3–4" (7.5–10 cm) up to allow room for the clipping and dropping of the bias piece (see bias circle skirt, pp. 100–101).

Step 5

- Clip and trim, allowing fabric to fall in folds at the hem, bringing fabric around the side and ending at CB. The true bias pencil line should be straight up and down at about the side seam.

Step 6

- Cut hem excess to even it out, but do not finalize until rest of blouse is ready.

- Tape neckline and armhole.

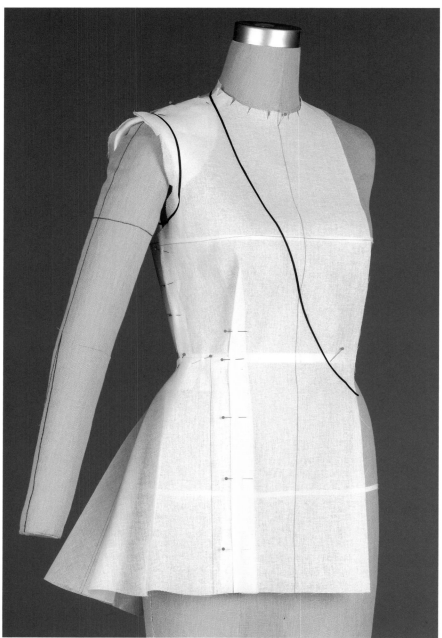

Sleeve draping order

As you begin the sleeve drape, remember to follow the basic draping order set out on p. 133:

1. Set proper angle

2. Pin crown

3. Set wrist

4. Set notch points

5. Work line from underarm to elbow

6. Trim excess and work lower sleeve curves

7. Finish underarm seam where it meets the armhole point.

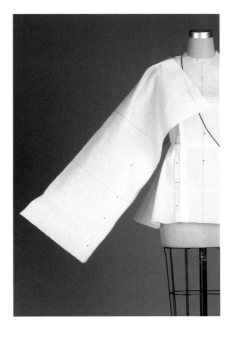

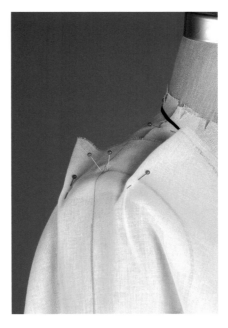

Step 7

- Align straight grain of sleeve piece with outer line of stuffed arm and pin at underarm line (not shown).

- Allow sleeve to angle slightly forwards as the natural hang of the arm, following the blue line on the stuffed arm.

Step 8

- Set crown volume by pinning in ease on upper edge at shoulder area. There will be about 1.5 cm (½") ease on both the front and the back.

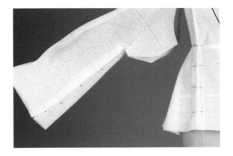

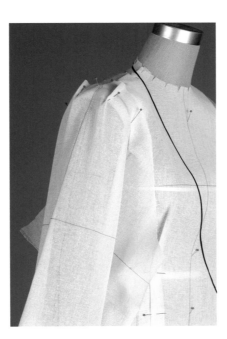

Step 9

- Starting at wrist, determine volume of lower edge. It is narrower at the elbow than at the wrist, so bring in seam at an angle, keeping wrist area as full as possible.

- Remember to match horizontal grains at underarm as you pin this area.

- Pin wrong sides together from wrist to elbow area. Clip to your pins.

Step 10

- Set notch points. Looking at sleeve from the side, determine volume around arm.

- Pin at notch points. Note that there is quite a bit more fullness in the bicep area than there was with the bell sleeve (see pp. 142–45). The actual crown ease will still be 1.5 cm (½") at both front and back, but there will be more as it travels down towards notch area.

- Pin firmly to about halfway down depth of armhole.

- Clip to the pin, and trim off excess triangle of calico above it.

- Repeat for back.

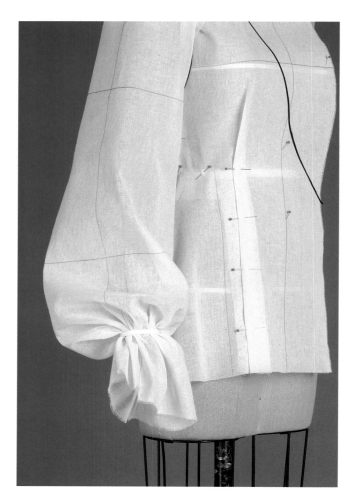

Step 11

- Turn underarm seam front over back from wrist to elbow, checking to see that horizontal grains are matching up. This is an awkward procedure. To make it easier, lean the fabric against the stuffed arm and smooth it out as you pin.

- Tie a twill tape or elastic around the wrist and adjust gathers.

- Check the photo for amount of blouson.

- As you adjust the gathers, note that in the photograph the back of the sleeve is longer than the front. This creates more ease for the movement of the elbow; also, a sleeve that is shorter in the front and longer in the back gives a more graceful, classic look.

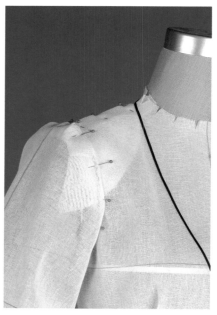

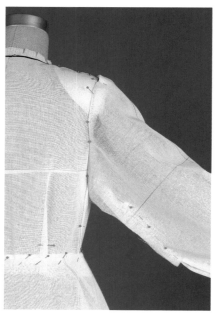

Step 12

- Finish crown area by adjusting ease and turning it under along armhole line.

- Trim away excess below notches at front and back, and turn to the inside.

Step 13

- Pin underarm seam up to armhole as you alternately pin the lower sleeve area down the armhole.

Step 14

- Pin lower front and back curves, raising and lowering the stuffed arm and studying the way the sleeve 'breaks'. Ideally, armhole seam should be covered by drape of sleeve, as seen here.

Step 15

- Drape collar by first folding bias section in half.

- Starting at CB neckline, pin to the halfway point. Pin straight for the first 2.5 cm (1"), clip, then continue clipping as collar rolls around shoulder area.

- Bring it down along the taped style line of the neckline.

- When you see the volume you want, pin it to the neckline, folding excess under.

Draping bias fabrics

Because the fabric is on the bias grain, it will stretch. Allow it to fall naturally without trying to stretch it. Notice how the bias grain lets the fabric follow the neckline curve without breaking or wrinkling.

Step 16

- Use a smaller scrap of bias to create a tie piece that will begin at the left side seam; create a bow with the piece that ends at the right waistline.

- This is your focal point, so look carefully at the proportion you are creating and coordinate with the rest of the blouse.

- Turn up the hem.

- Check your drape from a distance to see if the fullness of the sleeve flows well with the amount of flare in the peplum. The size of the bow should complement the volume of the other elements.

2.3
Trousers

History

Modern ethnic trousers echo the traditional forms pictured here. The woven panels are cleverly engineered to allow for maximum movement and economic utilization of the fabric. These elemental designs have endured because of their purity of form, simplicity and functionality.

Early trousers evolved over centuries and through many practical changes before arriving at what we consider today a well-fitting trouser. The contrast between the basic cuts of these trousers and the detail and finesse that go, for example, into the pattern for a modern designer jean is extreme.

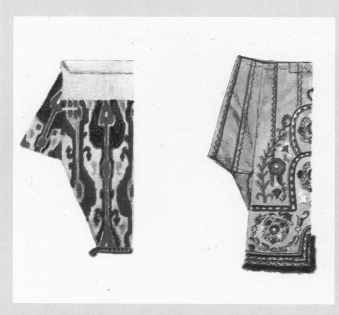

Top: Wide cloth trousers from Syria and Kurdistan. Note the geometric cuts of this traditional garment.

Above: Traditional women's trousers and riding pants from Turkestan. Note the geometric cut. The centre front gussets allow for freedom of movement.

With the advent of a shaped front rise, or crotch curve, the generously cut style of ethnic trousers gradually evolved to

the gentleman's fitted trouser, as depicted in this nineteenth-century portrait by François-Édouard Picot.

Today, trousers are an indispensable part of a woman's wardrobe. However, in historical context, they are relatively new. The modern garment as we know it did not come to widespread use until the early nineteenth century. Before that time, in Western culture, well-dressed men wore knee breeches with long stockings to cover the rest of their legs.

Knee breeches first gave way to pantaloons around 1792. These were made from a light-coloured cloth or cotton, covered the entire length of the leg and were cut on the bias to achieve a close fit. The pant or trouser, which evolved from a functional garment worn by sailors and was first adopted as seaside wear, gradually replaced pantaloons for daywear by the mid-1820s. In the United States, it was not until around 1810 that long trousers came into fashion. By 1850

Levi Strauss was producing the first denim, a sturdy cotton with a blue warp thread and a white weft, the origin of what now is almost an international 'uniform'.

For women, wearing trousers took much longer to become acceptable, due to social and cultural mores. One of the first innovators in women's trousers was the rebellious American Amelia Jenks Bloomer, a suffragette and champion of women's rights. In the 1850s she designed a loose-fitting pant, the 'bloomer', to be worn under a knee-length skirt. She and her followers were subjected to so much ridicule and harassment that it became apparent the world was not ready for women in trousers.

However, trousers were beginning to be worn regularly in work situations. Women working in British coal mines were reported wearing trousers in the 1840s, and women working the ranches of the American West needed the practicality of trousers more than they needed or cared to look stylish.

Marlene Dietrich was escorted off the streets of Munich for wearing trousers in 1932, and when Katharine Hepburn insisted on wearing trousers on her movie sets, there was no going back. In the 1940s, while men went off to fight in World War II, women began to take their jobs in factories and on assembly lines – wearing trousers. Money and materials were in short supply, so wives began to dress in their husbands' clothes to save wear and tear on their own.

By the 1950s, trousers were acceptable for gardening and beachwear. By the 1960s, they were fully accepted in society for any occasion.

The 1980s designer-jean trend brought trouser fit to an exact science, with the smallest incremental changes in the curves of the pattern causing sales to rise and fall as shoppers sought out the latest style and fit.

Different trouser types

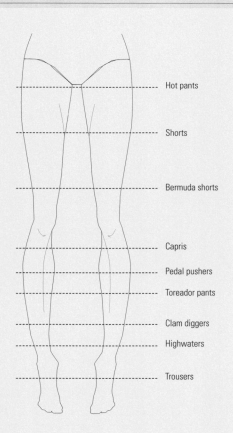

Hot pants

Shorts

Bermuda shorts

Capris

Pedal pushers

Toreador pants

Clam diggers

Highwaters

Trousers

Today there are a myriad of trouser styles for women.

Exercises
Draping and fitting trousers

Modern trousers are traditionally draped with the straight grain running vertically down the leg for maximum strength and a long, slimming line. The way the crotch area is cut away determines the fit of the trousers. The goal is to create a well-balanced combination of curves at the hip, crotch and inside leg seams so that no matter how wide or narrow the trousers, they fit well and fall smoothly.

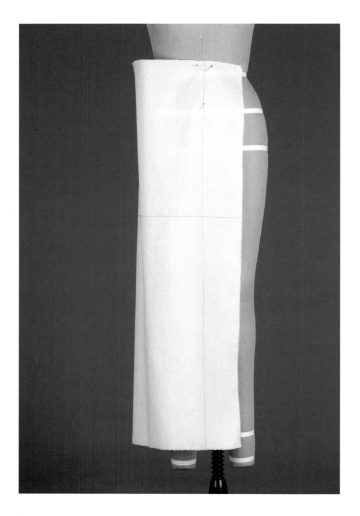

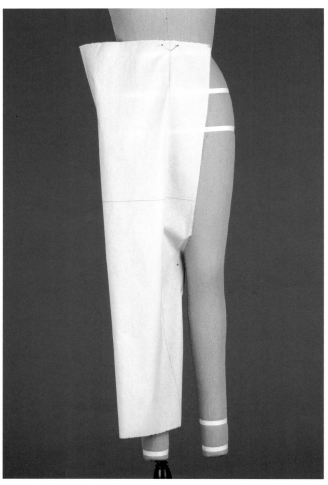

Beginning a pair of trousers

Observe the shape that is created when a simple rectangle of fabric is wrapped around the lower torso and leg.

Joining the inside leg seams

Note how the fabric wrinkles at the crotch when the inside leg seams are joined. Historically, this issue is addressed by adding more panels, as in the ethnic trousers on p. 158.

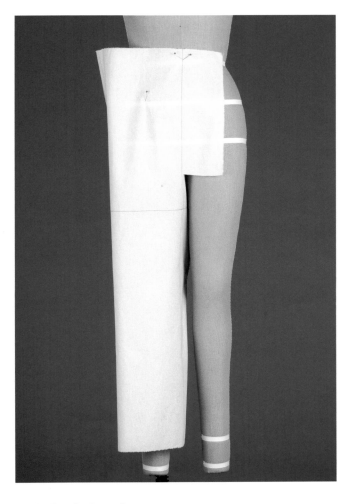

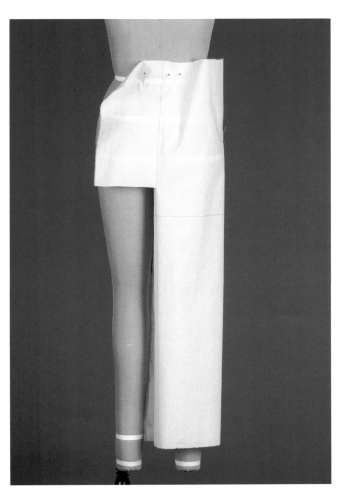

Beginning the front rise

To release the tension and wrinkling at the inside leg/crotch area, slash in horizontally about 10–12.5 cm (4–5"), allowing the fabric to lie smoothly as it wraps around the leg.

Beginning the back rise

For the back, a greater allowance is needed for the fullness of the back hip area.

Note in the photograph the difference between the front and back; there is a greater distance to travel at the back of the crotch than at the front.

Combination of curves

As with the join of the sleeve and armhole in Chapter 2.2, here again is a complex combination of curves, this time required to fit two trouser legs together.

There is an infinite variety of combinations that create the fit of a pair of trousers. The way these curves are engineered affects the fit at the hip, crotch and inside leg areas.

Generally, the wider and fuller the trousers, the longer the 'hook' or curve of the crotch seam extends. For narrow, close-fitting trousers, the back hook, usually much longer than the front, meets towards the front of the classic inside leg point.

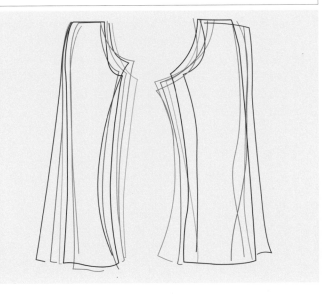

Harem pants

In 1910 the Russian painter and theatrical designer Leon Bakst created these harem pants, worn by Nijinsky in the Ballets Russes production of *Scheherazade*. This simply cut traditional pant is seen in many ancient cultures. It was revived by Yves Saint Laurent in the 1980s and continues to surface in designer collections periodically. It is also a staple of the modern belly-dancing costume.

In preparing the flat sketch, try to capture the fullness and also the straight look of the leg. It is gathered at the top edge.

There is no side seam, so, opened up, the pattern was probably cut from a simple rectangle of cloth with shaping for the crotch. The straight grain would be straight down the side seam and the horizontal grain perpendicular.

The fabric determines the volume

The final look and silhouette of these pants will vary according to the fabric used. If cut in chiffon, the thin, fluid quality of that fabric would drape very straight down the side of the leg. If a heavier silk or cotton is used, the volume of the pants will be fuller.

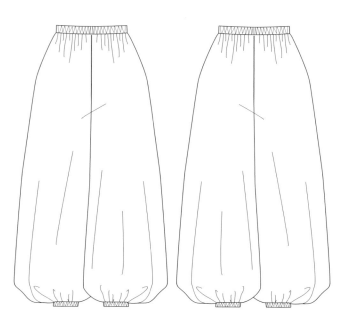

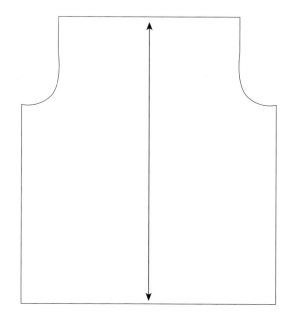

162

Crotch depth

To estimate where to draw the horizontal grain, which will be at about the crotch depth, or rise, have the wearer sit in a chair and measure from the waist to the bottom of the chair.

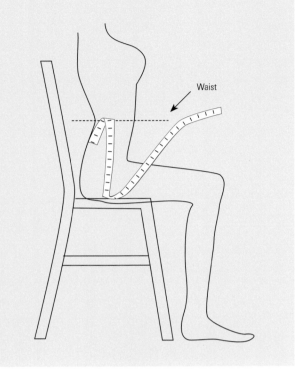

Visualizing the volume

When preparing your calico, the amount of fabric needed will have to be estimated.

Hold a tape measure around the hip area and try to estimate how full you want the pants to be. Stand at a distance before a mirror to make it easier to see how the proportions of the length and width are working. Visualize Nijinsky or your favourite dancer on stage and try to work out how much fabric they would like to have around their body as they extend their legs to leap and dance.

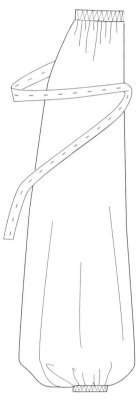

✏️ Calico preparation

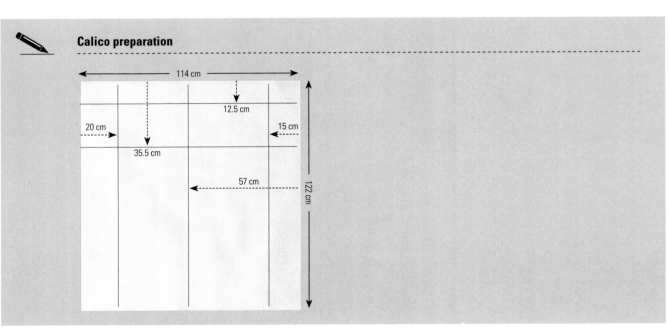

Step 1

- Because you are using the full width of the fabric, pin the inside leg seam together first.

- On the table, fold in 1.5 cm (½") or so seam allowance on the front and pin over back to about halfway up the leg. It helps to place a grading ruler under the seam to press against (not shown).

Step 2

- Align straight grain with side seam of mannequin, then CF line with CF of mannequin and CB straight grain with CB of mannequin.

- Tie a length of elastic or twill tape around the waist and adjust top edge so high hip horizontal grain is level with ground (not shown).

Calico vs fabric

Use your skills of visualization here. The calico will react differently from a soft silk or jersey, for example. Try to imagine how the volume of your drape would change when made up in a thinner fabric with a softer hand.

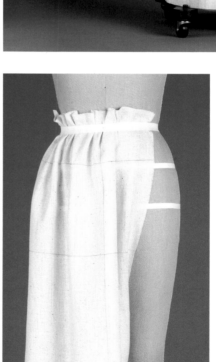

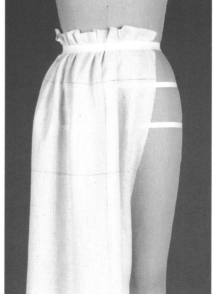

Step 3

- As gathers are adjusted at the waist, under the elastic, the straight grain of CF and CB should fall quite vertically, perpendicular to the ground.

Step 4

- Clip straight to CF at high hip line, then tape front rise, following curve of mannequin.

- Trim away excess fabric; clip as the seam falls in towards the inside leg seam (not shown).

- Cut away curve for the front crotch seam (not shown).

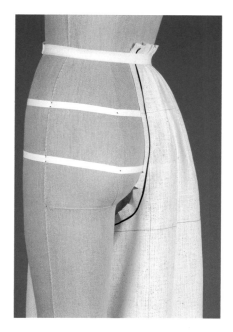

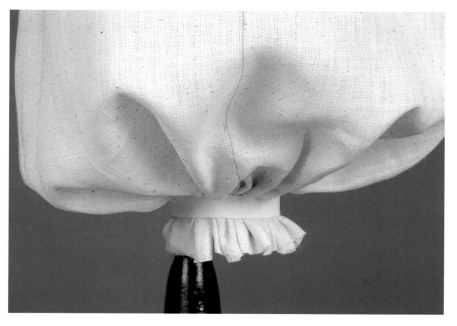

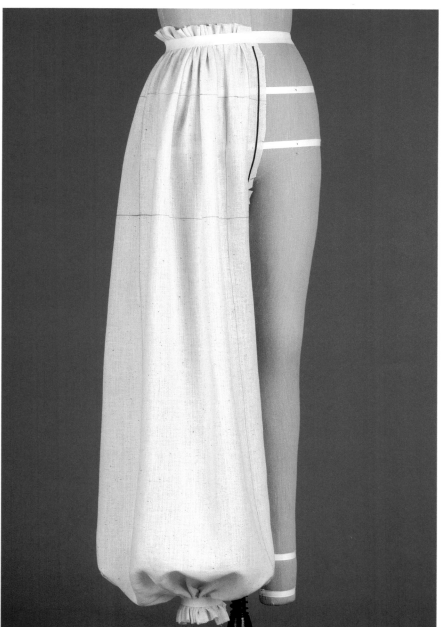

Step 5

- Repeat Step 4 for back, but note that the back hip area requires a deeper curve to be cut away than at the front.

- Trim back rise a little at a time until it smoothly follows the seam of the mannequin.

- Pin the inside leg seam above the knee.

Step 6

- Tie elastic or twill tape around ankle and adjust gathers until the look of the photograph is achieved.

Step 7

- Observe finished trouser drape and compare it to the photograph. Notice how the calico falls; it will be easy to see if you are off balance by looking closely at the grainlines. Practise your visualization skills by imagining what the pants would look like in a soft silk, like a chiffon or a crêpe de chine.

Hakama

The hakama is the traditional pant of the Japanese samurai. Originally, it was a heavy outer garment worn to protect the legs while riding through brush, similar to the chaps worn by Western cowboys. Now it is worn by men and women for the practice of *kyudo* and other martial arts.

Made basically of four squares – two fronts and two backs – the hakama has deep pleats that attach to a wrap waistband and side openings that are very low.

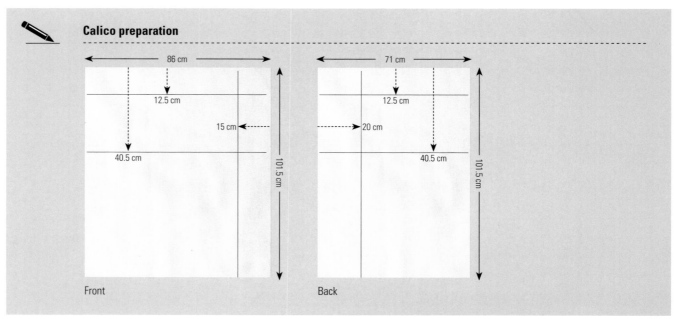

Calico preparation

Front

86 cm
12.5 cm
15 cm
40.5 cm
101.5 cm

Back

71 cm
12.5 cm
20 cm
40.5 cm
101.5 cm

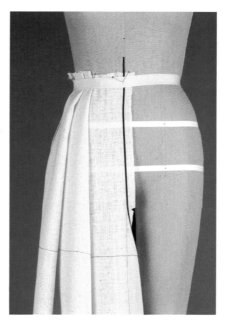

Step 1

- Align CF line with CF of mannequin, keeping horizontal grain level with floor.

- Tie a length of elastic or twill tape around the waistline to hold in the area that will be pleated.

- Pin at side seam to support pants.

- Tape crotch line. In the photograph it is quite low, probably 15–20.5 cm (6–8") from the actual crotch line.

Step 2

- Trim excess at front rise along twill tape and turn into the inside leg seam, clipping where necessary to allow fabric to lie smoothly.

Step 3

- Align CB line with CB of mannequin, keeping horizontal grain level with floor.

- Tie a length of elastic or twill tape around the waistline to hold in the area that will be pleated.

- Pin at side seam to support pants.

- Tape the crotch line, ending at the same depth as the front.

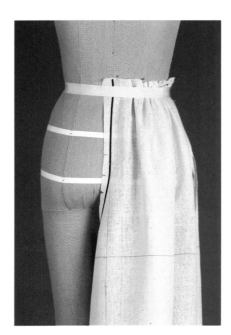

Step 4

- Trim excess from back rise along twill tape and turn into the inside leg seam, clipping where necessary to allow fabric to lie smoothly.

- Pin pant inside leg seam, keeping seam straight and grainlines horizontal.

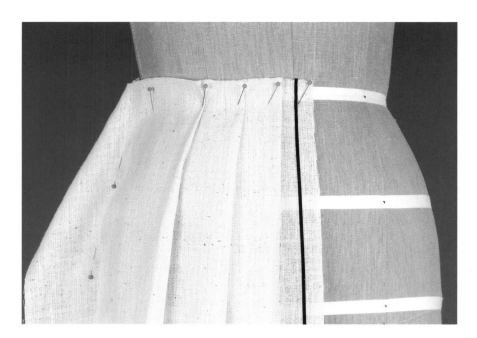

Step 5

- Study the photograph and form the pleats to achieve the linear and geometric look of the pants.

- In the front, the pleats fall vertically and are not angled at all; therefore, the top edge should be very straight.

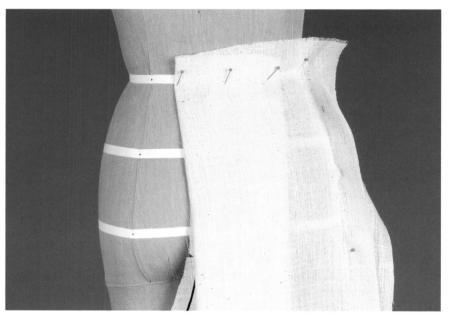

Step 6

- The back pleat angles strongly towards CB. Note how back waist pleat must end above waistline to achieve the look.

- As you form this pleat and set the waistline, check the inside leg seam. It should be hanging straight down centre of inside leg. If it is angling towards the back, back waist is being pulled too high; if it is falling towards the front, back waist is too low. Experiment with what happens to the inside leg seam as you move the back up and down.

Balance of the inside leg seam

The balance of the inside leg seam is critical in trousers. If trousers are torqued either to the front or back, the fit will not be right. It is important to develop your eye to see when this balance is achieved. Study trousers carefully and observe how moving the inside leg seam towards the front or back affects the hang of the trousers.

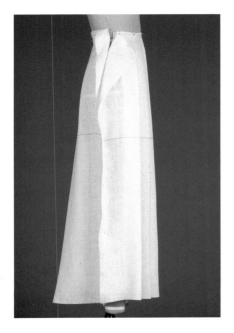

Step 7

- Pin sides so that seam hangs straight along side seam of mannequin. As in traditional forms of this pant, side seams will be perfectly straight on the grain.

- Note the interesting silhouette created on the side by the angled back pleat and the straight front pleats. The angle of the pleats forces the fabric out in the back.

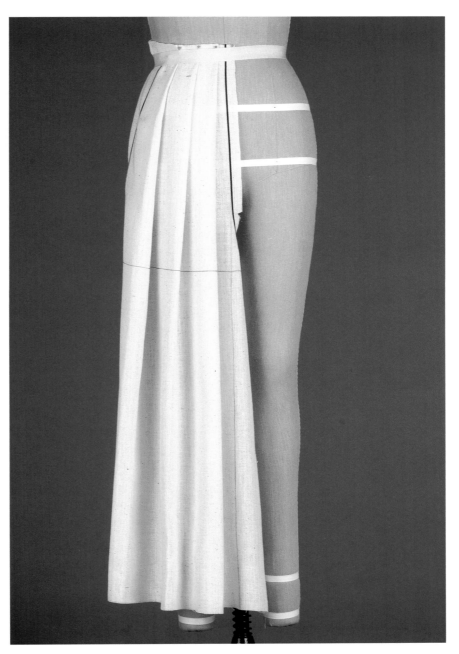

Step 8

- Turn front over back at side seam and pin.

- Tape side openings.

- The sides of traditional hakama are open to mid-thigh. In a modern version, this would be a great place to set in a deep side pocket.

- Pin a tape or ribbon around the waist to help mark exact waistline.

- Because the pants are voluminous and the angled tucks are important to the way they hang, this is a good time to view your drape from a distance in front of a mirror. Experiment with the balance of the pants by pulling up first the front waist, then the back. See what happens when one is dropped and the other pulled up.

Wide-leg trousers with front tucks

After Marlene Dietrich surprised the fashion world by wearing trousers, called slacks, in her early films, the style was embraced by Hollywood stars – most notably by Katharine Hepburn, who was seldom seen in a dress outside of the movies.

Draw the trousers, noticing how the proportion of details affects the look. The classic trouser will have some sort of pockets, a zip and often cuffed hems.

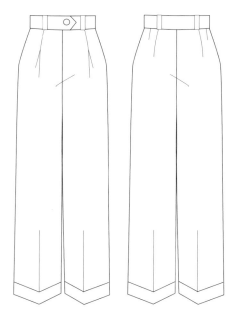

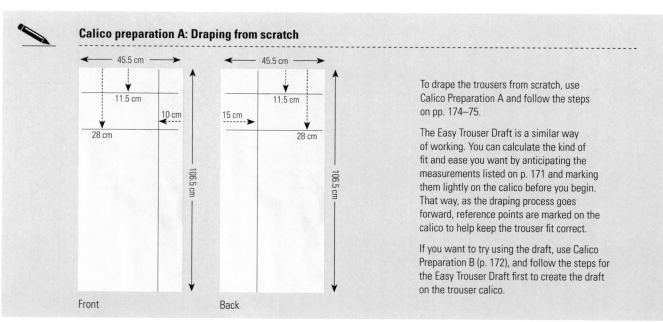

✏️ **Calico preparation A: Draping from scratch**

Front

Back

To drape the trousers from scratch, use Calico Preparation A and follow the steps on pp. 174–75.

The Easy Trouser Draft is a similar way of working. You can calculate the kind of fit and ease you want by anticipating the measurements listed on p. 171 and marking them lightly on the calico before you begin. That way, as the draping process goes forward, reference points are marked on the calico to help keep the trouser fit correct.

If you want to try using the draft, use Calico Preparation B (p. 172), and follow the steps for the Easy Trouser Draft first to create the draft on the trouser calico.

Easy trouser draft

There are many methods available to draft trousers by precise measurement rather than by draping. With draping, however, you have the advantage of being able to see the silhouette as it is created and the flexibility to refine the subtleties of its shape.

This particular method is intended to help you drape trousers. Having some measurements and a basic shape to follow is useful when starting the drape. It is not intended to be a final pattern, but rather a time-saving device to set the general parameters of the trousers' volume.

This draft can be done on paper and then transferred to a calico piece, or it can be drawn directly onto calico.

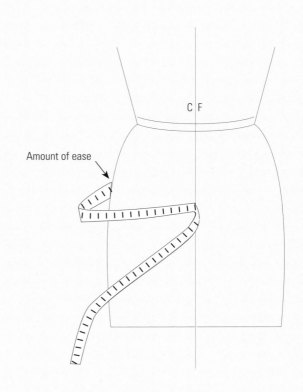

C F

Amount of ease

Measurements

Waist or high hip	66 cm (26")	This is where you want the trouser top edge to be.
Hip	101.5 cm (40")	This is probably the widest area of the trouser pattern.
		Determine the ease. For tight-fitting trousers, work with the exact hip measurement of the mannequin. For standard, more loosely fitted modern trousers, estimate 10 cm (4") around the hip. Although that sounds like a lot more than the 91.5 cm (36") hip measurement of the mannequin, it is only 5 cm (2") for each side, and only 2.5 cm (1") per front and back, which will be about right for a non-stretch fabric (see diagram above).
Crotch depth	23 cm (9")	Determine crotch depth using the method on p. 162, or measure down from the waist of the bifurcated mannequin to the crotch.
Length	96.5 cm (38")	Determine an approximate length by estimating an outside leg measurement. This is the measurement on the side seam of the bifurcated mannequin from the waist tape to the end of the leg.

Front and back rises

These two curves are critical to the fit of the trousers and have an infinite variety of settings. You will have to further determine this curve by working with the trousers on the mannequin.

It is a good exercise to study the front and back rises, or crotch curves, of different types of trousers. Notice how the shapes of these curves affect the fit of the trousers.

Drafting the trouser hem measurement

When adding to or decreasing the trouser hem measurement, a good rule is to do it equally from both the inside and outside leg seams.

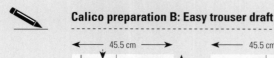
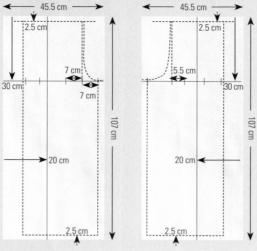

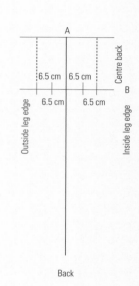
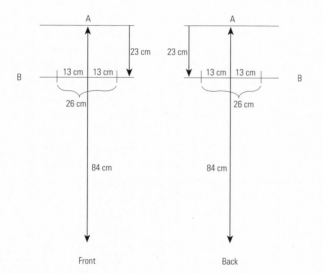

Step 1

- Draw a vertical line the length of your target trouser length and label it 'A'. This will become your straight grainline. Draw a line at 90° to the top of this line to mark the waist/high hip line. Repeat for back.

- Measure depth of crotch down the vertical. Draw a horizontal line and label it 'B'. This will become your horizontal grainline. Repeat for back.

- Divide your hip measurement in half: 52 cm (20") for the half trouser you will draft. Now divide that in half for the front and back sections: 26 cm (10") each. Now divide that measurement equally either side of the straight grain, and from line A measure out 13 cm (5") along line B to each side and mark two points.

Step 2

- Now divide the measurement between the two points into four, creating 6.5 cm (2½") segments, and mark the points along the horizontal grainline B.

- Draw two vertical lines up from the two outside points to the waist/high hip line. These two lines will become the centre front and back, respectively.

- Label inside and outside legs.

A ... A ... A ... A

B

Inside leg edge — C 6.5 cm — Outside leg edge

Front

Outside leg edge — C 11.5 cm — Inside leg edge — B

Back

D   D   D   D

Step 3

- To create front rise, add one increment – in this case, 6.5 cm (2½") – to the front inside leg edge, and mark it point 'C'.

- To create back rise, add two increments *less 1.5 cm (½")* – in this case, 11.5 cm (4½") – to the back inside leg edge and also mark it point 'C'.

- Keeping lower rise quite straight for the first 2.5 cm (1") or so in the front and 5 cm (2") in the back, blend line upwards.

Step 4

- Determine hem measurement. It is better to take a larger measurement than you actually anticipate and then finalize it during the draping process. For now, draw the lines tapering in only 2.5 cm (1") on each side and adjust it further on the mannequin. Measure hem out equally either side of straight grain at the bottom of line A and mark two points, labelling them 'D'. From points D, draw lines up to the points C on the inside leg and to the

bottom of the vertical lines you drew in Step 2 to create the outside leg seams.

- After filling in the outside and inside leg lines, the waistline is yet to be determined. This will largely depend on how you are treating the fit at waist and hip. You will need some sort of darting or tucking to create the fit at the waist; for now, just leave the waist and drape it on the mannequin.

Measurements for the wide-leg trousers with front tucks

Straight grainline A	108 cm (42")	These are looser-fitting trousers with pleats in the front, so allow that much ease.
Crotch depth for position of horizontal grainline B	28 cm (11")	They have a high waist and a waistband, typical of the 1940s vintage look. This measurement is, therefore, taken from crotch to waist plus about 2.5 cm (1").
Points C		When determining these points, allocate 56 cm (22") for the front trouser, because of the fullness of the front pleats, and 52 cm (20") for the back trouser. Points C, therefore, will be: *Front*: 28 cm (11") horizontal grainline, centred and divided into fourths = 7 cm (2¾") per increment = 7 cm (2¾") extra for front rise. *Back*: 26 cm (10") horizontal grainline, centred and divided into fourths = 2½" (6.5 cm) per increment. Add two increments, less ½" (1.5 cm) = 4½" (11.5 cm) extra for back crotch curve.

Creating new styles from established patterns

Often in the garment industry, basic blocks, or slopers, are used to create new patterns. A trouser company, for example, would have various blocks representing their different types of fit. When a new style is being created, one of the blocks would be used as a reference. That way, the designers know that the trouser hip, inside leg and front and back rises have been tested and can use that information to save time when developing the new style.

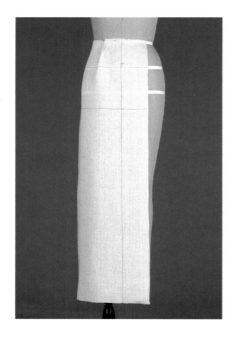

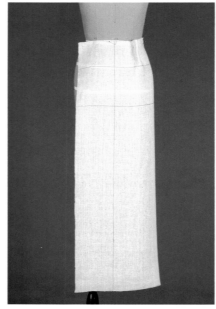

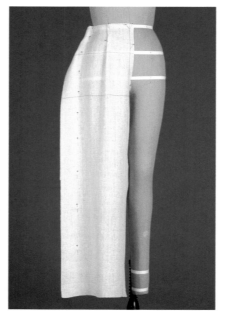

Step 1

- Align CF line with CF of mannequin, keeping horizontal grains level with floor.
- Approximate pleat point and pin pleat.
- Pin at side seam to support trouser.

Step 2

- Repeat Step 1 for back, making sure horizontal grains are on same level.
- Note how much more fabric is needed in the back than the front to create the back rise.

Step 3

- Using the Easy Trouser Draft to help find the right crotch depth, estimate hip measurement of trousers. In this case, the front trouser will be slightly larger than the back because of the pleat.
- Tape front crotch line and clip to CF grainline about 10 cm (4") down from waist. Continue clipping and trimming away excess, following curve of mannequin all the way to inside leg.
- Remove tape.
- Repeat Step 3 for back of trousers, as shown.
- The crotch depth should end at the same place as the front (horizontal grains should match at the inside leg).
- If you feel more comfortable draping the trousers without the draft method, drape curve by trimming and clipping until crotch line lies smoothly along crotch line of mannequin. For a classic cut, remember that the back curve will be a little less than twice the depth of the front.

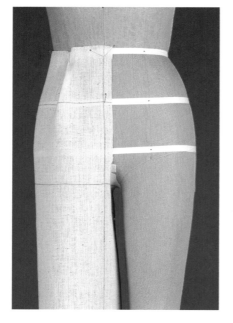

Step 4

- Pin inside leg front over back. If you have a two-legged mannequin it can be difficult to fold under and pin, so just pin the front over the back, laying the two pieces flat on a table. If you have a one-legged mannequin, pin front over back on the mannequin.

Step 5

- Pin side seams wrong sides together and check the silhouette of the photograph.
- Check that side seam is falling straight down side seam of mannequin.
- Check fullness of trousers. This garment is cut with a very straight, angular look, and the cuff ends at the top of the shoe.

- To help determine a target measurement for the cuff, study some of your own trousers and familiarize yourself with what a 61 cm (24") trouser hem looks like compared with a 45.5 cm (18") hem. This one looks to be about 50–60 cm (20–24") wide.
- Pin down side seams and adjust inside leg seam until balanced.

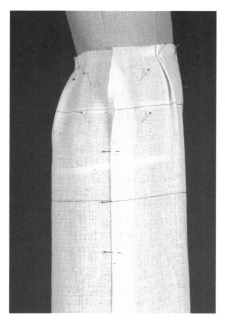
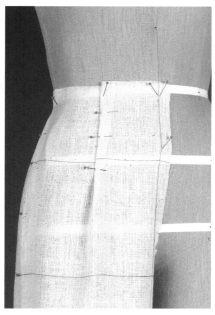

Step 6

- Once you feel you have achieved the look, pin front over back at side seam.

Step 7

- Once you have corrected the width of the trousers, find the centre of the front leg and check how your front tuck is angled. Correct it if you need to; it should angle slightly outwards to coordinate with the crease at CF of trousers.

- The tuck is stitched down 7.5–10 cm (3–4"), so pin down to where tuck stitch will finish.

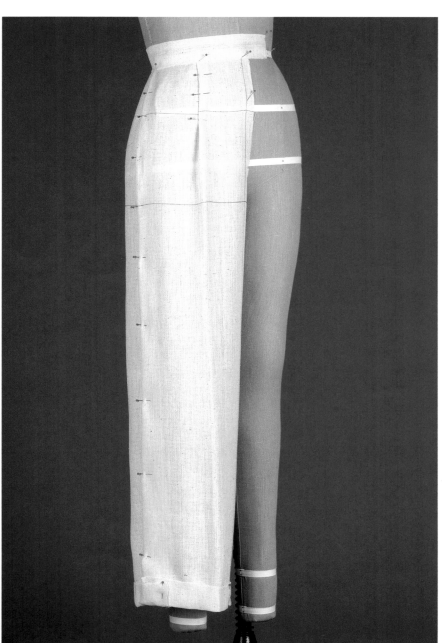

Step 8

- Determine width of waistband and wrap it snugly around the waist to make marking the waist easier. These are 1940s-era trousers, so the waist will be high.

- Turn up the cuff.

Draping project

This contemporary design from Nanette Lepore's Spring/Summer 2011 collection is cropped trousers with some flare at the hem.

The fabric in the photograph appears to be a Tencel, silk or soft cotton twill, as it has a gentle flow. The ease at the waist is taken in by small darts hidden at the flap-pocket line. Very little fit is needed in the waistband, as it sits at the high hip line about 7.5 cm (2–3") below the waist.

The attitude is of relaxed resortwear – casual, fun and chic. The trousers should have a modern fitted hip and fairly slim upper leg that flares just a bit at the hem.

For this style, use a hemp/silk blend. It has a softer drape than the standard calico and more closely resembles the look of the trousers in the photo. Also, because it has a looser weave, it is easier to see the grainlines, which is helpful in draping trousers.

If you use the Easy Trouser Draft (pp. 171–73), the approximate crotch depth will be 2.5–5 cm (1–2") shorter in the front than the back, similar to a jean cut. Calculate the hip measurement very close to the mannequin. For this project, the ease at the waist will be taken in by just one dart.

Slim-fitting styles

Often in a jean style or slim-fitting trousers, the back crotch is extended and the front shortened for a closer fit in the back high area.

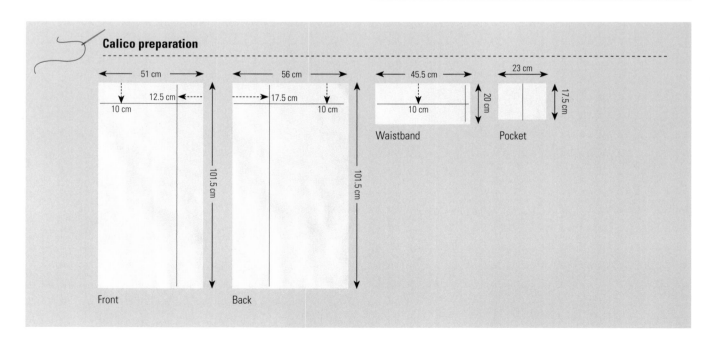

Calico preparation

51 cm · 12.5 cm · 10 cm · 101.5 cm · Front

56 cm · 17.5 cm · 10 cm · 101.5 cm · Back

45.5 cm · 10 cm · 20 cm · Waistband

23 cm · 17.5 cm · Pocket

Step 1

- Set front snugly around hip, keeping straight grain vertical.

- Fold in the front dart, keeping it as small as possible, just enough to take a little excess off the waist.

- Tape front crotch line.

Step 2

- Set back section, keeping grainline vertical below hip. Then, allow CB grainline to fall to the left of the CB of mannequin, smoothing fabric to fit over back high hip. Angling this CB grainline will allow for a more fitted back hip area. Also, because the CB is thrown onto a slight bias grain, this will give some stretch, allowing the piece to form fit over the body.

- Form a small dart to fit the top edge.

- Hold fabric in at thigh area.

- Form back dart.

Step 3

- Cut crotch-depth line in front and back; note that, as you follow the crotch line, you will be clipping beyond your taped line. As the trousers are quite fitted in that area and need to be draped close to the mannequin, it is acceptable to do this. Keep back thigh slim as you pull fabric around to inside leg.

- Pin inside leg area to mannequin. Again, because these are fitted trousers, the inside leg often goes towards the front. In this case, drape it about 2.5 cm (1") towards the front, which should allow you to keep the fit close to the thigh in the back.

- Make sure that your knee-line horizontal grains are matched at the inside leg. If you have a one-legged mannequin, this will be easy to do. If you have the two-leg mannequin, it is more difficult, so just pin the fabric to the inside leg of the mannequin as smoothly as possible.

Fitting the back thigh

You can shape the upper thigh by pulling more or less fabric into the inside leg seam.

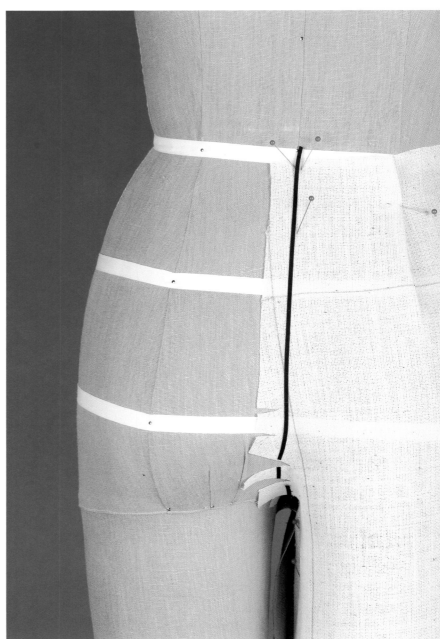

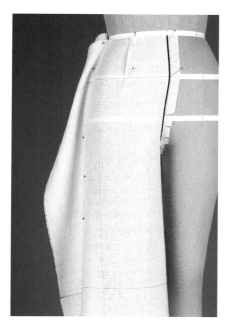

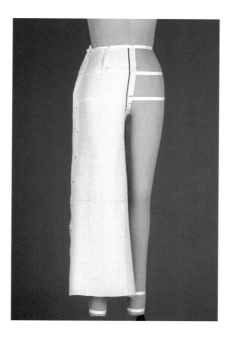

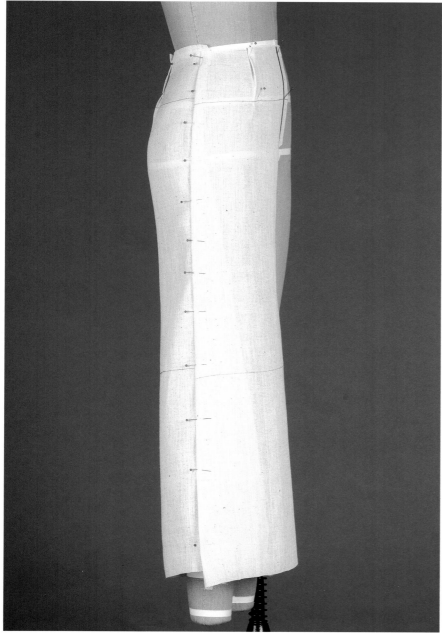

Step 4

- Check the photograph and start pinning side seams wrong sides out. When you get to the knee area, begin to flare out the leg.

Step 5

- Trim excess at hip area and continue pinning to the hem.

- Pin the inside leg seam at the same time, balancing the two flares and keeping grainline straight down the centre of the trouser front and back.

Step 6

- Turn side seam front over back and check silhouette.

- If you have a single-leg mannequin, you can pin the inside leg front over back as well. If you have a two-leg mannequin, pin by laying the front on top of the back.

Trouser flare

When working with trouser flare, the amount on the inside and outside leg should be fairly equal.

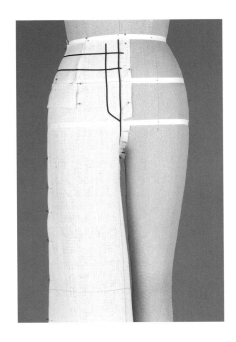

Step 7

- Determine set of waistband by first taping the position of the top and bottom edge.
- Drape pocket flap by creating a rectangle from fabric with the edges turned under.
- Tape the fly stitching or J-stitch.
- Check the proportions of all three details.

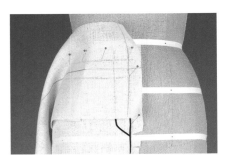

Step 8

- Start draping waistband at CF with horizontal grain centred on taped area and straight grain vertical to CF.

Step 9

- Pulling fairly tightly, wrap waistband around to CB, allowing grainline to drop as CB of waistband becomes bias. This will allow band to fit snugly around high hip.

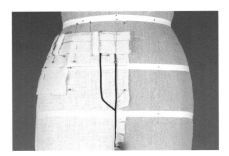

Step 10

- Trim excess from both sides of waistband and turn edges under along the taped lines. You can remove the tape so that it is easier to see the actual line.
- With small scraps of fabric, determine proportion and placement of belt loops.
- When positioning these details, note that even 0.5 cm (¼") larger or smaller makes a big difference in the look of the trousers. A 4 cm (1½") waistband has a completely different look to a 3 cm (1¼") waistband.

Step 11

- Turn up the hem.

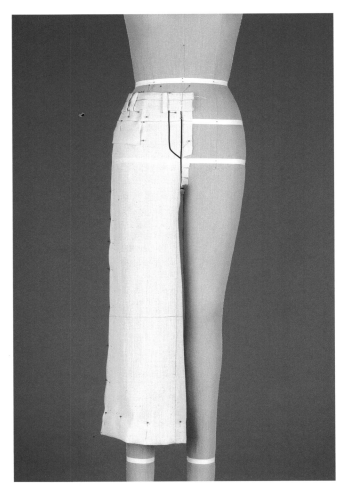

Marking and truing

Correcting lines

Use a red pencil for corrected lines, and blue if there are further corrections. That way, it is easy to remember that your pencil line is the original marking, and the two colours are the subsequent corrections.

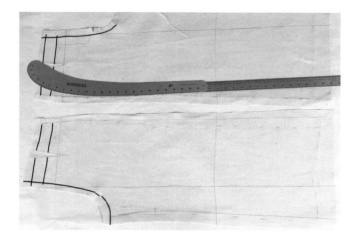

Step 1

- In truing up trousers, it is very important that the long seamlines of the outside and inside leg are smooth. The long metal hip curve is perfect for the job. Here it is combined with the metal ruler to create the line from hip to hem.

- Observe the two side-seam curves. The front section appears quite a bit wider than the back. It is possible for the back to be slightly smaller than the front trouser, but in this case it may have draped slightly off balance. It would, therefore, be sensible to even out the flares by taking a little bit off the front and adding it to the back.

Step 2

- At the point where the crotch seam flattens out, the inside leg seam will usually begin with a concave curve angling towards the knee.

- Here you can see the pencil lines are quite erratic. Draw a red line to start the correct angle, but then soften it with the further correction in blue.

- True up the waistline of the trousers from the bottom edge of the back waistband tape and align the small front darts with the position of the pocket flap.

Analysis ◉

- Do your trousers accomplish the look of the photograph? What kind of attitude do they evoke overall? Does the upper part look fitted and flattering? Are the legs flared enough to look playful yet chic?

- Look carefully at the hip area. The inside leg is pulling in the front or back crotch and creating a 'smile' effect. This will occur if your front or back crotch seam, or rise, is too short. Add to the crotch line where it flattens out, which means you will also have to widen your trousers slightly at the top of the inside leg. Just blend the line as it travels down towards the knee.

- If the back crotch is cutting in too much, your back curve is probably not concave enough. Carve out a little more, starting about 10 cm (4") down from the top edge, and observe the difference. Just 0.5 cm (¼") more out of that curve will change the fit.

- If the upper trouser seems to be sagging in the front or back, try pulling up first at the front waistband, then the back, and observe how it changes the tilt and look of the trousers.

- It is questionable whether there is enough fullness in the trouser leg. The fabric in the photographed design has a lighter drape than our hemp/silk blend. But some of the fullness here is in the back, unseen, while the photograph has some movement in it.

- If you want to add to or subtract from the width of the legs, remember to do it equally on the inside and outside leg seams, unless there is a balance issue.

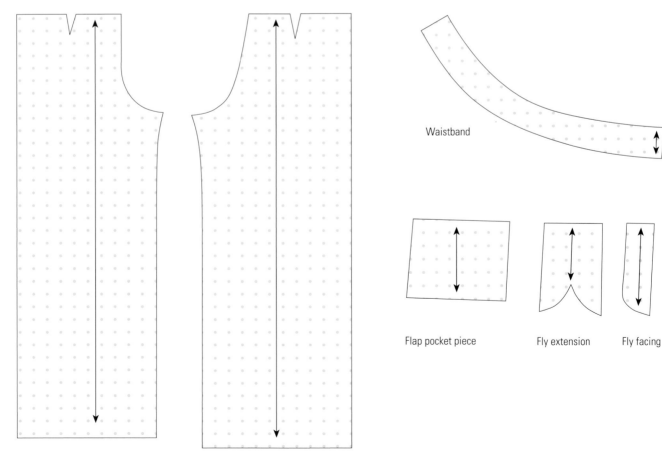

Waistband

Flap pocket piece   Fly extension   Fly facing

Front   Back

2.4
Knits

History

The beauty of knit is in its ability to stretch. Interlaced yarns comprise an entirely different structure than that of a woven fabric. The inherent give in the knit can create either a smooth, close fit or, when falling freely, a uniquely fluid drape.

The earliest knitted fabric is attributed to the Egyptians. Their style of knitting however, was closer to the way fishnets are made than to what we know as knitting today. Beaded dresses of this fishnet construction, when worn over a sheath-like garment made from linen, would create a figure-hugging silhouette.

Knitting with two needles probably emerged as a technique for making fabric around 1000 AD. Before that, textiles of similar structure were made using one needle. Evidence of knitting can be found in medieval paintings and in surviving garments – including jackets, caps and gloves – from the sixteenth and seventeenth centuries.

The mechanization of knitting began in 1589 with the stocking frame by the Reverend William Lee. Successive generations built on the machine's foundations, through to the Industrial Revolution in the mid-nineteenth century, when the industry gained in stature.

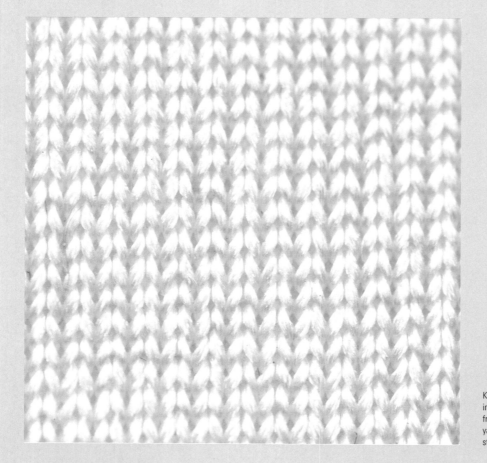

Knitted fabric is created by interlocked loops formed from a single piece of yarn, its structure giving it stretch in all directions.

Opposite page:
Left: Coco Chanel is seen here getting into her car, the model of the emancipated, mobile, modern woman in her knit ensemble. The knit skirt allows a freedom of movement that symbolizes women's forward progress.

Right: Like a second skin, painted and ornamented knit garments, such as this unitard, afford the acrobats and aerialists of Cirque du Soleil full freedom of movement.

The first designer to truly popularize the wearing of knits by women for daywear was the revolutionary fashion icon Coco Chanel. Early in her career, Chanel often borrowed garments from the men in her life with which to work. One of the first garments she experimented with was said to be a polo shirt cast off by a stable boy, which she cut up and tailored to fit herself.

After World War I, when textiles were in short supply, Chanel's ingenuity served her well. She fashioned knits that were more commonly used for undergarments into modern and comfortable tops, skirts and jackets, often with bright stripes and patterns.

Technological advances in yarns and knitting in the last half century have brought us from those old polo shirts to the state-of-the-art fabrics used for legwear and hosiery, swimming, and shaping and slimming, with such amazing qualities as moisture wicking and thermo-regulation.

Exercises
Cotton knit top with ribbed neckline

Creating fitted garments from knit fabric is more commonly done by pattern drafting than draping, because it is difficult to pin fabric to the mannequin while stretching it. If the garment is tight, and the stretch of the knit is being utilized, such as in swimwear, it is better to draft the pattern. If the knit fabric is intended to softly lie over the body, or to be draped in folds, then it works well to drape it.

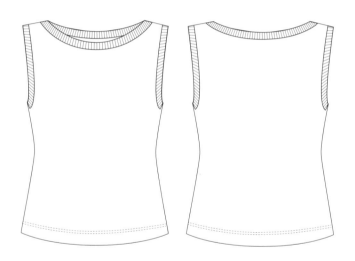

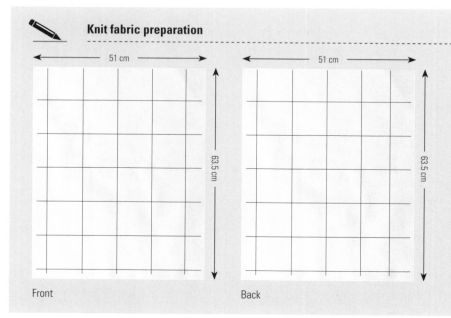

✏️ **Knit fabric preparation**

51 cm

63.5 cm

Front

51 cm

63.5 cm

Back

A problem that sometimes arises when draping with knits is that the knit may stretch out of shape during the process. When truing up, it becomes difficult to tell what the original measurements were. For that reason, it is helpful to draw a grid on the fabric before draping with it. This entails drawing additional grainlines on the fabric so that it can be re-blocked back into its original measurement after draping.

In the following exercise, you will draw a grid on the knit so that it can easily be re-blocked. This will make it easier to see where you are utilizing the stretch as the grid moves out of alignment.

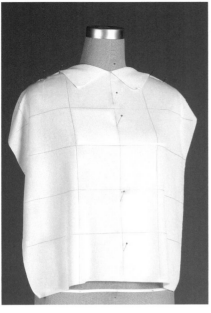

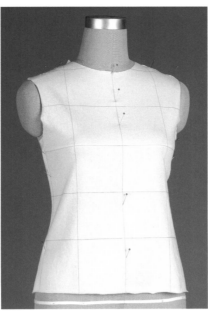

Step 1

- Align CF of knit piece to CF of mannequin; pin down CF and at shoulders. Keep the gridlines as close to vertical and horizontal balance as possible.

Step 2

- Cut away CF at neckline to allow fabric to lie smoothly.

- Pull equally on both sides at bust to determine how much of the stretch will be utilized. The goal is to pull it tightly enough so that the dart usually used for the bust ease will not be needed.

- Pin at bust and down sides until the front has the look you want. It should lie smoothly with very little wrinkling.

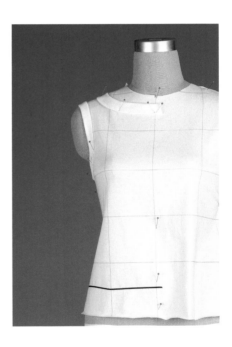

Step 3

- Repeat from Step 1 for back.

- To drape the rib neckline piece, first determine a width and fold a piece of rib fabric in half against the rib. If you don't have rib, a small piece of your horizontal-grain knit will work as well.

- Starting at CF, pull rib piece around neckline towards the back, stretching slightly as you go. Observe how, at the shoulder, the cut edge needs to be stretched more until the folded edge lies flat.

Step 4

- Drape rib piece around armhole, as you did with the neckline.

- Tape the hem length.

Draping a knitted garment

With knits, it is best to drape a full front and back instead of only half the garment. This will help keep the knit stable as you are working with it.

Strapless knit top

This classic strapless style can be done in any fabric, but works particularly well in knits. The fabric is stretched over the bodice, resulting in beautiful gathers that conform to the shape of the body and are then tacked lightly to the lining to keep them in place.

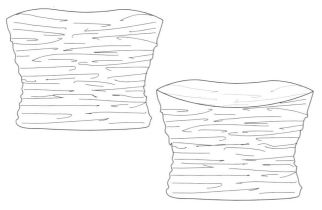

Utilizing the stretch of knit fabric

This is a style that utilizes the full stretch of the knit fabric. When you pull the knit firmly over the mannequin, observe how the gathers seem to fall naturally into place.

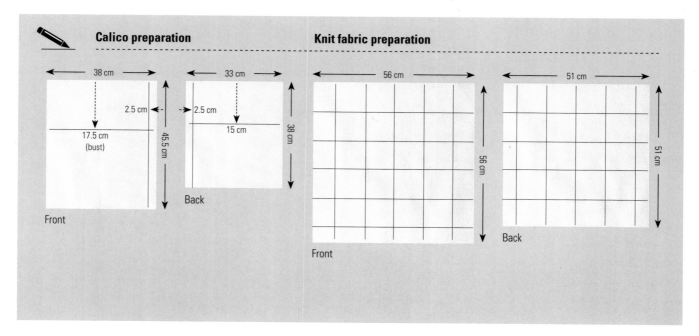

Calico preparation

38 cm

2.5 cm

17.5 cm (bust)

45.5 cm

Front

33 cm

2.5 cm

15 cm

38 cm

Back

Knit fabric preparation

56 cm

56 cm

Front

51 cm

51 cm

Back

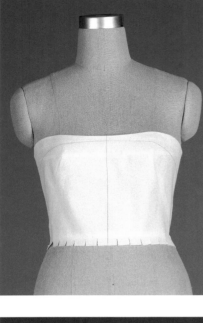

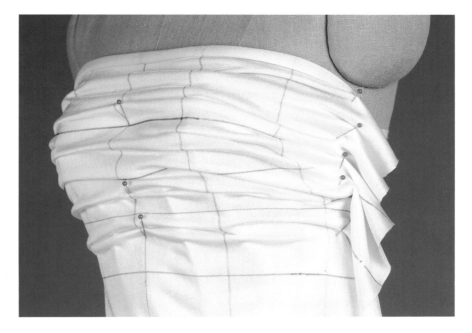

Step 1

- Set a woven bodice on the mannequin to use as a base for the gathers. Try using the bodice draped on pp. 46–47.

Step 2

- Pin CF to CF of mannequin, and left side of the knit to side seam of mannequin.
- Start gathering up the sides, pulling fabric evenly over bust.

Step 3

- Tape top edge and hem.
- Pin to hold gathers in place.

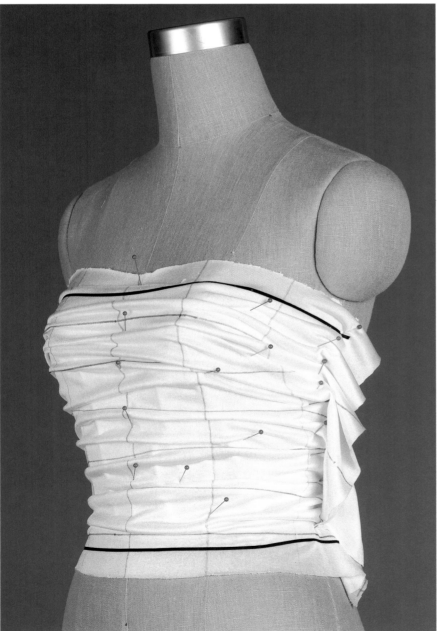

Draping project

This halter-neck knit top from Nanette Lepore's
Spring/Summer 2011 collection exhibits a
sporty chic and whimsical attitude.

The multiple neck straps are not necessary to hold up
the top, but they serve well to keep the top edge even
since there is no understructure to support the light
knit. A halter-style neckline is created by the ring of
knit that holds the straps.

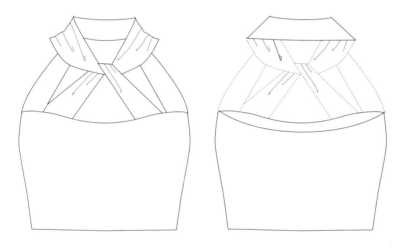

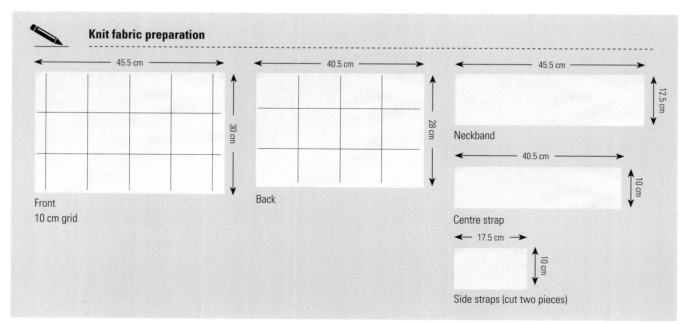

Knit fabric preparation

45.5 cm

30 cm

Front
10 cm grid

40.5 cm

28 cm

Back

45.5 cm

12.5 cm

Neckband

40.5 cm

10 cm

Centre strap

17.5 cm

10 cm

Side straps (cut two pieces)

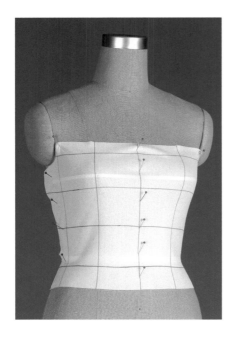

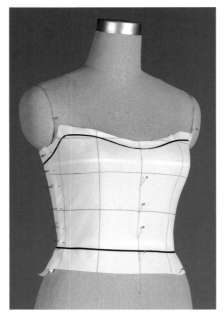

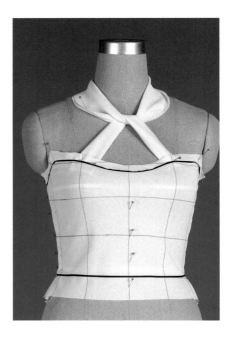

Step 1

- Set front by pinning CF to CF of mannequin.

- Smooth fabric equally towards both sides.

- Pull slightly over the bust to determine how much of the stretch you need to utilize to eliminate the need for any darting or seaming.

- Repeat for the back.

Step 2

- Turn front over back and pin side seams.

- Tape neckline. Take care to keep side bust area high before sloping down at the back. Top edge of back should cover bra line. Check photograph to determine top edge of front. It is a little bit lower in the centre.

Step 3

- Set neckline halter drape and CF straps.

Step 4

- Set side straps.

- Re-adjust neckline drape so it looks like the photograph – not too tight, not too loose.

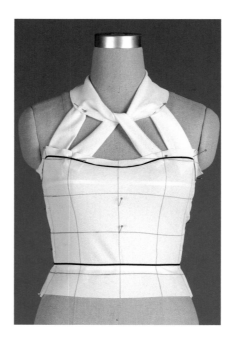

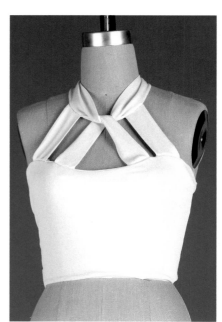

Marking and truing

Step 1

- Mark knit top with pencil or chalk before removing it from the mannequin (not shown). Sometimes with knits, the pencil or chalk does not give enough definition. If so, try a felt-tip or gel pen, taking care it does not bleed through to the mannequin.

- Crossmark more frequently with knits than with woven fabrics (not shown).

- Remove the tape (not shown).

- Re-block onto paper grid to the original measurement.

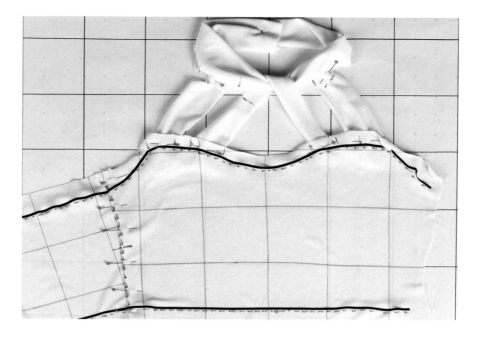

Step 2

- True curves as marked, and correct against the photograph.

- Mark seam allowances, which on knits are often 1 cm (⅜") to allow for overlocking.

- Use V-notches, rather than cutting in on knit fabrics.

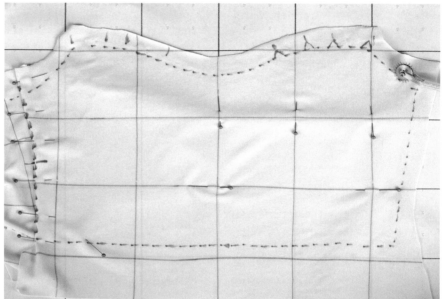

Analysis

- Compare the fit of your knit top with that in the photograph. Does it lie smoothly over the front torso? If it is too tight, it will wrinkle at the underbust or waist. If it is too loose, it will sag slightly.

- The right degree of utilization of stretch takes some experience. Study this by making the top both slightly smaller and larger, and observe the differences in the fit.

- Visualize the top on a muse. Is it low enough in the neckline to be fun and flirtatious? Are the straps spaced in an interesting way?

- When looking at the straps, pay attention to the negative spaces. Rather than looking at the straps themselves, focus on the spaces between them, and then compare those shapes to those on the photograph. This may help you determine whether you have spaced them correctly.

Analysis of the ensemble

This top is paired with the trousers you draped in Chapter 2.3: Trousers (see p. 176).

- When working with ensembles, the challenge is to coordinate the overall look and sizing of the pieces. If the top is too fitted and petite, or the trousers too oversize, the proportion will look askew. When draping two pieces to be worn together, it is important to view them on the mannequin at the same time, to make sure they look as if they belong together. Here, the sizing is similar to that in the photograph.

- The details are important. The size of the neck and shoulder straps must relate to trouser details such as the belt and pocket flap. They do not need to be the same size, but if they are of the same level of volume, they will flow together. Be aware of details that stand out too much; this may signal that they are out of proportion within the ensemble.

- Detailing such as topstitching is important here, too. Remember that the delicacy or boldness of the stitching needs to match the tone of the garments.

- Wide belt loops create a broken-line effect that is echoed in the neckline straps. The gaps are not the same size, but they tie the two pieces together, drawing the eye smoothly over the ensemble.

- It is a little hard to tell from the photo exactly where the body rise, or crotch depth, ends, and the legs on the trousers seem a bit longer. It could be that the model's very tall proportions are giving a more elongated look to the leg. Also, the movement in the trousers is bringing the flare forwards, whereas the leg here is static and the flare is partly in the back where you do not see it. Visualize the trousers in movement to determine whether you have achieved the right amount of flare.

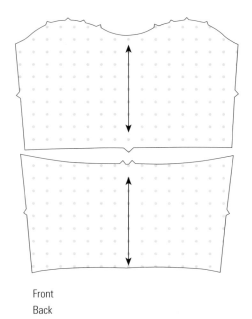

Front
Back

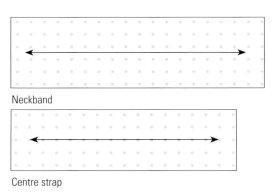

Neckband

Centre strap

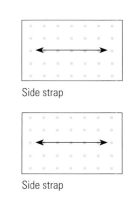

Side strap

Side strap

Variations
Top with batwing sleeves

The knit used in this blouse utilizes stretch only in the sleeve lift. The fabric is a rayon that has a heavy drape, which works well with the volume in the peplum. The term 'batwing' is used for a sleeve that is cut in one piece with the bodice.

For this drape you do not need grids on the peplum pieces, as you are not utilizing the stretch in those areas.

The character of draped knits

This style shows off the beauty of draped knit fabric, which tends to fall and flow heavily and evenly. It is a good exercise to study the many different weights and fibres of knit fabric and familiarize yourself with the different looks they create.

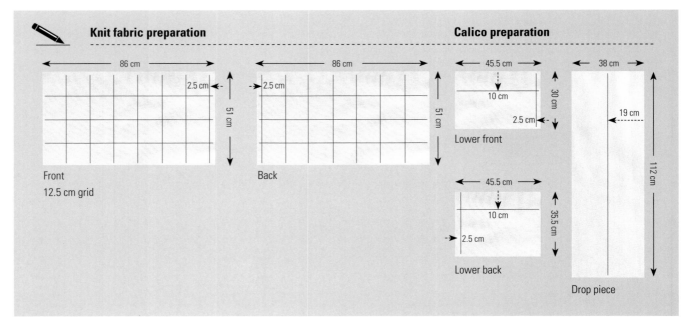

Knit fabric preparation

86 cm
2.5 cm
51 cm
Front
12.5 cm grid

86 cm
2.5 cm
51 cm
Back

Calico preparation

45.5 cm
10 cm
30 cm
2.5 cm
Lower front

45.5 cm
10 cm
35.5 cm
2.5 cm
Lower back

38 cm
19 cm
112 cm
Drop piece

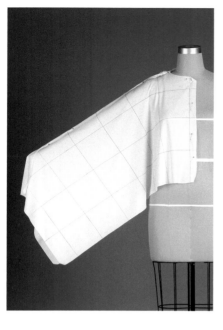

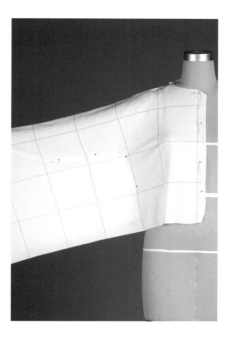

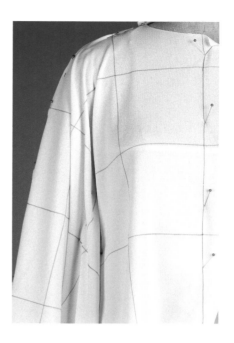

Step 1

- Set front section by pinning down CF, trimming and clipping neckline as needed.

- Pin across shoulder area and at bust line.

- Tie a length of twill tape around the wrist (not shown). Set the stuffed arm at a height you would consider optimal lift.

Step 2

- Determine depth of batwing sleeve. Test the lift by draping high and then dropping the arm to check amount of fabric at underarm. Pin side and underarm seams.

Step 3

- The sleeve set at this lift results in quite a bit of fabric under the arm.

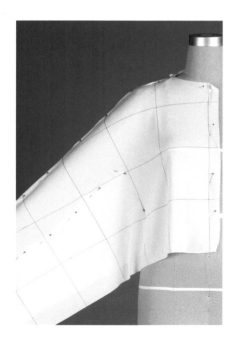

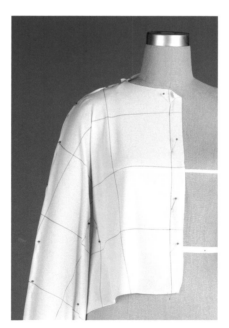

Step 4

- Try testing the lift at a lower angle.

- Set this low, the sleeve has no lift and will not be comfortable.

Step 5

- Try to arrive at a height that seems like a comfortable compromise.

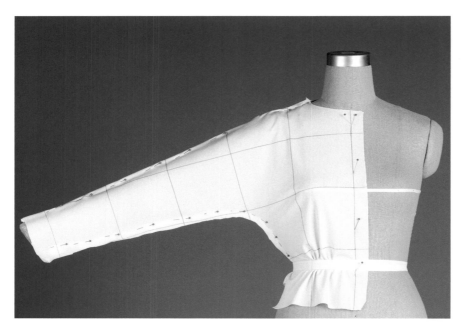

Step 6

- Set the stuffed arm at desired height and pin shoulder area wrong sides together. Trim excess fabric, leaving about 2.5 cm (1") seam allowance.

- Pin underarm curve wrong sides together. Trim excess fabric, leaving about 2.5 cm (1") seam allowance.

- Tie a length of wide elastic around waistline and check balance.

Step 7

- Set wide elastic at the waist.

- Set lower front drape. Start in CF with top edge of fabric about 7 cm (2–3") above the waist. Trim and clip as you did with the bias skirt to create the flare. Here you will also gather in the fabric as you go to create more fullness.

- Set lower back drape in the same way.

- Join side seams of peplum drape (not shown).

Setting the sleeve angle

The angle of the batwing sleeve determines how the underarm drape of the blouse will look. There is an infinite array of shapes to choose from, and there is no right or wrong way here. It depends on the look you want and the degree of lift you need.

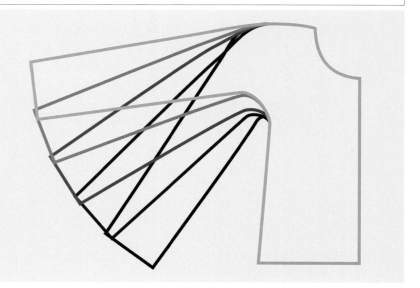

Step 8

- Trim hem of peplum, following the line of the photograph as it slants down from front to back.

- Turn waist edge under top edge and set wide elastic onto the outside.

Step 9

- Drape shoulder piece by tucking it into the elastic and looking at the shape it creates at the waist. It should gently fall over the elastic, but not too much.

- Practise draping this piece while looking in the mirror from a distance until you arrive at a look with which you are satisfied.

Working with a mirror

Remember that the mirror is your secret weapon! Designers tend to look at their work at very close range, but clothes are not usually seen that way – others see us at a further distance. Even when conversing with friends, we are often 1.5–2 m (5–6') away. This is the perspective you need to consider when you make the final adjustments to your drapes. Position yourself with a mirror so that you can continually look up and get that helpful perspective.

3

Advanced Draping

3.1 Coats and Jackets
3.2 The Grand Gown
3.3 Draping on the Bias
3.4 Improvisational Draping

With these advanced draping exercises, your eye will become more highly trained in recognizing subtleties in shape and form. Attention is given to 360° awareness of the drape, crucial to recognizing when a silhouette becomes new.

You will learn to map out the energetic flow of a garment, using grainline placement to support emotional content.

You will practise the designer's skill of visualization, critical in maintaining the essence of inspiration while draping larger shapes, such as a gown, or while working with support elements such as shoulder pads, foundations and petticoats.

You will continue to train your hand in the skills of sculpting through use of more complex seaming and shaping, learning to understand the power of emphasis and focal point and how slight differences can shift the atmosphere and mood of a garment.

Once you are able to focus more on the abstract, the ultimate goal of creating a signature look begins to be emerge, communicating not just a garment, but a consciousness.

3.1

Coats and Jackets

History

The inherently balanced drape of a simple square-cut panel of woven fabric can be easily seen in outerwear pieces such as cloaks, capes and mantles.

A classic example of the elegance of this elemental form can be seen in the royal robe. Throughout history, kings and queens were pictured with majestic lengths of fabric trailing behind them. The wealthier the family, the more fabric could be afforded, along with more elaborate embellishments.

Because they needed to be large enough to cover other garments, these panels of heavier fabrics — woollens, linens and, later, heavy velvets — often worked best when simply shaped, draped over or seamed at the shoulders.

Left: Queen Victoria wears a long cape of golden cloth in this nineteenth-century portrait by Charles Robert Leslie.

Above: A wool aba, chiefly worn by the Bedouins of Syria, is a simple outerwear garment made of woven panels pieced together at the shoulders.

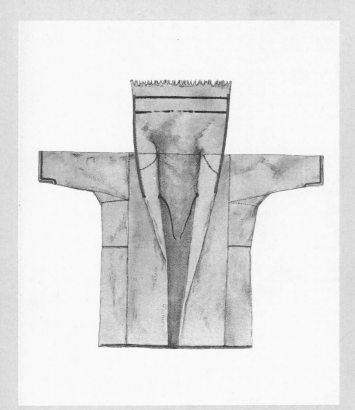

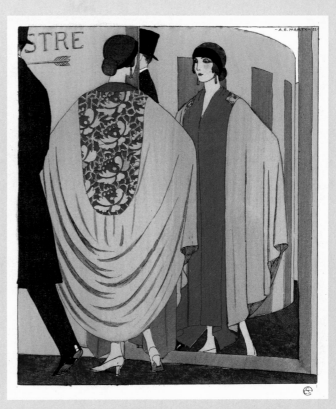

Garments recognizable as the ancestors of the coat and jacket began to evolve well before the Renaissance. The ancient Persians are credited with developing the first seamed coat with sleeves. For women, it was not until the mid-nineteenth century that coats and jackets were worn as fashionable daywear, as capes and mantles remained more practical for covering the voluminous garments worn for so many centuries.

Many of the coats and jackets worn today are modern adaptations of cuts whose construction template has endured and evolved over long periods of time. The original trench coat, peacoat, Spencer jacket and tailcoat are some examples of these classic coat styles.

When creating a coat that has older origins, be aware of references that may arise. For example, a woman's jacket with a fitted bodice and gathering in the crown of a fitted sleeve might remind one of the Victorian era, imparting to the garment the flavour of the posture, attitude or sentiment of that time.

Another example is that timeless classic, the trench coat. Countless versions have been designed, yet they always have a certain cachet. The collar with the high stand gives protection from rain, but also imparts a mysterious chic. The storm flap, deep pockets and shoulder epaulettes remind one of Humphrey Bogart and his unflappable cool.

Collars and shoulders tend to be focal points for jackets and coats. The collar frames the face – from demure lace to fur collars to the huge ruffs of the seventeenth century. Since the working man's frock coat was adopted into fashionable attire in the 1730s, the notched collar and lapel have become a timeless template, even as proportions constantly change with fashion trends.

Above left: This shepherd's cloak of Finnish/Asiatic origin is made of a series of square-cut woven panels and can be seen as an early example of a modern coat.

Above right: This cloak by Paul Poiret from the 1920s is a modern example of the timeless elegance of a simple drape.

Exercises
Understanding shoulders

The shoulder as focal point dates back to the ancient Greeks, whose peploses and chitons were fastened at the shoulders. Historically, in the military, the shoulder held the rank – it is where epaulettes are worn and where sashes and awards are hung. Coats and capes often have embellishments at the shoulders.

Various types of padding have been used over time to give the shoulder area more strength and volume, as a strong shoulder tends to give one more stature, dignity and even a sense of power. In the 1980s, the American television series *Dynasty* popularized women's suits with huge shoulder pads, dubbed 'power suits'.

However, the curve of the shoulder line is important to consider, as this is where the front and back fabric balance. If the shoulder line is off-balance, the front and back of the dress or jacket will kick out in the front or back, pushing the drape of the fabric towards the centre front or back.

Since many garments are supported by the shoulders, it is important to understand their structure. The outer shoulder is round, dips down in the centre and curves up at the neck. In simple clothing construction, this seam is often drawn as a straight line.

Study the shape and silhouette of clothing with different shoulder treatments, noticing the effect of a well-fitting shoulder.

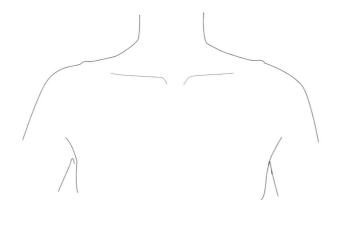

The curved shoulder shape holds the balance and must support the weight in many types of garments.

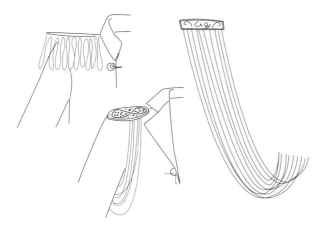

The decorated shoulder imparts a sense of dignity.

208

Kimono sleeve

The classic Japanese kimono is an example of a completely unstructured shoulder. The construction is completely geometric, the woven panels maintaining their balanced purity.

With this kimono sleeve construction, the fabric falls over the natural shoulder line unsupported, creating many folds and drapes at the underarm area. Because of the perfect balance of the front and back, the look is graceful and relaxed.

Shoulder pads

As a counterpoint to the kimono, the shoulder here is at its most constructed. With the help of a fitted shoulder pad, the fabric is shaped and moulded closely over the shoulder, eliminating all excess from the underarm area. There are no soft folds here, the line is trim and crisp. The front of the garment fits smoothly over the figure.

The large shoulder pad here, typical of the 1940s, makes it an obvious focal point. The height and angular shoulder line create a strong and sexy look for Lauren Bacall, the ultimate modern woman of her time, both beautiful and powerful.

Chanel-style jacket

The famous fashion innovator Coco Chanel popularized the fitted tailored jacket for women. She distilled the modern jacket of her day into a timeless classic that became her signature look.

The original Chanel jacket was short, with no collar, and typically boxy in shape. One of the key features of the tailored jacket is the three-panel construction.

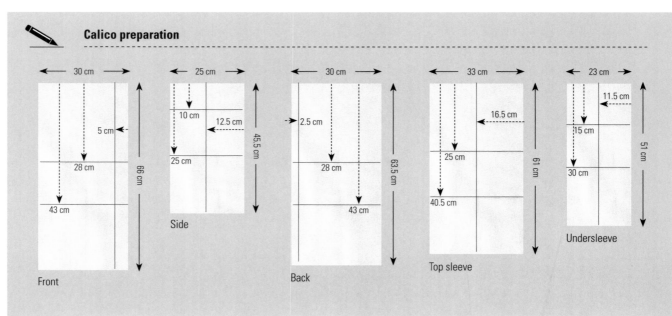

Calico preparation

Front — 30 cm, 5 cm, 28 cm, 43 cm, 66 cm

Side — 25 cm, 10 cm, 12.5 cm, 25 cm, 45.5 cm

Back — 30 cm, 2.5 cm, 28 cm, 43 cm, 63.5 cm

Top sleeve — 33 cm, 16.5 cm, 25 cm, 40.5 cm, 61 cm

Undersleeve — 23 cm, 11.5 cm, 15 cm, 30 cm, 51 cm

Today, Karl Lagerfeld designs for the House of Chanel. Many of his jackets still reflect the classic Chanel look – the boxy shape and short length with the three-panel construction. Other elements that reflect the look are the flap pockets, the bound edges and the finishing touch, the signature strand of pearls.

As jackets are intended to be layered over other garments, they need to have a comfortable amount of ease, which requires draping away from the mannequin. The sculpting of the shape and sensitivity to the contour of the lines becomes more challenging and ever more important.

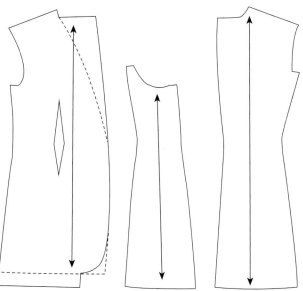

The classic three-panel jacket has a side section that eliminates the side seam and sits between the princess lines in the front and back. The two-piece sleeve angles slightly forwards for the natural hang of the arm, and has a closer fit at the inside of the arm and more room at the elbow.

Balancing the three panels requires 360° awareness of the shape, so that it looks flattering from every angle.

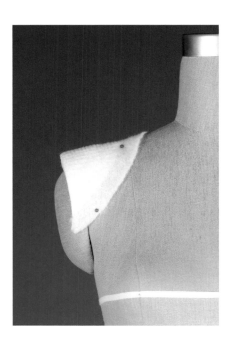

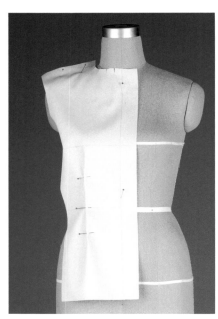

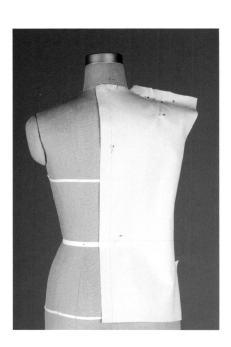

Step 1

- Begin by draping without the stuffed arm; it is much easier to see the balance of the three panels without the arm in the way.

- Pin shoulder pad firmly in place at the two lower corners and centre of the shoulder area. Make sure the pins are stuck all the way into the mannequin so they do not interfere with the drape of the calico.

Step 2

- Set front panel by aligning CF of calico with CF of mannequin. Trim and clip neckline until it fits smoothly.

- Pin across bust and into shoulder area lightly, leaving a little ease in the armhole and taking care not to pin too tightly.

- Pin at side to prepare for the volume you want. Because this first panel extends further towards the side than a princess line, you will need a dart to pull in the waist shape.

- Fold in a vertical dart with a fairly small intake; 1.5 cm (½") at the waist is about standard.

Step 3

- Set back panel by aligning CB of calico with CB of mannequin.

- Pin across back shoulder, keeping horizontal grain level by giving some ease at the armhole and shoulder area.

- Drape a very small dart into shoulder-seam area, and also pull in a little extra ease along that seam. It makes a better fall in the back at the hem if the shoulder is properly draped with the horizontal grain close to level and some ease on that seam.

- This ease and shoulder dart may be eliminated later depending on how the fabric reacts to shaping. Many weights of wool can be steamed and shaped to create room over the shoulder blade.

Armhole ease

Note that as you drape the ease in the body pieces that you need, it will naturally result in some armhole ease. Don't pin the tops of the side panel too closely; allow about 2.5 cm (1") extra in the front and back.

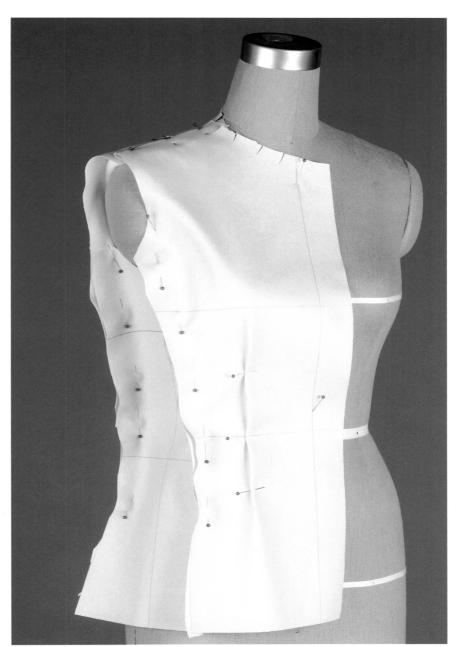

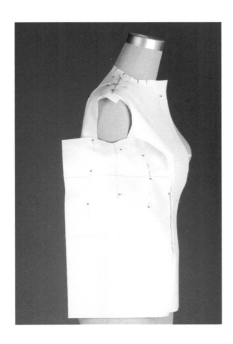

Step 4

- Set side panel piece by centring the piece in the side seam.

- First lay this panel on top of the front and back sections and try to get a feel for how much volume you would like to have.

- Pin down as you experiment with the amount of ease.

Step 5

- Keeping horizontal grain level, pin wrong sides out along back and front, joining the seams.

- Trim away excess leaving about 2.5 cm (1") seam allowance.

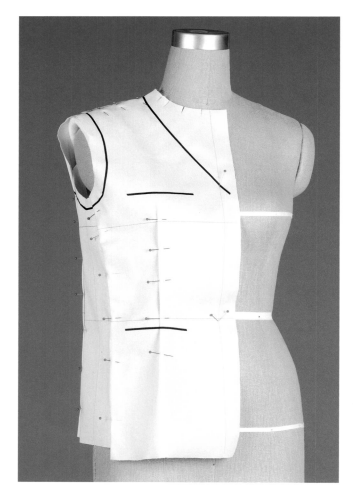

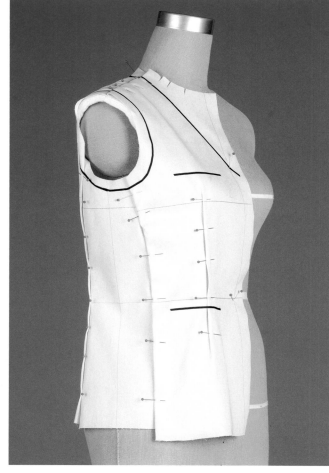

Step 6

- Turn seams to the inside, front over side and back over side panel.

- Tape armhole and neckline.

- Position pocket to help you set the proportions.

- Study the balance of the three sections. Do all three pieces have an even look? What does the contour of the jacket look like? Is it similar to the photograph? Does it look good from every angle?

Step 7

- Look closely at the back side seam. It is forming a straighter line than the front seam, which has more of the contour of the body.

- Try unpinning the back waist area, then clip more at the waist and re-pin a little tighter.

- Note how this correction changes the look of the jacket. The back panel seam now subtly shapes out at the shoulder blade where more room is needed and gently shapes in at the waist.

Studying through 360°

Look at the jacket through 360°, as you would if it were being worn by a person. The jacket needs to be well shaped from every angle, not just from the front and back.

The two-piece sleeve

Another basic construction element of the classic tailored jacket is the two-piece sleeve. Imagine that you have a basic blouse sleeve on the mannequin and you want it to be shaped more ergonomically to the arm. One way to do that is to pin a dart from the front underarm area to the wrist, pinning out more at the elbow where the arm curves in. Then pin the back sleeve area in above the elbow, letting out at the elbow where you need the room and pinning in again towards the wrist. Essentially, these darts made into seams are what form the two-piece sleeve.

The construction of two seams is a practical way to create a more comfortable shape to the sleeve by following the natural hang of the arm. Ideally, the seams should be minimally visible, falling to the inside of the arm and hidden in the folds of the fabric.

The seams traditionally do not match at the armhole. It is tempting to draw them that way when designing, because it makes sense for seams to match. However, in reality, four seams meeting at one point of the armhole would create too much bulk. ◉

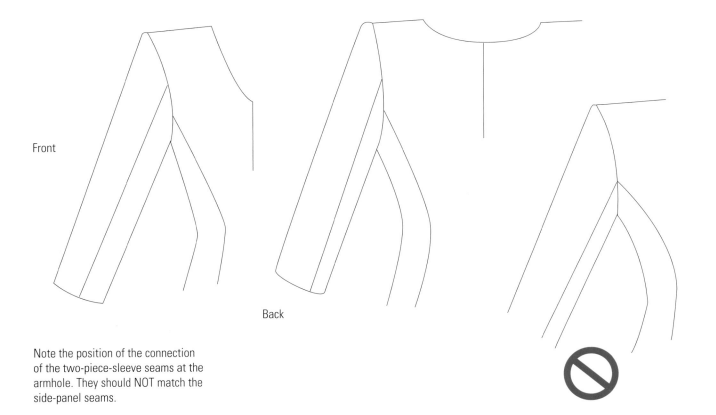

Front

Back

Note the position of the connection of the two-piece-sleeve seams at the armhole. They should NOT match the side-panel seams.

Easy two-piece sleeve draft

There are many methods for drafting sleeves using precise measurement rather than draping. With draping, however, you have the advantage of being able to see the shape you are creating as it develops and the flexibility to further refine its subtleties.

This particular method is intended to help you drape the sleeve. Having some measurements and a basic shape to follow is useful when starting the drape. It is not, however, intended to be a final pattern, but is rather a time-saving device to set the general parameters of the sleeve's volume.

This draft can be done on paper and then transferred to a calico piece, or it can be drawn directly on calico.

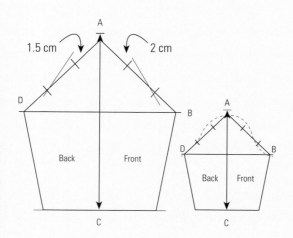

Step 1

- Begin with Step 5 from the Easy Sleeve Draft (see pp. 124–25).

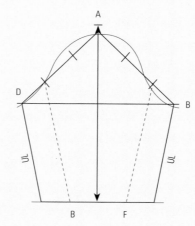

Step 2

- Divide hem into quarters, and mark new point at the front 'F' and new point at the back 'B'.

- Draw dotted lines from the lower marks on the back and from armhole down to the new points B and F on the hem.

- Notch the dotted lines to keep the fronts and backs from getting mixed up, with two notches on the back and one on the front.

- Label the underarm lines 'UL'.

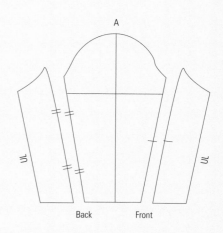

Step 3

- Cut the sleeve pattern apart on dotted lines from F and B.

- Notch the cut lines on the smaller pieces to match with the larger piece.

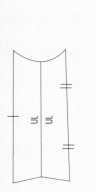
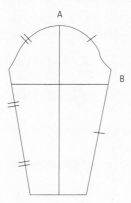
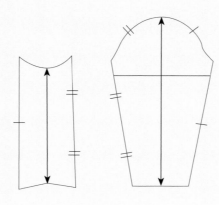
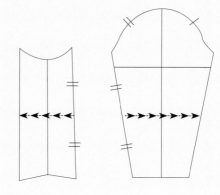

Step 4

- Tape the two smaller pattern pieces together along the UL lines.

- Now you have the two basic pattern pieces for the two-piece sleeve: the smaller one is commonly called the 'undersleeve'; the larger one is the 'top sleeve'.

- Mark the remaining marks on the back armhole curve with a double notch and on the front with a single notch.

Step 5

- Mark the taped UL line as the straight grain of that piece and the centre line of the top sleeve as the straight grain.

Step 6

- Now add some shape to the elbow area to follow the natural hang of the arm.

- Draw an elbow line about 17.5 cm (7") below the underarm line on both pieces.

- Slash and spread the elbow line of both pieces open about 1.5 cm (½").

Step 7

- Then add shape to the bicep area.

- Add a further 1.5–2 cm (½–¾") to the bicep area of the top sleeve and a little less to the undersleeve.

- Blend lines into a curve, smoothing out the elbow line.

- It is preferable that the front seam of the two-piece sleeve is not too visible from the front. Adjust pattern slightly by adding 2.5–4 cm (1–1½") to lower front edge of top sleeve; remove the corresponding amount from undersleeve.

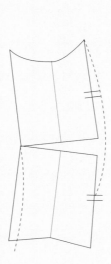
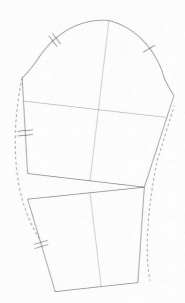

Four sleeve types and their pattern pieces

Note how the two-piece sleeve pattern can be adjusted to create various sleeve shapes.

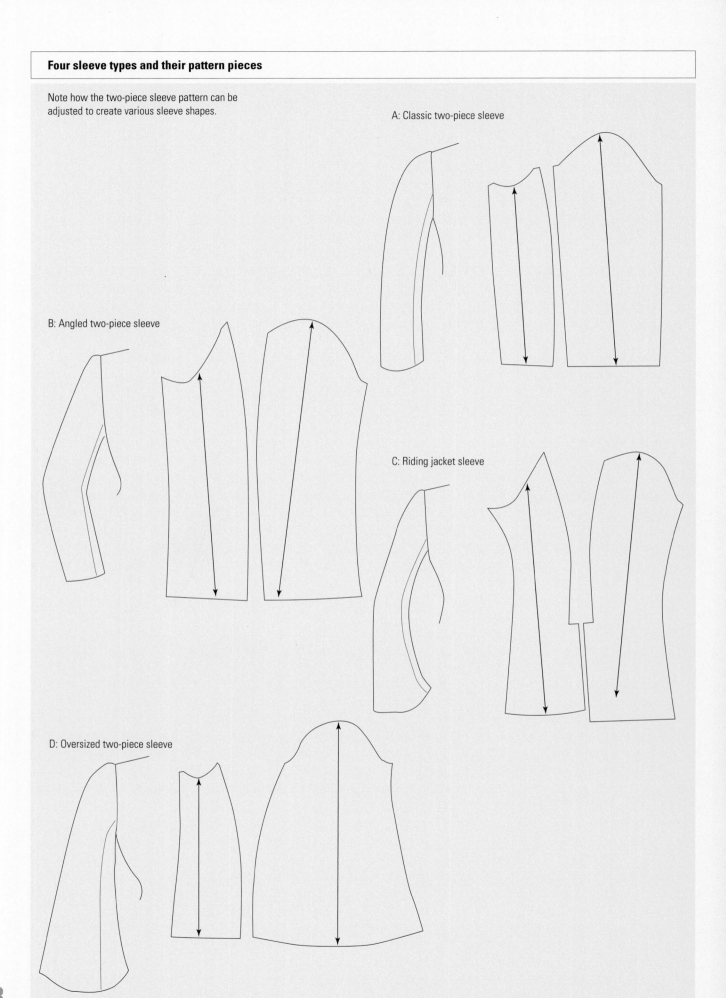

A: Classic two-piece sleeve

B: Angled two-piece sleeve

C: Riding jacket sleeve

D: Oversized two-piece sleeve

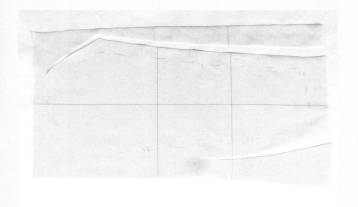

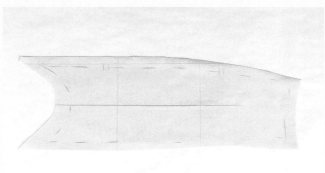

Step 8

- Using the shape from the two-piece sleeve draft, trace top sleeve paper pattern lightly with chalk onto prepared calico piece.

- Cut around the line leaving about 2.5 cm (1") seam allowance.

Step 9

- Repeat Step 8 for undersleeve pattern piece.

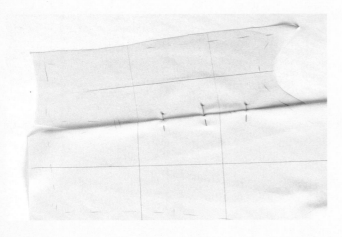

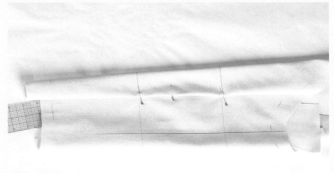

Step 10

- Pin top sleeve over undersleeve on seam lines.

Step 11

- Use a clear grading ruler to help you pin the second seam, as shown.

Step 8

- If not already attached, pin the shoulder pad to the toile. Gently remove the jacket drape with the pad from the mannequin.

- Attach the stuffed arm.

- Replace the drape and pad in the same position, pinning again down CF and CB.

- Chalk armhole and remove tape so it is easier to pin on the calico sleeve.

- Set the two-piece sleeve onto the shoulder, starting at the crown and angling it slightly towards the front, following the natural hang of the arm.

Step 9

- Note how the sleeve puffs out slightly at the crown area. This indicates that there is significant ease at the crown area. It should be no more than about 2 cm (¾") per front and back. Because the final jacket fabric will be wool, this amount of ease can be steamed and shaped to fit the armhole.

- Now check the position of the two sleeve seams. They should be slightly hidden by the drape of the sleeve.

- Here it looks as if the front undersleeve is angling too far to the front; use tape if necessary to re-mark the new lines.

- Readjust angle of sleeve drape and/or height of notch points so seams are either hidden or hanging in an unobtrusive way. Re-pin if necessary.

Step 10

- Adjust and distribute ease of sleeve crown. Finalize position of notch points.

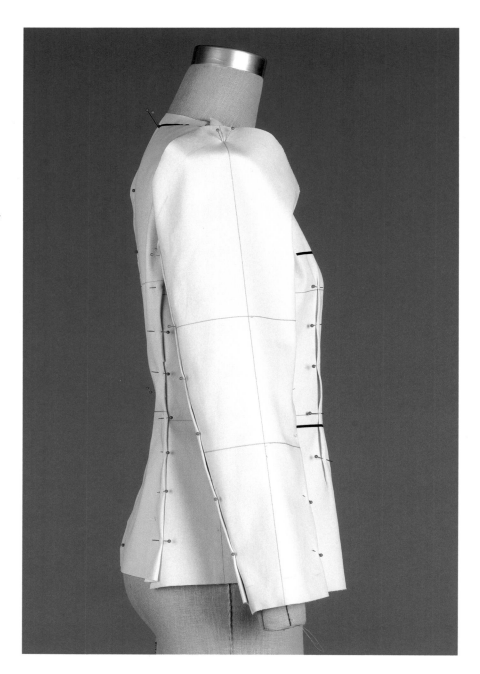

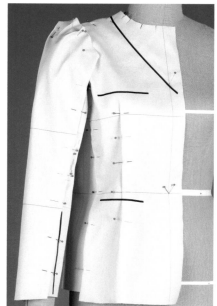

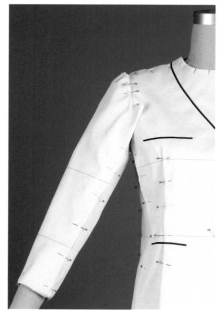

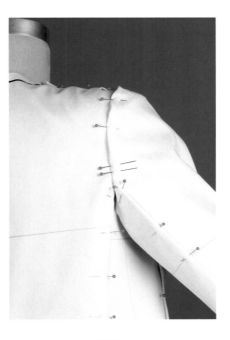

Step 11

- Allow excess at lower armhole of sleeve to fall towards inside of armhole.

- Pin it into a smooth curve, raising and lowering armhole as you go to find the right balance aesthetically and for movement.

Step 12

- Repeat from Step 9 for back, remembering that sleeve should be hanging slightly towards the front, following the natural fall of the arm; therefore, there will be slightly more ease in the back of the sleeve and a little less fabric in the front, especially at the lower parts of the curves.

Step 13

- Complete the drape by adding the finishing details, taping the pocket flaps, buttons and sleeve vent.

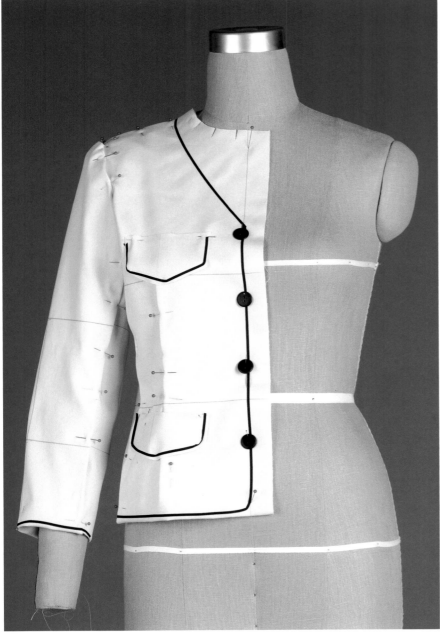

Aesthetics vs movement

There is a happy medium to be found in the sleeve lift. If the lift is very high, there is freedom of movement, although more fabric under the arm. If the lift is low, and all the ease has been draped out, raising the arm will cause the entire jacket to ride up.

Draping project

This Dolce & Gabbana tuxedo jacket, worn by Rihanna, is a perfect balance of masculine and feminine. The body of the jacket is the epitome of classic menswear tailoring with its fitted shape, welt pockets and peaked lapels, while the rounded, Victorian-style leg-o'-mutton sleeves are soft, light and feminine.

When preparing your flat sketch, try to capture the angular look of the body and the contrasting soft curves of the sleeves. To help you visualize the volume, find a sleeve as close as possible to this one. Studying this reference will help you decide how much larger or smaller your actual sleeve needs to be. Calculate measurements for the largest sleeve you think you may want, so that you do not run short on your fabric pieces while draping.

For this drape, use a heavier fabric, such as a cotton twill, or simply fuse your regular calico. The weight will help the definition of the body shape and sleeves.

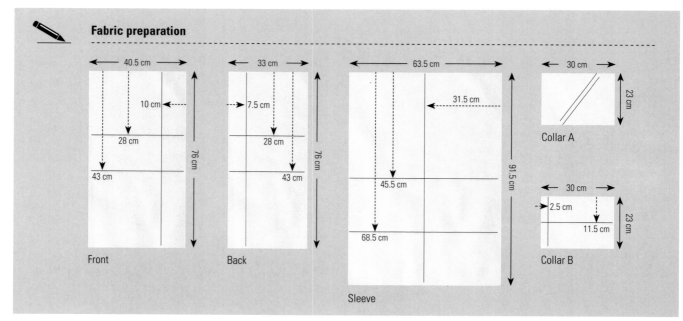

Fabric preparation

Front

- 40.5 cm
- 10 cm
- 28 cm
- 43 cm
- 76 cm

Back

- 33 cm
- 7.5 cm
- 28 cm
- 43 cm
- 76 cm

Sleeve

- 63.5 cm
- 31.5 cm
- 45.5 cm
- 68.5 cm
- 91.5 cm

Collar A

- 30 cm
- 23 cm

Collar B

- 30 cm
- 2.5 cm
- 11.5 cm
- 23 cm

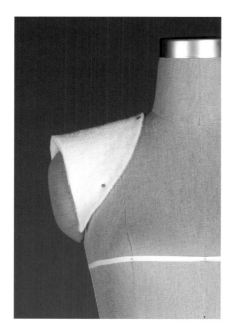

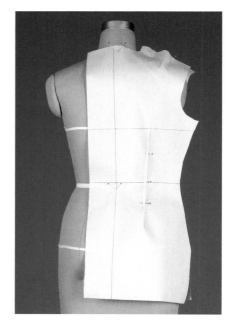

Step 1

- Study the silhouette of the jacket and determine which shoulder pad to use.

- Set shoulder pad onto shoulder, extending it about 2 cm (¾") beyond armplate.

- Compare it to the Chanel-style jacket on pp. 212–13; note that its look is more square than the softer Chanel.

Step 2

- Pin CF. Trim and clip neck, but only exactly where it hits the mannequin's neck. Leave CF high for the peaked lapel.

- Form a neckline dart that starts about 2.5 cm (1") from the shoulder line and parallels what will be the roll line. This will help keep horizontal grain level, and will transfer some of the neck ease to bust area. It will also help the lapel to curve a bit and roll more smoothly.

- Trim shoulder and armhole area.

- Form front vertical dart. Check silhouette: if it seems that the dart needs to be very deep to create the fitted waist, form two darts instead. The second dart should be midway between first dart and side seam, and shorter than main dart.

- Pin at the side.

Step 3

- For the back, align horizontal grain across shoulder blades and pin.

- Note the long angular look necessary to keep the jacket long and slim.

- Pin a vertical dart.

- Shape CB seam in at waist and out at shoulder blades.

- Wrap shoulder seam towards front, trimming and clipping neckline, and pin.

- There should be ease in the back shoulder area. (This will be shaped in during sewing.) Allow about 0.5 cm (¼") for a satin and up to 1.5 cm (⅝") for a loosely woven wool.

- If necessary, fold in a small shoulder or back neckline dart to hold the ease.

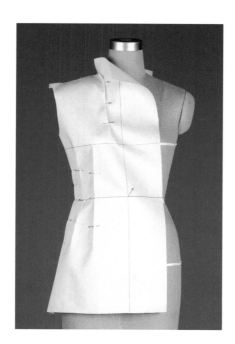

Step 4

- Clip curve of side seam all the way to sew line at the waist and turn front over back.

- Check the shape: the contour of the side seam is very important in achieving the look. It is long and slim, gently curving in so that it is not too exaggerated or sharply hourglass in shape.

- Remember to check your drape in the mirror from a distance. Look at the side seam in the photograph; it has a very sleek look. Observe any difference between your seam and that of the jacket in the photograph and adjust it if you need to. Add another dart at the waist if it brings you closer to the look of the photograph.

- Remember to look at the jacket through 360° degrees and even out the fit between all the darts and the side seam.

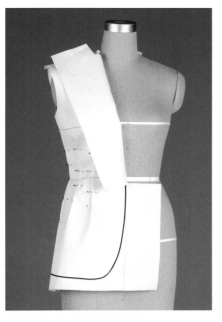

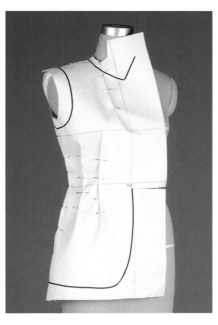

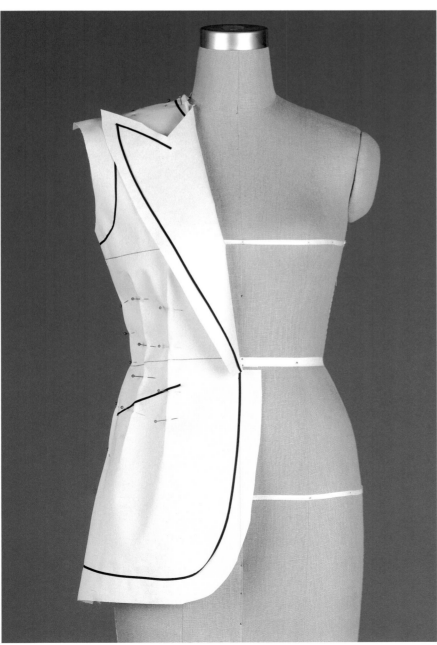

Step 5

- Determine roll line and break point of lapel and collar, which is the exact point where the front of the jacket turns over to become the lapel. Check the photograph.

- Anchor-pin the point at which the closure will sit at the waistline. It is important to finalize this break point now; moving it later will affect the collar drape.

- Tape lower hemline to help determine proportions.

- Clip to waist and turn back lapel area.

Step 6

- Tape the armhole.

- Tape the neckline. Start from CB and bring tape around to front in a fairly straight line, then angle up for the peak of the collar and lapel.

Step 7

- Turn lapel over at break point and tape style line.

- You will need to see the neckline from both sides of the fabric, so re-tape from the underside as well, making a smooth connection with the lapel and creating the angle you want.

- If you need to adjust the tape on the other side of the fabric to match it, do so now.

- Trim excess fabric and tape the welt pocket line. This detail will help you see whether you have achieved the right proportion.

- Study the silhouette. Compare it to the photograph, and check it in a mirror.

Draping the notched collar

The notched collar is draped from the opposite direction to the collars draped previously in the book. Instead of starting at the centre back, start at the front and roll the fabric piece towards the back. It is crucial that the collar flows with the roll line of the lapel as it travels around the neck towards the back. First connect the two pieces and then work with the height of the stand and the width of the collar.

The grainline of notched collars is at the discretion of the designer. It is most commonly placed with the straight grain matching the grain of the centre back.

If there is a pattern to the fabric, it is important that it match there. The straight grain placed vertically at the centre back also gives the strongest line to the collar and a crisper roll around the neckline. For a softer look, the collar may be draped on the bias.

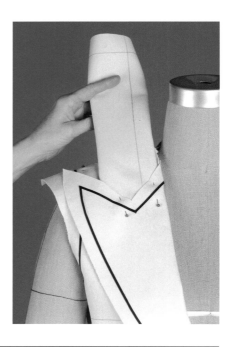

Step 8

- Start the collar drape at the front by folding fabric piece with the straight grain and laying it under the lapel. Keeping the folded edge on an exact line with the roll line, pin it to the top part of the lapel.

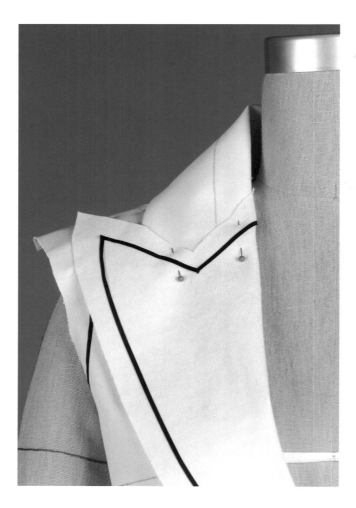

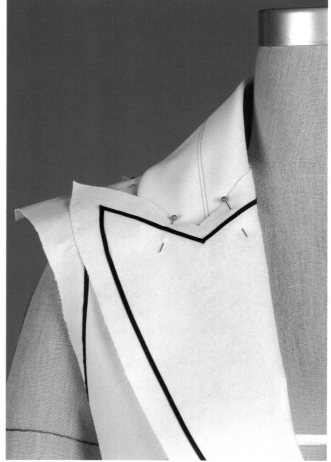

Step 9

- Now wrap collar piece around the neck towards the back.

- Observe the nature of the fold: it appears crisp and has quite a high stand.

Step 10

- Test the bias grain to see if it works better: fold the fabric with bias grain running parallel to foldline and place that piece against the lapel edge. Drape it around the shoulder towards the back.

- See the subtle difference between this fold and that created with the straight-grain piece in Steps 8 and 9. The bias rolls around the neckline very smoothly while the straight-grain piece breaks as it travels around the neckline, making a harder fold, like a crease in the fabric.

- The bias grain always tends to look softer. In this case, the stronger look of the straight grain in Step 9 is more suited to the masculine, angular jacket.

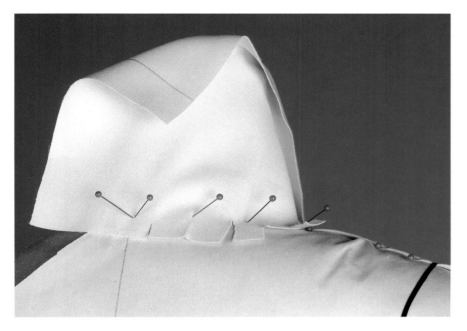

Step 11

- Once you are happy with the look and proportion of the collar, carefully turn it up and begin pinning it to the back neckline, clipping as you move towards the shoulder.

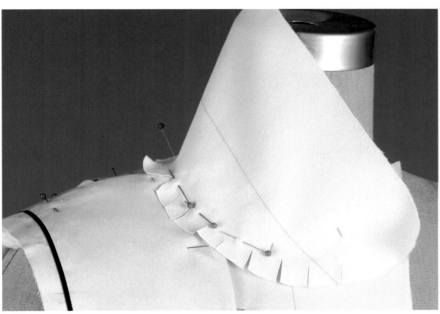

Step 12

- Continue pinning collar to neckline all the way to the front edge, checking the style line you taped beneath the lapel.

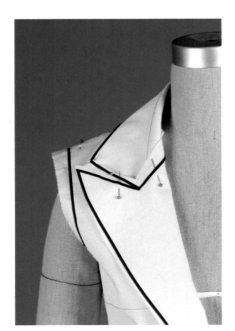

Step 13

- Fold collar down and check that it is smooth, with no breaks around neckline.

- Tape the style line along the outer edge, comparing it to the photograph and finding a good balance to the peaked lapel.

Draping the sleeve

For this sleeve, use the Easy Sleeve Draft (pp. 124–25). The sleeve here is so large and cumbersome to drape that it will be easier to do it in one piece and form the two seams as darts.

Alternatively, you can follow the instructions for the Easy Two-piece Sleeve Draft (pp. 216–19) and proceed, creating the two seams now.

You can also drape it from scratch – it is awkward, but not hard.

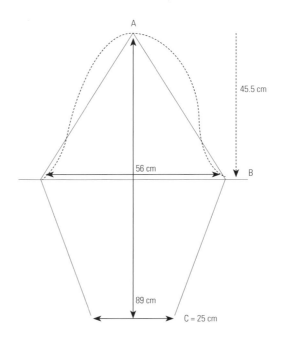

45.5 cm

56 cm

B

89 cm

C = 25 cm

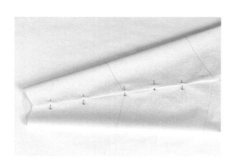

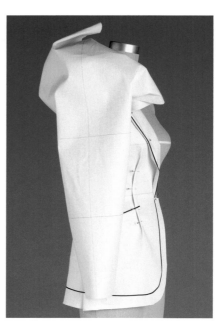

Step 14

- Chalk armhole and remove tape so it is easier to pin the sleeve (not shown).

- Attach the stuffed arm if you have not already done so (not shown).

- On the table, pin underarm of sleeve up to elbow area, front over back. Use a clear grading ruler inserted inside the sleeve to help you avoid inadvertently pinning to the other side of the sleeve.

Step 15

- You will need some support for the fabric at the crown area. Pin a ruffle of crinoline or extra fabric onto the top of the arm or the seam allowance of the armhole.

- Whether or not you need to incorporate this ruffle in the final garment will depend on the main type of fabric being used and how much body it has. It is likely, however, that some type of support will be needed.

Step 16

- Start by setting sleeve piece at crown area, angling the grainline slightly towards the front. Pin to armhole a few centimetres to the front and back of the shoulder point.

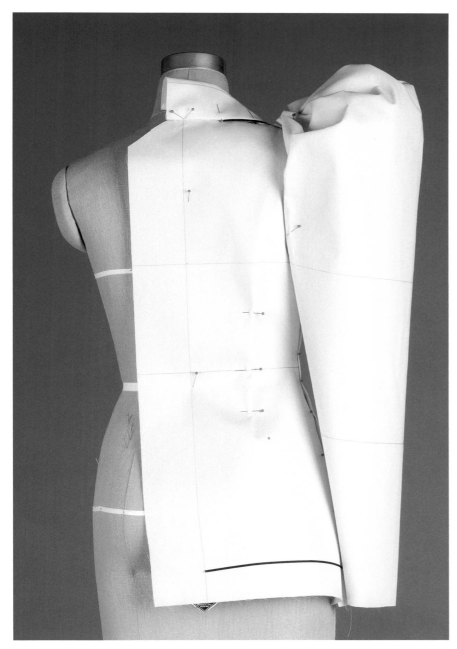

Step 17

- Set notch points at back and front armhole by checking height of crown and checking circumference of that area against the photograph. Pin firmly in place.

- The notch points will help you determine the amount of lift. Test lift by moving the stuffed arm up and down until you get a look you like.

- Finalize crown height and pin edge of sleeve to armhole. The fullness of the sleeve will be accommodated by gathers on the top edge. You will need to pin every 1.5 cm (½") or so to keep the heavily gathered fabric in place.

Step 18

- Create a dart in the front of the sleeve in the position of the front seam for the two-piece sleeve. Take fabric out from the wrist to the elbow to shape the sleeve, creating a forwards bend and a more slimming and flattering look for the front of the arm.

- Remember that with a two-piece piece sleeve, you want the seam to fall towards the inside of the sleeve so that it will not be seen from the front.

- Cut or clip the dart if necessary.

Step 19

- As with the front, create a dart in the position of the back seam for the two-piece sleeve, this time creating a line that will fall to the inside back of the sleeve.

- You will need a vent at the back of the wrist; determine its length and mark it.

- Here the dart has been taped to check the position of the seam from a distance.

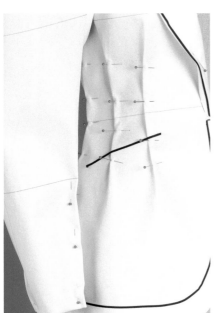

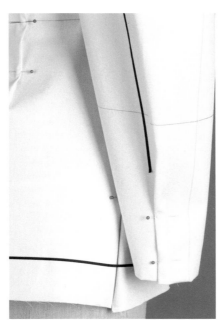

Shaped darts

Subtly shaping the darts to fit the figure more precisely would improve the look of this jacket. Work the darts carefully, pulling in just a bit more fabric at the underbust area and letting out some at the high hip. This shaping will also help the end points of the darts to smooth into the jacket without puckering.

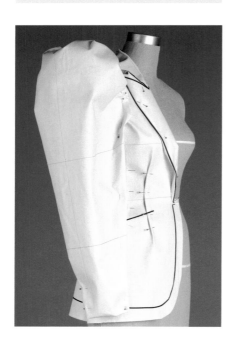

Step 20

- Check drape from all angles, and how it works through 360°.

- Check all darts and refine their shapes. They can be moulded in at the underbust area and slightly shaped out below the waist at the high hip.

- Check position of the two-piece sleeve seams, making sure they flow with the sleeve and fall towards the underarm area.

Step 21

- Determine the finishing touches: what will the front closure be? It could be a large hook and eye, or perhaps two buttons linked by a cord.

- Decide whether you want to include the chest welt pocket and side pockets of the classic tuxedo style. The jacket in the photograph appears to have a binding trim on the outside edge of the lapel; this would be a good time to check the proportion and determine its width.

Marking and truing

Step 1

- Mark the fabric along all sew lines, taking extra care to crossmark frequently on sleeve crown area (not shown).

- Clearly mark break point at the waist; its position is very important in keeping drape of collar intact (not shown).

- Mark roll line on collar and lapel with needle and thread for precision.

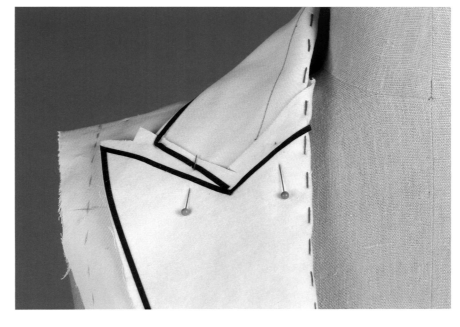

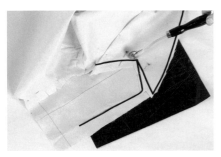

Step 2

- Remove drape from mannequin and mark the lines of the collar and lapel on both sides of the fabric using carbon paper.

Step 3

- Mark the neckline with pencil.

- Use lots of crossmarks on the darts where you have shaped them (not shown).

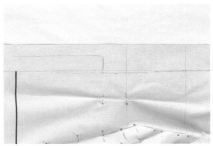

Step 4

- Mark the CB seam line; note that it is not a straight line.

- Draw in the shape of the vent.

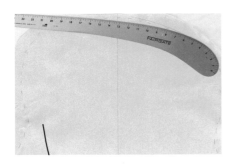

Step 5

- True up sleeve crown shape using round end of hem curve.

- Keep in mind the classic shape of a sleeve: the back curve is wider but softer; the front curve is wider at the top for the bone just below the shoulder line, but then curves down more sharply to remove excess fabric from front of sleeve.

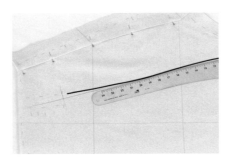

Step 6

- Smooth the lines of the two-piece sleeve seams.

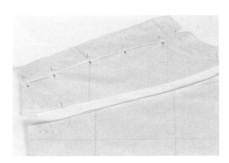

Step 7

- Crossmark the two-piece sleeve seams before cutting seams to create the two pieces of the sleeve.

Analysis

- Compare the look of your drape with that of Rihanna's jacket in the photograph. Imagine your jacket in a different fabric, a silk satin perhaps, and imagine Rihanna wearing it. Does it convey the right attitude? Do the contours of the lines have that crispness and slim angular look? Is your waistline too hourglass shaped? Is the sleeve soft and elegant?

- It is helpful when analysing your work to start systematically at the top and work your way down. After assessing the overall look, carefully study the lines of the collar, then the lapel. Then move to the sleeves and their seams. Check the fit of the waist and hip and then the length of the jacket to see if it is all in balance.

- Remember that proportions are very important. If you do not like the look of your jacket but cannot quite work out why, try working with the sizing of the pockets, or the width of the lapel until everything feels more harmonious.

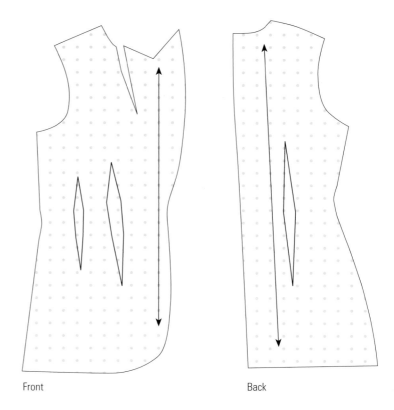

Front   Back

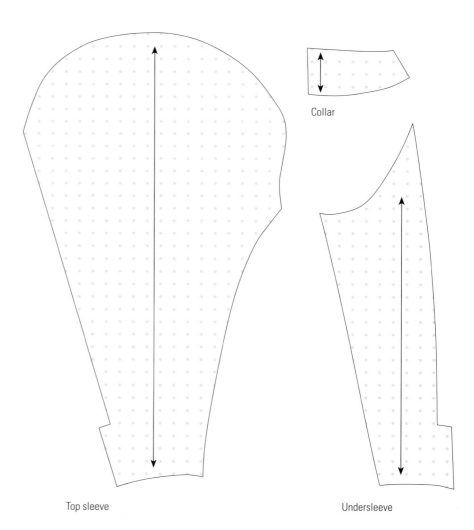

Collar

Top sleeve   Undersleeve

Variations
Raglan jacket

The raglan sleeve was created by a tailor who fashioned the looser-fitting armhole for the 1st Baron Raglan, who had suffered an arm injury at the Battle of Waterloo. This sleeve extends at a diagonal from the underarm to the collarbone, often with a dart at the shoulder line.

The jacket draped here is modelled after one from the 1940s, an era when the raglan's soft shoulder line gained popularity in womenswear.

✏️ **Calico preparation**

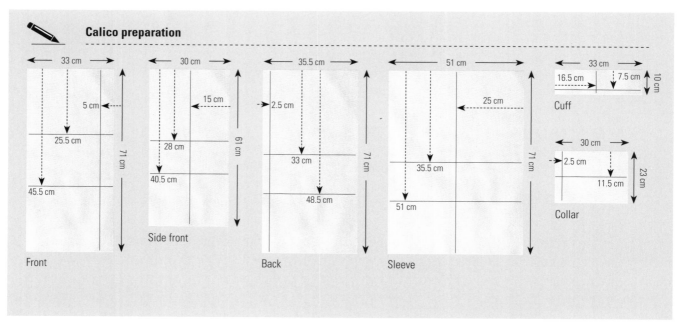

Front: 33 cm, 5 cm, 25.5 cm, 45.5 cm, 71 cm

Side front: 30 cm, 15 cm, 28 cm, 40.5 cm, 61 cm

Back: 35.5 cm, 2.5 cm, 33 cm, 48.5 cm, 71 cm

Sleeve: 51 cm, 25 cm, 35.5 cm, 51 cm, 71 cm

Cuff: 33 cm, 16.5 cm, 7.5 cm, 10 cm

Collar: 30 cm, 2.5 cm, 11.5 cm, 23 cm

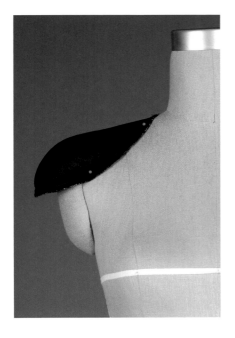

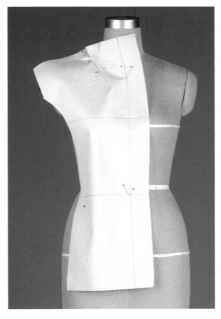

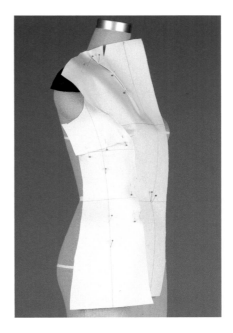

Step 1

- Prepare mannequin by setting a shoulder pad. The classic raglan pad extends over the shoulder with a soft curve. If you do not have a raglan pad, tack some cotton wadding or felt over a classic pad.

Step 2

- Set front by aligning CF grainlines with CF of mannequin and keeping horizontal grain level. Smooth shoulder area and neckline, clipping and trimming only enough to allow shoulder to lie smoothly.

- Do not cut top part of CF calico; it will be needed for the collar.

- Form a dart along the neckline where the fabric seems to fold in on itself. This is the beginning of your undercollar shape.

Step 3

- Set side front piece and form a side bust dart.

- Keep side bust dart small: you want to distribute the ease and fit over the whole front, not fit the bust area too specifically.

- Remember you are draping a jacket that needs to have ease. Try pinning with fewer pins and let the fabric fall away from the mannequin as you work the shape.

- The only part that needs to be firmly pinned is the area of the shoulder where it meets the rise of the neck, about 2.5 cm (1") out from the neck seam of the mannequin. This is the crucial point from which coats and jackets balance, so do not let it get loose and undefined. Be clear about where that point is and pin it decisively.

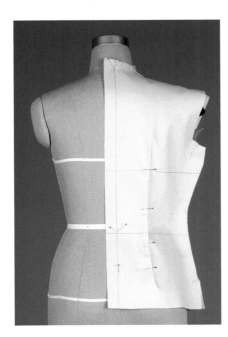

Step 4

- Set back piece by aligning CB grainline with CB of mannequin.

- Set width by pinning lightly at the side seam area.

- Trim and clip neckline and shoulder to fall smoothly, but not too tightly over the mannequin.

- Form the vertical dart in the centre of the back panel.

- Pin back side seam to front side seam, wrong sides together. Check the amount of ease. The fit is shaped to the figure, but not tightly.

Step 5

- Turn front over side front at the princess line. Turn front over back at the side seams and at the shoulder.

- Although the raglan sleeves will drape over the shoulder area, leave the shoulder seam in place for now to maintain stability in the drape.

- Check the silhouette. Compare it to the photograph: does it have the same fit? Do the lines have the same soft contour?

Step 6

- It appears that the waistline in the photograph is more shaped in than the toile. Try pinning a dart in the side front panel between the side seam and the princess seam. This will help fit the waist a little more closely. Do not make it too tight; remember that this jacket needs some ease.

- Observe the subtle difference in bust shape and waistline with the addition of the dart.

Step 7

- Tape the roll line. It will angle towards the break point where the first button will go.

- Tape it firmly. This part is on the bias and will stretch easily. Often in tailoring, this tape will pull in a little bit of ease so that the front of the jacket gently cups over the bust area.

- Tape the hemline.

- Prepare for the raglan sleeve by taping the armhole. You will not have to adhere to this as your final line, but it will help by giving you a target line for which to aim.

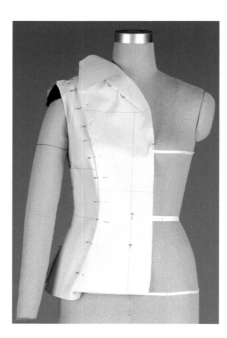
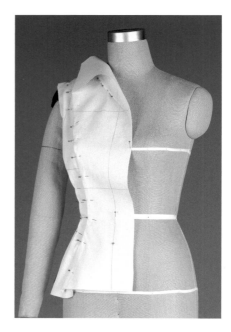
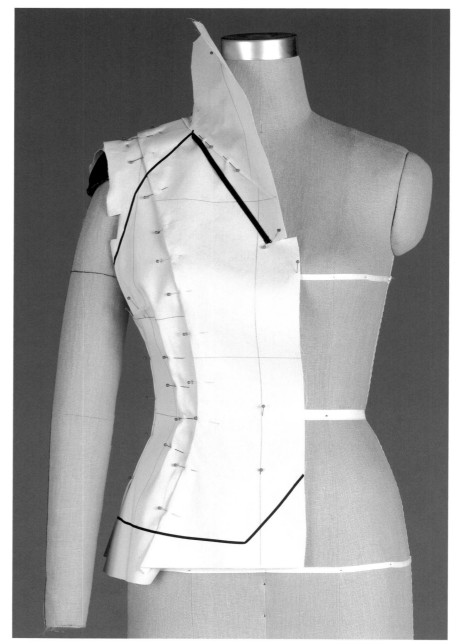

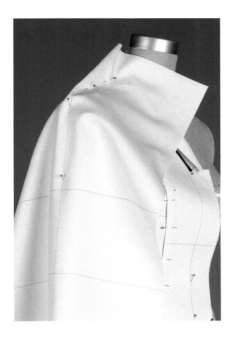

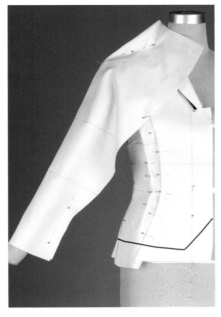

Step 8

- Start by setting the sleeve at crown and shoulder area.

- Form the dart with the excess fabric created by the shoulder curve.

Step 9

- Review the Sleeve Draping Order (see p. 133). Next determine circumference of wrist. Pin wrong sides together about 7 cm (2–3") up.

- Trim the excess from wrist to elbow area, leaving about 2.5 cm (1") seam allowance.

Step 10

- Set the notch points by determining volume of sleeve around bicep area. Pin firmly.

- Working with the stuffed arm, raise and lower sleeve until you have found optimum lift point.

- Trim the excess triangles below the raglan seam tapes (not shown).

Step 11

- Continue pinning raglan seams.

- Trim the dart.

- Finish shaping sleeve by pinning underarm seam to armhole, wrong sides together.

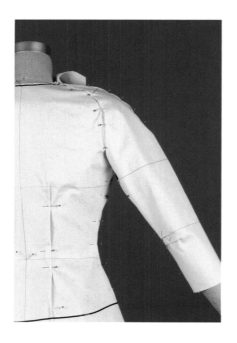

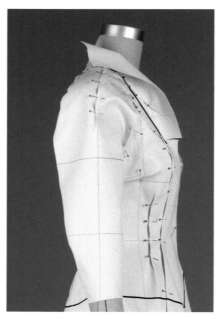

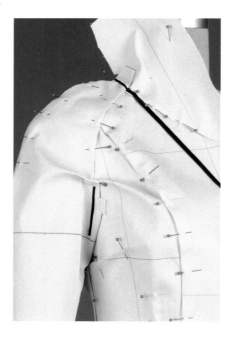

Step 12

- Turn raglan seam allowances over the armhole line.

- Finish underarm seam by turning seams to the inside and pinning as far as you can up the underarm.

- Notice the shape of the sleeve in the photograph: it is angled forwards at the elbow. Pinning one or two darts at the elbow will give that curve to the sleeve.

Step 13

- Check the side view to make sure the sleeve is hanging towards the front and the back is draping slightly larger and lower than the front.

- Here the front does not seem to have a good drape; it is sagging at the front raglan line and must be corrected.

Step 14

- To work out how to correct that sagging, try pinning various darts in different directions to determine where to correct it. Observe how the sleeve changes as you take in or adjust the angle at various different points.

- A horizontal dart on the raglan seam lifts the sleeve towards the front, allowing it to fall without wrinkling and sagging, so that is where to make the correction.

> ### Fitting a jacket
>
> Fitting a jacket is a complex skill and takes experimentation. If something does not look quite right, trust your eye. Go back to the photograph and follow the contours, trying to see where it differs from your drape. Having the patience to re-pin and adjust the drape is critical to the learning process.

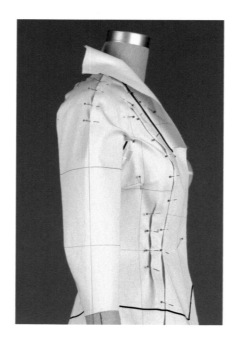

Step 15

- Study the corrected angle of the sleeve.

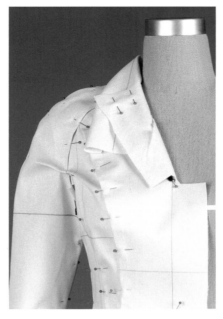
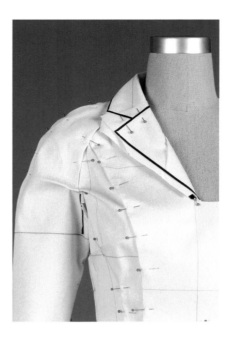

Step 16

- Start collar by pinning at CB, clipping at neckline and bringing it around the shoulder, controlling the stand with the angle of the collar piece.

- Bring collar to front, aligning roll line of collar with roll line on jacket front.

Step 17

- Turn lapel section over draped collar piece. Trim excess of neckline section so it lies smooth OVER the collar.

- Roll line of collar should blend with roll line of lapel. When it is lying smoothly, pin the two pieces together.

Step 18

- Create style line by taping outer edge of the lapel and continue that line as it falls to the inside and becomes the neckline.

- Create style line of collar from CB to where it connects to the lapel.

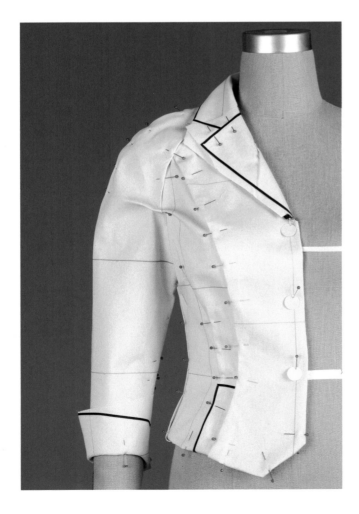

Step 19

- Create the cuff by draping the calico piece around hem of sleeve, letting it angle out slightly in the back. Trim lower edge even with the hem, clipping if necessary, and turn it under. Tape or fold under top edge.

- Finish the details, taking extra care to balance the proportions: tape front pocket; set button placement; and trim hem, turning it under to check the shape.

Step 20

- Check the final drape against the photograph. Scan contours and check proportions. Do the lines of the notched collar and lapel complement the soft roundness of the raglan shape?

- The toile doesn't quite have the sensual quality of the photo. The break point is too high, which is making the jacket seem too conservative. Remember that you are communicating an attitude.

- To lower the break point, you will need to change the collar drape and pull in some excess fabric where the collar joins the top of the lapel.

Trench coat

This is a classic trench coat as defined by the elements historically associated with that style. It is belted, roomy and knee length, with a storm flap at the front and back, a high stand and collar, pockets and epaulettes. The coat has a no-nonsense, utilitarian feel, yet its directness and clarity of purpose impart a modern, chic and stylish look.

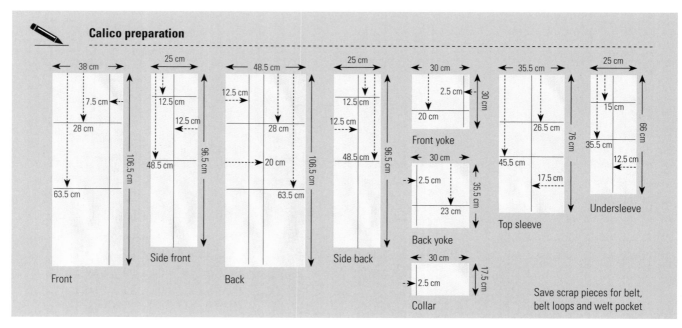

Calico preparation

Front — 38 cm, 7.5 cm, 28 cm, 63.5 cm, 106.5 cm

Side front — 25 cm, 12.5 cm, 12.5 cm, 48.5 cm, 96.5 cm

Back — 48.5 cm, 12.5 cm, 28 cm, 20 cm, 63.5 cm, 106.5 cm

Side back — 25 cm, 12.5 cm, 12.5 cm, 48.5 cm, 96.5 cm

Front yoke — 30 cm, 2.5 cm, 20 cm, 30 cm

Back yoke — 30 cm, 2.5 cm, 23 cm, 35.5 cm

Top sleeve — 35.5 cm, 26.5 cm, 45.5 cm, 17.5 cm, 76 cm

Undersleeve — 25 cm, 15 cm, 35.5 cm, 12.5 cm, 66 cm

Collar — 30 cm, 2.5 cm, 17.5 cm

Save scrap pieces for belt, belt loops and welt pocket

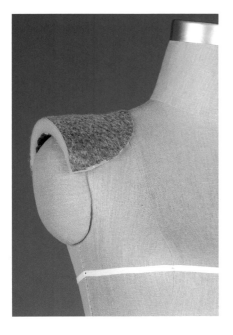

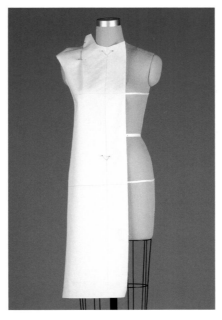

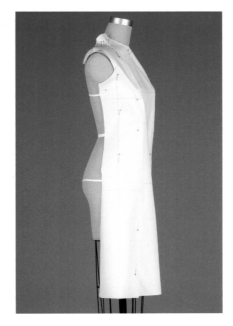

Step 1

- Set the shoulder pad.

Step 2

- Set the centre front section by aligning CF grainline with CF of mannequin. Note that the grainline placement here leaves excess at the left side of the mannequin for the large placket.

- Pin a vertical shoulder dart to accommodate the bust and keep the coat from flaring out in the front.

Step 3

- Set the side front panel by centring the grainline between the princess line and the side seam. Keep the grainline vertical.

- Trim the excess above the waist, and make sure to leave plenty of room for the fullness below the waist towards the hem.

- Note that in the photograph there is a gentle A-line swing to the lower coat, yet it is not full at the waist. This tells you there are princess seams that are shaped in at the waist and flare out towards the hem. This has been done to keep the extra folds of the fabric away from the waist, where they would add extra bulk.

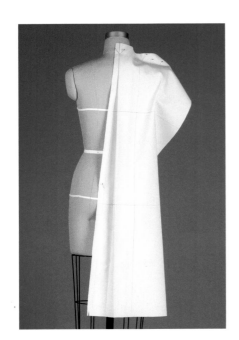

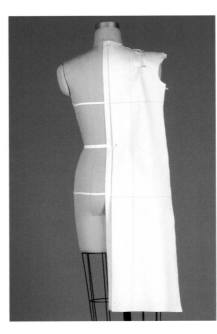

Step 4

- Set CB panel by aligning CB grainline with CB of mannequin. As with the front panel, the grainline is drawn inside the panel to allow extra calico in back that will accommodate the deep CB pleat.

- Form CB pleat by folding excess fabric towards CB, keeping the foldline vertical. This is called an 'inverted pleat'.

Step 5

- Set the back at waist, checking volume.

- Form the shoulder dart, easing in a little bit of the volume.

- Trim and clip neckline and smooth shoulder under front shoulder piece, pinning front over back.

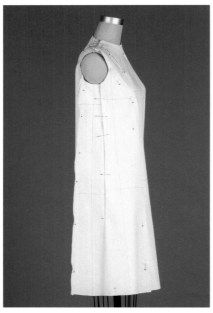
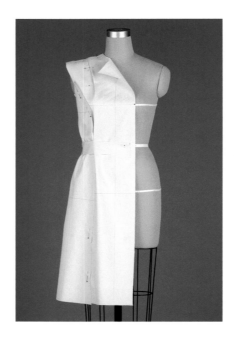
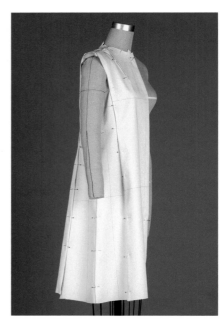

Step 6

- Set side back by centring grainline of piece between back princess line and side seam.

- Pin to the side and back pieces.

Step 7

- Turn side seams to inside, front over back.

- Tie belt around waist to check volume.

- If hem flare is not wide enough, adjust pinning of the two princess-line seams.

Step 8

- Check the balance of all four pieces; they should be shaped in at waist and flared at hem.

- Turn front and back over side front and back pieces.

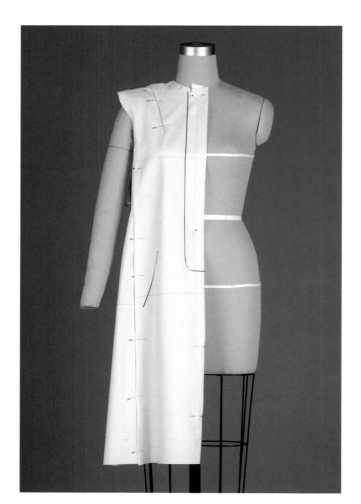

Step 9

- Now that the body is set, start filling in some of the details that will help you confirm whether your silhouette is correct.

- Tape the placket line to prepare for the front yoke piece.

- Place pocket line below the waist.

- Turn front placket to the inside to determine its width.

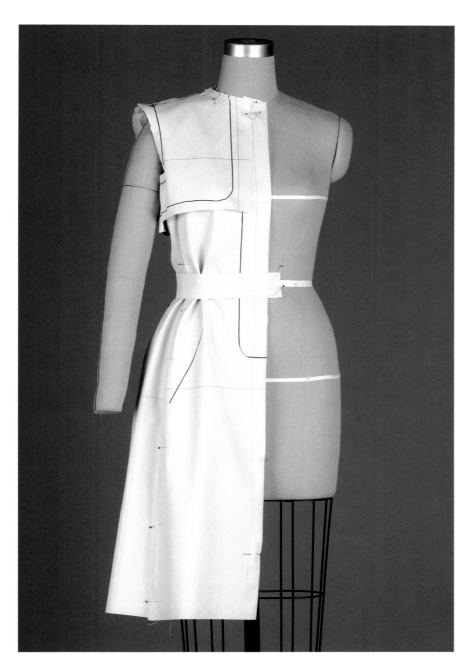

Step 10

- Set front yoke by pinning along shoulder line and armhole. The shape is flat; it will lie smoothly over the bust.
- Set back yoke the same way.
- Join the two yokes at the side seam, noting amount of ease over body sections. It should stand away, as in the photograph.
- Tape hems of yokes and mark armhole.
- Add belt again to check the silhouette.

Step 11

- Drape the collar starting at the CB.
- Pull the piece around to the front and check the height of the collar and the distance from the neck.

Step 12

- Finish collar by trimming excess and turning under the outer edge.
- Flip collar up again; make sure it is trimmed and clipped smoothly and pinned to the neck edge without any concave areas.
- If any areas are caving in, clip a little more and pull collar piece out slightly. Very small amounts here make a big difference.
- You may want to trim or turn under the yoke hems to help you visualize the proportions.

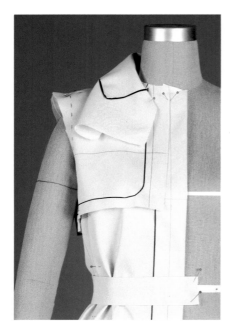

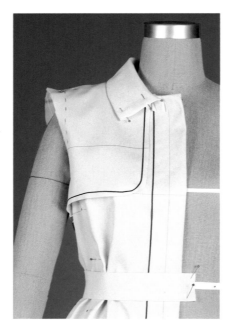

Draping the sleeve

Step 13

- Before beginning the sleeve drape, review the Sleeve Draping Order (p. 133). If you feel it will be easier, use the Easy Two-piece Sleeve Draft (pp. 216–19) to set your parameters.

- Starting the sleeve drape with the calico placed at the proper angle is crucial.

- Set the crown. On this coat, there is no gathering to help you fit the shape into the armhole, which always makes it a little more difficult. There is probably about 2 cm (¾") of ease in the front and back curves.

Step 14

- Setting the notch points is also key. This will determine how much ease is left to work into the upper crown area and how the sleeve falls below those points.

- Also analyse the lift. Decide how much fabric to leave in the underarm area and the degree of lift you want.

Step 15

- Work the lower curves of the front and back sleeve. Keep them pulled up and the line crisp and clean.

- Review the classic shape of the sleeve as you refine these lines. You will be pulling more out of the front than the back.

- Raise and lower the stuffed arm continually, studying the way the fabric falls as you adjust this important combination of curves.

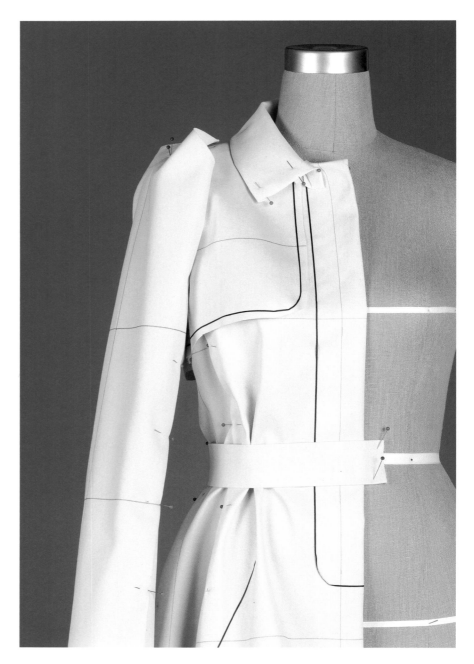

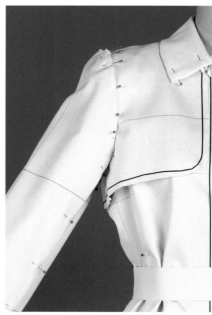

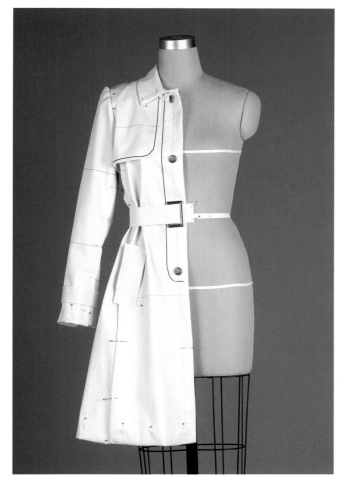

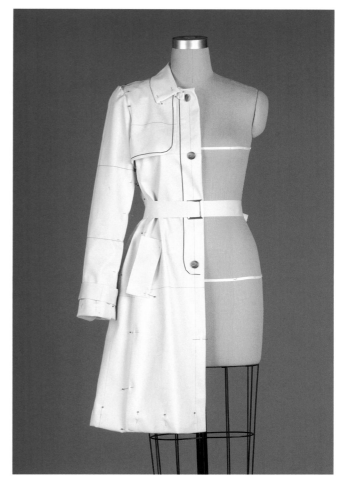

Step 16

- Turn up the hem and belt the coat.

- Place the epaulettes and sleeve band.

- Place the buttons.

- Now analyse the proportions and details. Here it appears from a distance that the belt is too prominent. Notice how it is making the whole coat appear chunky and wide in the middle.

Step 17

- Place a narrower belt with a smaller buckle on the coat. The proportions are now correct.

- Notice how such a small adjustment suddenly brings the proportions of the piece into balance.

Swing coat with shawl collar

The swing coat came into vogue in the late 1940s, its full volume a reaction to the austerity of the war years. As Dior's New Look gained popularity, wider coats that flared away from the hips and legs were needed to cover the full skirts. Here, the full sweep of the hem adds a flirty, stylish attitude.

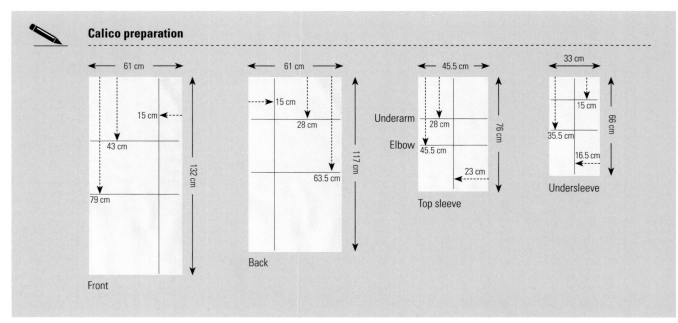

Calico preparation

Front

Back

Top sleeve

Undersleeve

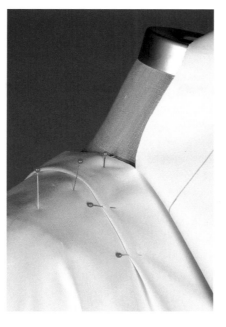

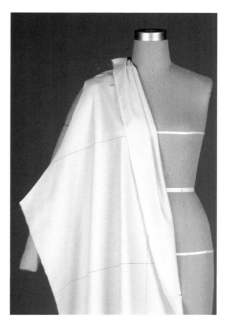

Step 1

- Prepare mannequin by setting a shoulder pad. You can use a rounded pad similar to the raglan pad, but it needs to be a little more substantial to hold the weight of the wool from which the finished coat will be made.

- Begin coat by setting front section onto mannequin, aligning CF grainlines and pinning at bust line and shoulder.

- Now drape the flare. Notice how you can control the direction and volume of the flare by the way you hold the shoulder line. Find the point that secures the flare that you want. Keep in mind that the weight of the coat will be supported from that shoulder area, so pin firmly.

- Keeping the horizontal grain level, fold in a shoulder dart to accomodate the ease from the bust.

Step 2

- The awkward part of a shawl collar is determining where to slash at the shoulder. Find the point at which neckline needs to be clipped to allow the collar fabric to lie smoothly over the shoulder, with the excess fabric towards the front and rolling towards the back to create the shawl collar.

- Slash fabric into the shoulder line.

Step 3

- Prepare to drape the front by cutting away excess fabric from the shoulder line to the high hip line.

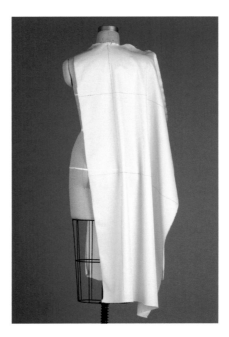

Step 4

- Drape back piece by manipulating the shoulder area in the same way that you did the front until you achieve the right amount and direction of flare.

- Cut away excess from the shoulder to the high hip line.

Step 5

- After cutting away the excess, note how the fabric now falls naturally at the side seams. It should fall unobstructed from the shoulder area. If the stuffed arm is restricting it, cut away more until it is falling freely.

- Pin front over back at the shoulder.

- Cut hem to approximate length, levelling it against the bars of the mannequin cage.

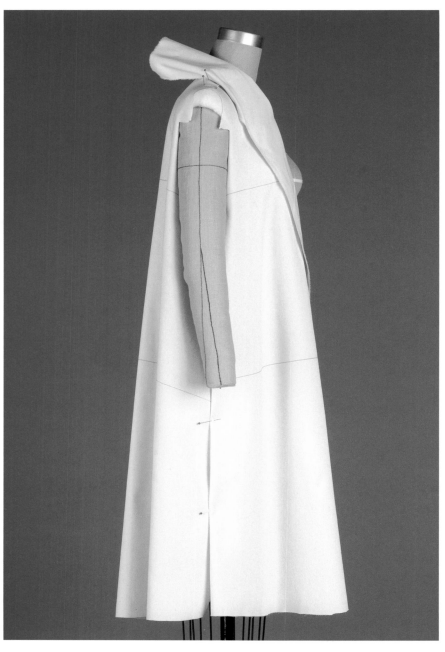

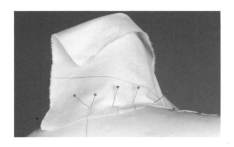

Step 6

- Pin side seams together. Use the method of simply folding back seam allowance on the front section and letting it fall over the back section until it balances. Then pin front over back.

Step 7

- Lift shawl collar and pivot it at the clipped point. Continue to clip as you pull it around to CB, pinning as you go. Check it a few times to make sure you have a finger's distance between coat and neck of mannequin.

- Adjust outer edge/hem of collar and set it firmly at CB.

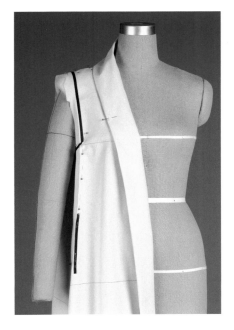

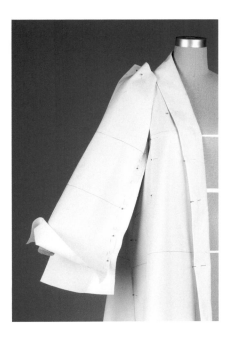

Step 8

- Form the dart that runs from armhole to top of pocket area. This will pull in a little extra fabric at the armhole area, but take care not to reduce the amount of fabric needed to accommodate the bust comfortably.
- Tape the armhole.
- Tape the pocket line.

Step 9

- Start sleeve by preparing the calico, following the Easy Two-piece Sleeve Draft on pp. 216–19.
- Trace around the pieces leaving about 4 cm (1½") seam allowance.
- Pin sleeve seams together as on p. 219.
- Chalk armhole line and remove tape to make sleeve piece easier to pin on.
- Align sleeve section from the crown, angling forwards slightly.
- Pin at the crown area, accommodating about 2.5 cm (1") of ease.

Step 10

- Pin out crown ease, distributing it evenly.
- Set the notch points, checking circumference around top area of sleeve.
- Trim excess triangles at top of sleeve.
- Check sleeve angle again to see where the two-piece sleeve seams are hitting. If they intersect with the front armhole seam, shift it up or down a bit to avoid too much bulk.
- Check the volume of the sleeves and adjust if necessary.
- Turn sleeve seams to inside and pin.

Draping the sleeve from scratch

If you prefer not to use the sleeve draft, drape the sleeve from scratch following the basic Sleeve Draping Order (p. 133).

Step 1

- Pin crown and angle it towards the front. Then determine where the seams will go; they should fall towards the inside and be as hidden as possible.
- Now determine total measurement of hem at the wrist. Also determine measurement of undersleeve.

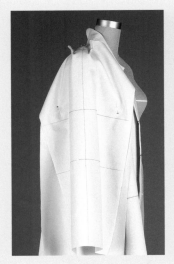
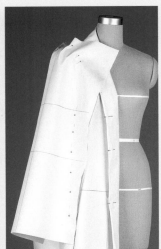

Step 2

- Set the notch points as in Step 10.
- Pin top and undersleeves wrong sides out. Shape the sleeve, working from the wrist up.
- Trim excess triangle sections at top of sleeve.

Step 3

- Turn seams to inside and pin.
- Continue with Step 11, p. 250.

Step 11

- It will help at this point to use a tape to hold up the arm as you check the notch points to achieve the optimum lift point.

- Work with the ease created when the arm is dropped. Here it seems as if there is too much; pull in more fabric at notch points until you feel you have a good balance.

Step 12

- Finish the lower curves at front and back and check the lift.

Step 13

- Check sleeve proportion with coat volume.

- Pin up the hem.

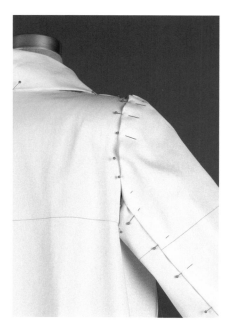

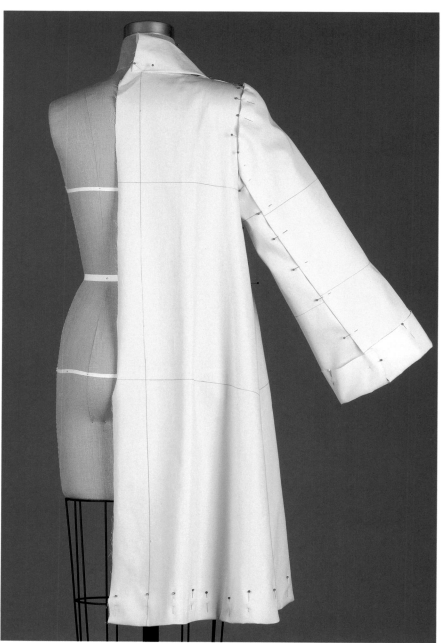

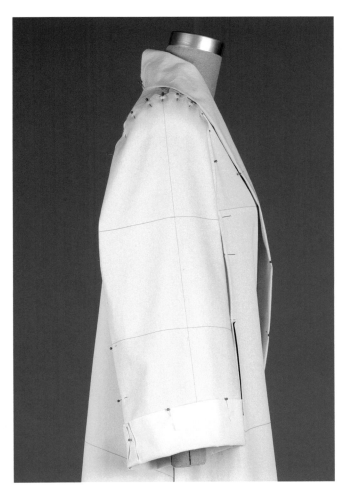

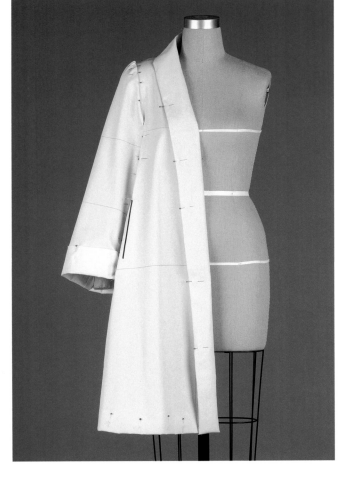

Step 14

- Check the coat through 360°. The break of the sleeve should be lower in back than in front and should angle forwards. Here the sleeve silhouette has a break just below bust-point level at the back of the arm.

- Turn up hem at the sleeve cuff.

Arriving at your signature look

Study your drape next to the photograph. Look at it in the mirror from a distance and visualize it being worn by someone strolling down a busy boulevard. Think about what you could do to bring it closer to your 'signature look'.

For example, the length could move up or down, the fullness in or out. The look would change if the collar became much wider or narrower. Would the addition of pockets change the focal point?

Arriving at your signature look is allowing yourself to express what YOU like, the proportions that please YOUR eye. Go for it!

Coat with egg-shaped silhouette

This coat from the DKNY Spring/Summer 2011 collection envelops the model with its high funnel collar, tapered sleeves and pegged-in hem. The shoulder is a rounded/kimono style, which supports the look of the egg-shaped silhouette. The diagonal seam from the neckline to pocket allows shaping in the front and fit for the bust.

The silhouette, along with the soft, thick wool, adds to the sense of warmth and protection of this garment. Anchor this feeling and the visualization of the shape before you begin draping.

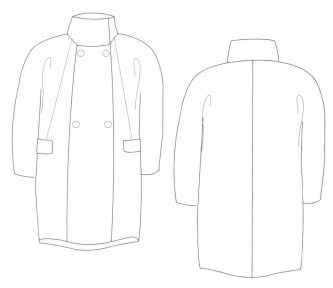

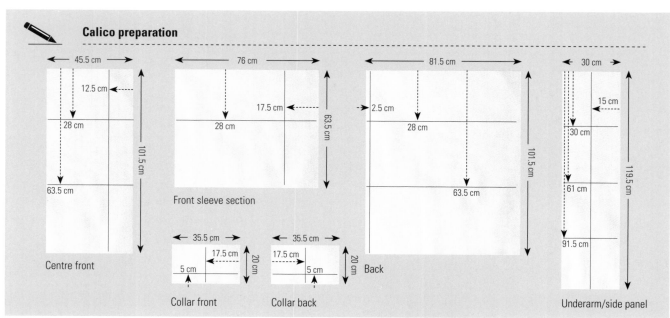

Calico preparation

Centre front: 45.5 cm, 12.5 cm, 28 cm, 101.5 cm, 63.5 cm

Front sleeve section: 76 cm, 17.5 cm, 28 cm, 63.5 cm

Back: 81.5 cm, 2.5 cm, 28 cm, 101.5 cm, 63.5 cm

Collar front: 35.5 cm, 17.5 cm, 5 cm, 20 cm

Collar back: 35.5 cm, 17.5 cm, 5 cm, 20 cm

Underarm/side panel: 30 cm, 15 cm, 30 cm, 61 cm, 119.5 cm, 91.5 cm

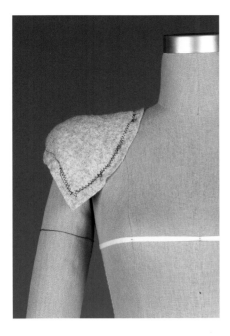 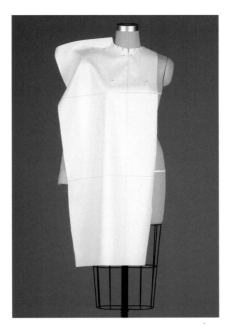 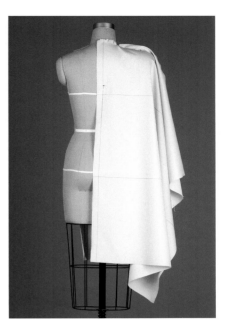

Step 1

- Set a raglan, or dropped shoulder, pad. This one is soft but has some lift, as it will drop a little with the weight of the wool.

Step 2

- Set front by pinning down CF and across shoulder and bust.

- Trim and clip neckline to fit smoothly.

- This is a coat, so remember to keep the drape light and roomy.

Step 3

- Pin at CB, across shoulder and shoulder-blade area.

- Form a small dart at neckline to keep grain horizontal; if collar is set low enough, or the coat is made from a wool that can be moulded and eased, the dart can be eliminated later.

Balancing from the shoulders

When setting the shoulder seams, pay close attention. Properly set, the ease or dart in the back shoulder seam will allow the horizontal grain to remain level, keeping the coat from kicking out in the back.

The angle of the front shoulder seam will control the hang of the front of the coat. The point about 2.5 cm (1") from the neck of the mannequin will hold most of the weight of the coat. Make sure it is pinned firmly and decisively. Then check that the front and back of the coat are balanced.

Step 4

- Pin the shoulders.

- Check the drape from all angles.

- Clip about halfway along shoulder and turn front over back.

- Remember that coats hang from the shoulders. It is important at this point to stop and check the balance. The horizontal grains should be fairly level.

- Recall the visualization of the volume and shape of the coat. It will help you when draping such a large piece away from the support of the mannequin.

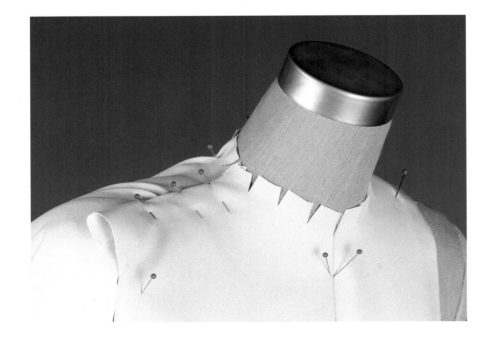

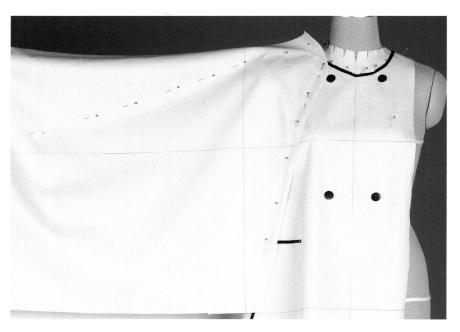

Step 5

- To determine the placement of the front seam, it can help to set some of the other details in place so you can start coordinating the proportions.

- First, tape the neckline, setting it low to allow for the funnel collar and also making it a little wide to allow for other garments to be worn beneath.

- Set the buttons, two below the collar line and two just above waist.

- Tape the pockets at the high hip line.

- Now tape the front seam.

- Trim away excess above the seamline, leaving fullness at hem below pocket line.

Step 6

- Set front sleeve piece by aligning horizontal grains.

- Pin across shoulder and down the twill-tape line.

- Trim away the excess (not shown).

Step 7

- Now set sleeve height by setting the stuffed arm at about a 45° angle and pinning across the shoulder area, keeping grains horizontal and balance between front and back.

- Take time to consider the amount of ease you want under the arm: the higher the lift, the more fabric you will need under the arm; the lower the lift, the less you will need.

- Pin back to front at top of the sleeve.

- Trim away triangles of excess fabric at the top edge.

Step 8

- Set the underarm height and clip all the way to underarm area.

- Set the hip width and trim the excess.

- Tape seamline in front and back as preparation for side panel.

Step 9

- Turn the front sleeve piece seam over the coat front.

- Turn the shoulder and top sleeve seam front over back.

- Now check the silhouette: note that the coat shapes in very slightly at the waist. Pull a little fullness out from the diagonal sleeve seam to help make that shape (not shown).

Step 10

- Set the side panel. Start by pinning the approximate centre of the panel to underarm areas.

- Make sure horizontal grains on side panel section remain level with the floor.

- Pin wrong sides together, working back and forth, from underarm towards wrist and from underarm towards hem.

Step 11

- Turn front and back over side panel. This is a difficult and awkward operation, so be prepared to spend some time with this. Set the arm at about 45°; as you pin, continue checking side panel from underneath to make sure it is smooth and balanced. Do not worry about keeping the straight grain centred. As you will be draping with the arm angled towards the front, the grainline may shift as it moves towards the wrist.

- Check the proportions against the sketch. It will help to finalize the shape by doing some of the finishing work: attach pocket flap; turn up hem of sleeves and lower edge of coat (not shown); remove twill tape and turn under edge of front facing.

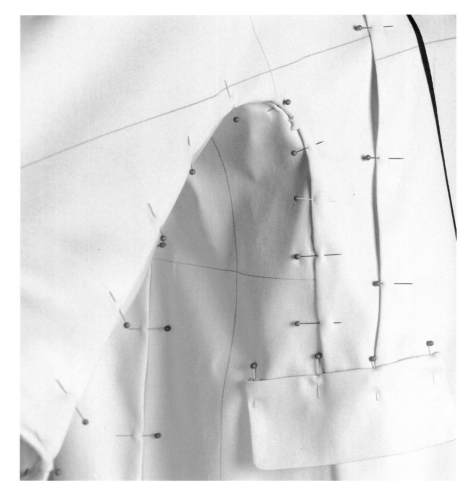

Step 12

- Look at the coat in the mirror and check though 360°, with the arm up and down.

- Once you are satisfied with the drape, remove twill tape and mark neckline with chalk to prepare for the collar drape (not shown).

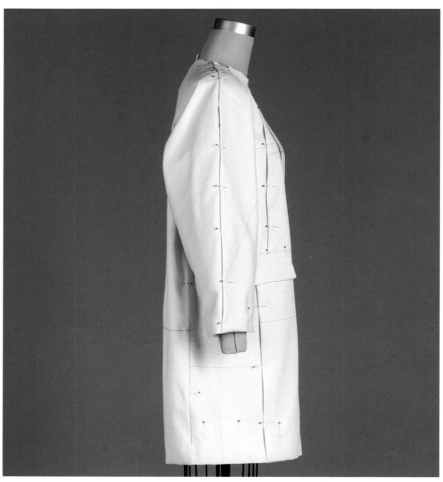

Draping the standing collar

To determine the collar's construction, first consider its grainline. The standing collar's strong vertical shape tells you that the stronger straight grain must be at the centre front and centre back.

It will need side seams. If the centre back is on the straight grain, as it needs to be, then, as the piece wraps towards the front, the centre front will end up bias, which would soften the grain too much to keep the strong standing shape. Also, adding a side seam will give you more freedom in determining the angle of the collar as it travels upwards from the shoulder.

Because of the large size of the collar, it will be helpful to drape the full piece rather than half the front and back. That way, as you drape, the collar piece will help support itself. If your calico is soft, stiffening it with a fusible interfacing will help it hold the shape.

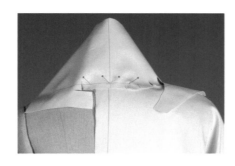

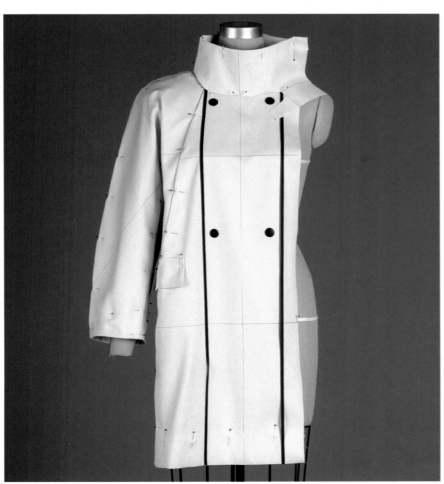

Step 13

- Start the back collar by pinning centre line and horizontal grainline to CB of coat.

- Clip and trim as you bring the piece around to the shoulders, working both sides.

- Follow the neckline you have chalked, but if you feel it is not giving you the look you want, move the collar away from the line.

- The collar should stand away from the back neck.

Step 14

- Begin draping the front collar by pinning intersection of straight and horizontal grainlines at front of chalked neckline.

- Trim and clip the back as you pull collar piece around towards the shoulder.

- The front collar will also stand away from the neck, even more so than at the back. Check the photograph: note how the model's chin just meets the edge of the collar.

- Also note that the collar is not really round, but is broad at the front and then angles strongly towards the shoulder.

- Pin side edges and trim the excess.

Step 15

- From the side, the front collar should angle significantly more forwards than the back.

- When you feel you have it right, turn front collar over back collar at sides and pin.

- When refining the shape of the collar, you only have to perfect one side. Make sure you keep the CF and CB straight grains vertical. The side that has been perfected can be transferred to the other side of the pattern afterwards.

Step 16

- Turn under neckline of collar and pin to neckline of coat.

- If the collar is collapsing in areas, rework the clipping; clip little by little, pulling out collar seam until it lies smoothly.

- Remember to take care when marking the collar. The line may have shifted while you were focusing more on achieving the shape of the collar than sticking with the original neckline.

- Turn down top edge of collar to determine its width.

3.2
The Grand Gown

History

The 'grand gown' is not so much a fashion term as a statement. It describes a dress that is a grand gesture: the wedding gown, ball gown and evening gown. These clothes are about presence, about making an impact.

The grand gown is worn by a woman when she is at her most highly ornamented. It employs the highest quality fabrics, most advanced draping and couture sewing techniques, and the most precision of fit. This genre of clothing represents the very best artisanship that a culture is able to produce. Fashion history is full of stories of scores of seamstresses working night and day on elaborate gowns for their wealthy clients.

Intriguing in their display, enchanting by their sheer beauty, these dresses are beguiling to men and women alike. There are the legendary gowns: Empress Elisabeth's famous wedding dress; Marie Antoinette's outrageously ostentatious court dresses; Scarlett O'Hara's romantic and seductive antebellum ball gowns. Glinda the Good Witch of the North from *The Wizard of Oz* was magical because her dress was.

In many cultures and eras, the volume of the gown was a display of wealth. Multiple yards of silk in a skirt were an indication of a comfortable position in life. In the medieval and Renaissance periods clothes were worn in layers, each of which was cut to reveal the richness of the fabrics beneath. Slashing was used from around 1480 to 1650 to add decorative pattern and also to reveal coloured linings.

The origins, or elemental structures, of these dresses hark back to simple shapes – the multiple panels of a large skirt, and bodices and sleeves that were darted and fitted.

The basic construction of women's clothing remained unchanged for many centuries. The large skirt and

The artistry of Charles Frederick Worth: silk satin, trimmed with pearl embroidery and lace, lined with silk, the bodice supported with whalebone struts, machine and hand sewn, c. 1881.

embellished bodice was the uniform of Western culture. Styles and silhouettes often changed in reaction to social, economic and cultural developments, although the antecedents of these new styles were often already in existence. One example is the extreme opulence of the dress of Marie Antoinette and the women of the court of Louis XVI that gave way to a slimmer silhouette after the French Revolution. That silhouette, ironically, was borrowed from the chemise dress popularized by Marie Antoinette herself in the 1780s.

The voluminous ball gowns of the 1950s became dated as soon as Marilyn Monroe appeared in *Gentlemen Prefer Blondes* wearing a narrow sheath dress. Jacqueline Kennedy's inaugural gowns as First Lady of the United States in 1961 were slim and fitted, paving the way for a new trend in silhouette.

In draping, the larger the panels of fabric involved, the easier it is to get lost in the details and lose sight of the overall form. The study of the grand gown is important in learning how to hold a vision of the final outcome and then express it – to materialize the grand gesture. It is essential to have clarity of intent and the skills to realize it.

Top: Elizabeth Taylor's Renaissance-style costume for *The Taming of the Shrew* has been slashed to reveal multiple layers and colors of fabric in an ingenious display of wealth.

Above: Evening dress in the early nineteenth century reflected the simplicity of the fashionable shapes of that period, but still employed elaborate fabrics and trimmings.

Exercises
Supporting the skirt

Creating a gown with large volume of fabric is never a simple endeavour. It takes skill to engineer the support and then sculpt the shape that lays over it. The silhouette of a full skirt is dictated by the type of fabric used, but also by the under-structure. Throughout history, as styles changed, so did the under-structures that created them. Mechanical miracles were accomplished with bustles and crinolines, hoop skirts and panniers, whalebones, wire and even wooden pulleys.

The softer petticoats that were worn over them (and sometimes under them) were made of ruffles of fabric layered onto an underskirt base, until the desired silhouette was achieved. The type of fabric used for the ruffles helped determine the shape of the petticoat and ultimately, the final outcome of the skirt.

Crinolines

'Crinoline' was originally a term for a stiff linen fabric with horsehair weft, starched and ruffled, which was used for petticoats. As skirt volumes increased, more support was needed, and by the 1830s whalebone or cane was used to help hold the skirts up and out. The famous dome-shaped 'hoop' skirt undergarment was patented in 1846. It allowed women to wear fewer petticoats and lightened their skirts considerably.

The crinoline was not an entirely new concept. The 'farthingale', worn in the fifteenth and sixteenth centuries, had also been stiffened with subtropical cane and, later, whalebone.

The term 'crinoline' is now understood to be simply a structure that supports a large skirt.

A fashion icon of her time, Austrian Empress Elisabeth is pictured here in 1867 in one of her grand gowns.

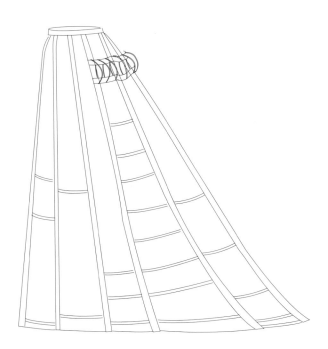

Panniers

The 'pannier' is an undergarment similar in construction to the crinoline. Also made of whalebone and linen fabric, it held the fabric of the skirt out on the sides, while remaining relatively flat in the front and the back. Popularized in the Spanish courts of the seventeenth century, they reached their most extreme during the reign of Marie Antoinette in the French court of 1774 to 1792.

Sometimes as wide as a metre (about 3') on each side, the width of the skirt provided a surface for the rich embroideries and elaborate embellishments the wealthy classes favoured.

Kirsten Dunst, in a costume from the film *Marie Antoinette*, wears panniers under her skirt to create the volume typical of the eighteenth century.

Corsets

The support of the skirt is only half the story. The other element is the foundation piece — a corset or bodice.

Unlike coats and jackets, where the weight of the garment hangs from the shoulders, many modern-day gowns are supported at the waist by this foundation garment. The weight of the skirt and any lower under-structure is held by the tightly fitted waist, while the foundation also supports the bodice from the waist up. The foundation needs to have either a very fitted and shaped waist or a ribbon or tape sewn at the waistline to keep it in place.

The corsets in Chapter 1.3 are constructed with boning and a fairly substantial outer fabric, fused to give body and strength. A lighter-weight lining fabric would be used to simply finish the inside of the piece.

With a foundation piece for a gown, the concept is the opposite. The under-layer has the stronger, heavier, usually boned construction, and the outer layer (the actual bodice fabric of the dress) lays gently over its support piece, relieving any stress on the lighter outer fabric. Because fine-quality silks or brocades can be delicate and easily bruised, the undergarment will do the support work and protect the more expensive fabric from damage.

This top layer of fabric sets the tone for the dress. Heavy, luxurious velvet will create an entirely different effect, even on the same under-structure, as a light and crisp organza.

Fabric as inspiration

Often the inspiration for a dress comes from the fabric. Many designers begin by pinning fabric to the mannequin and observing how it drapes.

Effects of different fabrics

This silk gazar wedding dress stands out on its own with the help of only a light net petticoat (left). Note the different effect of four-ply silk crêpe as it falls heavily in deep folds from a supporting bodice.

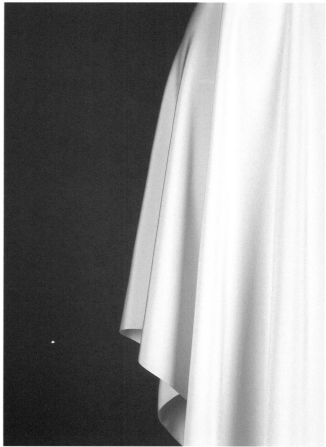

Study the two fabrics on the previous page. Practise visualizing what they would look like draped over Lady Gaga's foundation/crinoline structure (left). The line drawings below show the different silhouettes and moods the two fabrics would create.

The drawing on the left shows what shape the dress might be if constructed of silk gazar: it is crisp and light and the energy of the dress is perky, light, and uplifting.

The drawing on the right shows what would happen if the dress was made of the four-ply silk crêpe: the heavy fabric falls with gravity and the energy pulls downwards, creating a grounded, sensual mood.

Lady Gaga at the 2010 Grammy Awards, wearing a dress reminiscent of a boned bodice with wire crinoline under-structure.

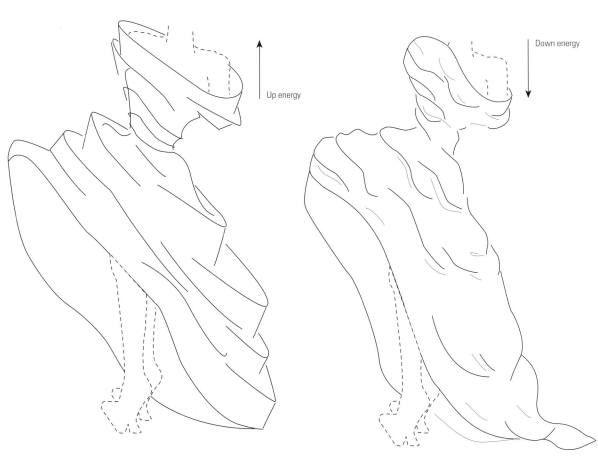

Up energy

Down energy

Gown with ruffled petticoat

Glinda the Good Witch in *The Wizard of Oz* wears a huge tulle and organza skirt with a fitted bodice. The skirt will be built of layers of ruffles engineered to create the silhouette of the photograph and to create a natural flow when in motion.

Hoop-skirt mannequins are available for use in making this skirt, but they often look stilted or forced. Various weights of fabric can be used to drape this dress. Experiment to discover the effects ruffles of different weights create.

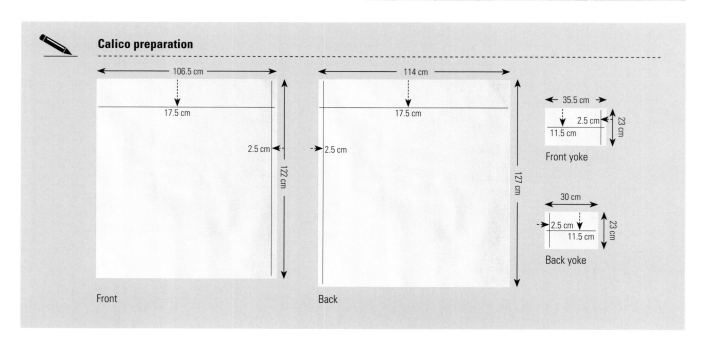

Calico preparation

106.5 cm

17.5 cm

2.5 cm

122 cm

Front

114 cm

17.5 cm

2.5 cm

127 cm

Back

35.5 cm

2.5 cm

11.5 cm

23 cm

Front yoke

30 cm

2.5 cm

11.5 cm

23 cm

Back yoke

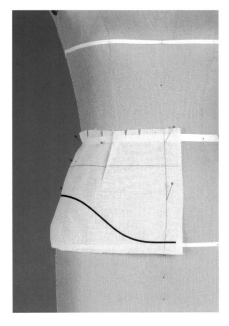

Step 1

- Set front yoke by aligning CF of calico with CF of mannequin. With the yoked skirt in Chapter 2.1 (see pp. 110–11), the waistline was simply clipped and the fabric allowed to wrap around the high hip area. For this piece, drape a dart into the waistline to keep the horizontal grain level and give it the strength to hold the heavy skirt it will be supporting.

- If the horizontal grain remains level, then the side seams will stay on the strong straight grain, again offering more support. If the fabric is wrapped towards the side without a dart, the side area would then be on the bias, giving too much stretch to the support piece.

Step 2

- Set the front skirt piece by aligning CF lines and then gathering in the calico at the top edge to form the gathers.

- Pin along the yoke, allowing lower edge to flare out.

- Trim the triangle formed between hem and high hip line.

- Repeat from Step 1 for the back.

- Turn side seams to the inside.

- Level the hem.

- Mark the yoke line and true up (not shown).

- Sew yoke darts and side seams.

- Sew side seams of petticoat skirt.

- Sew petticoat skirt onto yoke.

Step 3

- Topstitch a length of grosgrain or Petersham ribbon to the waistline to give it some strength.

- Sew a width of horsehair braid into the hem to help it stand out.

Step 4

- In the same way you draped the first petticoat skirt section, drape a new panel onto the high hip line to create a base for the next set of ruffles.

Step 5

- Cut a width of crinoline and gather it up fairly tightly.

- Working from CF to CB, pin the crinoline ruffle onto the outer layer, levelling it from the hem.

Step 6

- Create two overlapping layers of crinoline at hip.

Step 7

- Drape an organza layer over the two top crinolines and attach by hand-sewing onto the yoke seam.

- Note how the silhouette continues to evolve as you add the layers, slowly building out the volume and trying to achieve the effect of Glinda's silhouette.

Step 8

- Study the photograph and try and work out how to achieve the exact silhouette of the skirt. It appears here that the petticoat still needs to be built out a little more at the hip line.

- Working with the fine tulle, create another layer and tack it onto the organza at the level where you need the extra width.

- Lastly, add more fine tulle ruffles about 30 cm (12") above the hem to make the lower edge kick out a little more.

Step 9

- Drape the overlayer of sparkle organza onto the petticoat in as many panels as you need to create the fullness. It will be shaped down for the front yoke, so do not forget to gather it in and mark the angle of the yoke onto the gathered piece.

- Join the panels, gather up the top edge and hand-tack to the yoke.

- Trim the hem even with the floor.

Draping project

This gown was designed by Oscar de la Renta and worn by Gwyneth Paltrow at the 1999 Oscars. Its beauty is classic: the simple lines are flattering, the full skirt is showy and luxurious but not overly opulent. There is a feel of cool elegance and restraint. The light, crisp, silk taffeta brings out the young, princess-like quality of the dress.

One of the challenges of working with large skirts is determining the seaming. First you must consider the width of the fabric being used, and then calculate how many widths of the fabric will be needed to go around the finished hemline.

A large skirt such as Empress Elisabeth's (p. 262) must have had eight or more widths on each side. When seaming them, the rectangles of fabric would require far too much gathering at the waist, so the panels were probably cut in wedge-shaped pieces, with a small amount of gathering at the waist to create the small waist with fullness at the hem.

In this dress, the deep tucks that are released at the waist create the fullness of the skirt. The hem circumference is large, but probably not more than four panels per side.

The fitted bodice has delicate lines; the straps are quite thin and set wide apart. The dress must have a foundation for the thin silk taffeta that lies on top. The foundation will not only support the bust and shape the torso, but will provide a base for the petticoat to be sewn onto, which gives the full skirt its shape.

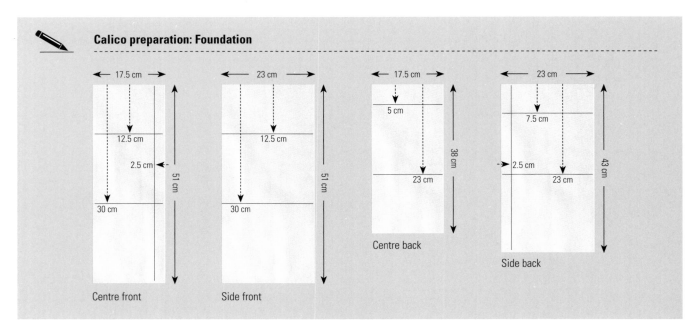

← 17.5 cm →

12.5 cm

2.5 cm

30 cm

51 cm

Centre front

← 23 cm →

12.5 cm

30 cm

51 cm

Side front

← 17.5 cm →

5 cm

23 cm

38 cm

Centre back

← 23 cm →

7.5 cm

2.5 cm

23 cm

43 cm

Side back

Draping the foundation

Review Chapter 1.3: Corsets to prepare for this drape.

Step 1

- Set CF piece of bodice by aligning CF grainlines. Form a horizontal dart at the bust line. This serves to fit the CF of the corset against the figure between the bust points.

Step 2

- Set side front piece as for the princess-line corset in Chapter 1.3 (see pp. 72–73).

Step 3

- Set CB and side back as for the princess-line corset in Chapter 1.3 (see p. 73) (not shown).

- Pin an additional dart on side front panel to pull waist in further.

Finish foundation

- True up by cutting both sides and sewing foundation pieces together.

- Mark lines for boning.

- Mark top edge.

- Mark hem.

Step 4

- Sew the full foundation together.

- Turn under a top edge on what will be the preliminary top edge of the dress.

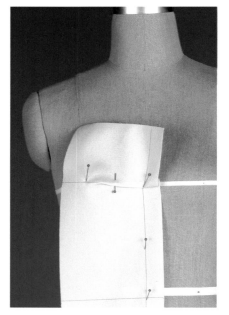

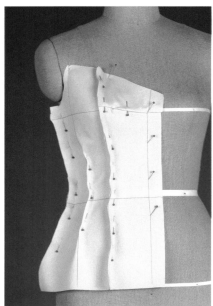

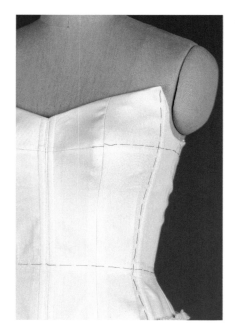

Step 5

- Stitch a length of grosgrain or Petersham ribbon onto waistline inside foundation. When fitting on your model, this will be fastened first to hold up the weight of the dress. A hook-and-eye closure is recommended.

←———— 114 cm ————→

←———— 114 cm ————→

2.5 cm ◄— —►2.5 cm

30 cm

30 cm

112 cm

117 cm

63.5 cm

Front

Back

Lower ruffle

Length to be
determined during
actual drape

Draping the petticoat

Step 6

- Drape the petticoat following the method on pp. 267–68.

- Finish the petticoat base and sew horsehair braid to inside of hem to help hold it out.

Step 7

- Attach a tulle ruffle to give the lower skirt some lift.

Draping the gown

Step 8

■ To begin the gown drape, first experiment with draping some of the silk taffeta that will be used for the dress. This will help you visualize the volume and decide how wide the sweep of the hem should be and how deep the tucks.

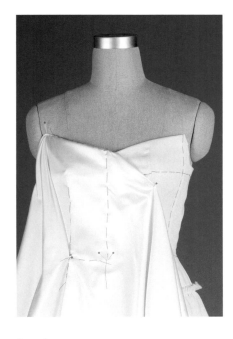 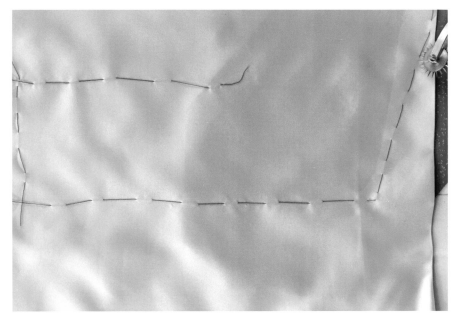

Step 9

- The front bodice will have a deep tuck at the waist. Study the effects of the tucking in the taffeta fabric to determine how deep the tuck will be.

- Thread-trace the bodice as you have draped it, the tuck and the top edge.

Step 10

- Remove the taffeta from the mannequin.

- Placing the thread-traced area of the taffeta over the calico section, trace the line with carbon paper and a tracing wheel onto the calico to help set the CF drape.

Now use the information you have gleaned from the actual fabric drape to help set the measurements and proportions of the calico pieces for that drape. The measurements taken from the above exercise will determine the size of the pieces to prepare.

Calico preparation: Gown

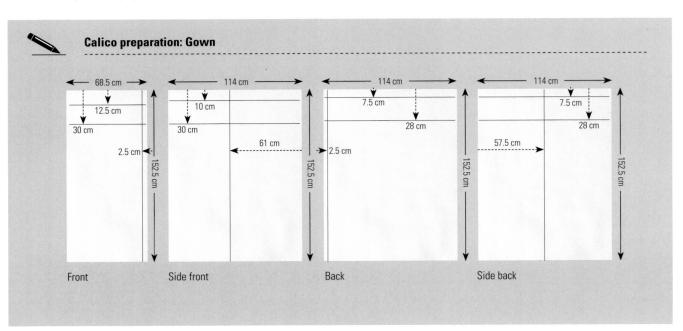

Front   Side front   Back   Side back

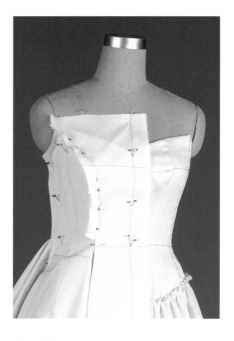

Step 11

- Set CF section by aligning CF grainline with CF of mannequin, following the lines created by the tracing of the fabric drape.
- Set the top edge along top edge of foundation.
- Fold the calico at the tuck point.
- Allow calico to drape over petticoat with as much fullness as you can.

Step 12

- Set side front piece by centring grainline between the princess line and side seam of the mannequin.
- Pin to the front section as for the princess-line corset in Chapter 1.3 (see p. 73).
- Trim excess triangle of calico above waist.

Step 13

- As you set the princess line, check the photograph and note that the straps are set very wide, at what should be the widest point of the foundation.

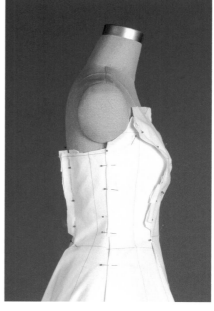

Step 14

- Set back section by aligning CB with CB of mannequin and allowing full width of calico piece to spread out over petticoat.

Step 15

- Set side back section by centring grainline between the back princess line and side seam of the mannequin.

Step 16

- Beginning with the side seam, turn seams to the inside, giving as much fullness as the fabric width will allow to the skirt.

Step 17

- Pin CF front section over side front.
- Pin side back over back.

Marking and truing

- Mark the calico with pencil or chalk.
- If you were draping in taffeta, thread-trace and tailor-tack your sew lines.
- Unpin and gently press out the pieces and true the lines.
- Cut two of each of the sections and re-pin or sew to test the pattern.

Analysis

- First analyse the overall effect of your drape. Does it have the light, young and pretty feel of the photograph? If not, try to work out why. It may be a proportion issue. Perhaps the straps are too narrow on the chest, or the tucks too close to the centre of the bodice.

- Now check all the lines and balance of the drape. Starting from the top of the shoulder, carefully compare the contours of your drape with those of the photograph. Train your eye to see subtle differences, and how they affect the overall look.

- Note that the angle of the 'V' neckline is shallower in the drape. It is making the bodice look heavier and slightly more elongated. It will need correction.

- What is successful about your drape? Does it accomplish the intent of the sketch or photo? How would you characterize the attitude it conveys?

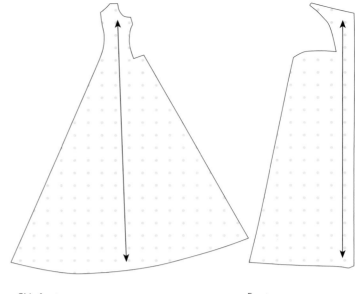

Side front   Front

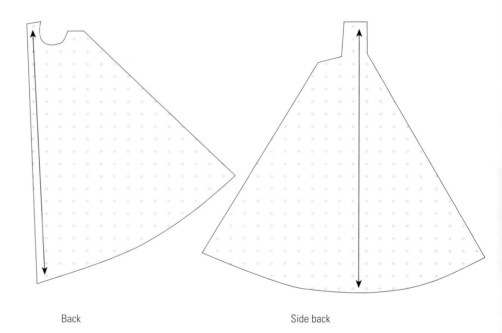

Back   Side back

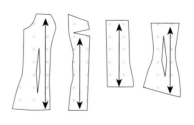

Side front   Front   Side back   Back

Variations
Royal wedding gown

The exquisite gown Catherine Middleton wore at her wedding to Prince William, Duke of Cambridge, in April 2011 showed off the very best of British craftsmanship. Designed by Sarah Burton and made by the House of Alexander McQueen, the dress was made of ivory silk satin gazar with a bodice appliquéd in an Irish Carrickmacross pattern with English Cluny and French Chantilly lace. The 2.7-metre (9-foot) train was accented with a subtle ruffle treatment at the back waist that you will drape here.

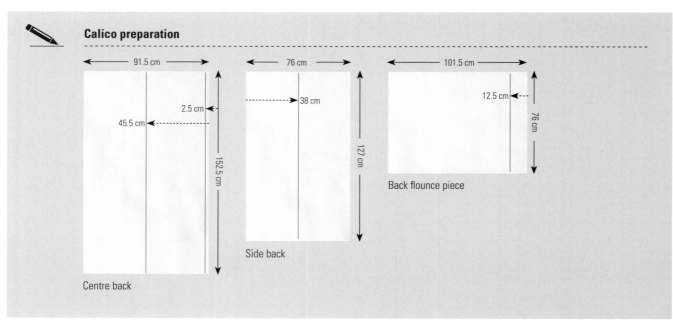

Calico preparation

91.5 cm

2.5 cm

45.5 cm

152.5 cm

Centre back

76 cm

38 cm

127 cm

Side back

101.5 cm

12.5 cm

76 cm

Back flounce piece

Step 1

- First, create the dress back to use as a base for the ruffle drape. The actual train was 2.7 m (9') long, but here you just need some length and width to get a sense of proportion.

- Start by draping CB piece at the waistline, letting it stretch out past the floor.

- Drape a side back panel and pin the two together to support the overdrape.

- Pin firmly along back waistline.

- If it helps, place some weights on the hem area to help keep the train fanned out.

Step 2

- Set back drape piece high to give plenty of extra calico for the flare in the back. Pin at the waist about 30 cm (12") down from the top edge of the calico section.

Step 3

- Cut down vertically to the waist and let back fall to hem of draped piece. You will see that this creates a cascade drape.

- Pin a deep pleat that folds towards the side, as in the photograph.

Step 4

- Note that hem of draped piece is now falling quite straight across back of train.

- Cut hem of draped piece so it angles up in the centre of the pleated area, leaving longer areas in CB and side back.

- Check the photograph for proportion.

Step 5

- Check the angle of the tucks. Look at the photograph and note their direction.

- Re-pin and adjust the angle until you achieve the look that you feel is right.

- Note that the shape of the back ruffle drape is controlled by how much flare is worked into the actual piece and also by the length of the ruffle piece. If you want more flare, which will result in more folds, study the cut that you made in Step 3. Practise visualizing how the drape would change if the cut was made with more fabric falling into the drape.

3.3
Draping on the Bias

History

A bias-cut garment is cut with the warp and weft threads at a 45° angle. This allows the weave to open and spread, giving the fabric the soft drape that characterizes the bias cut. At the same time, the stretch enables the fabric to mould to the curves of the body.

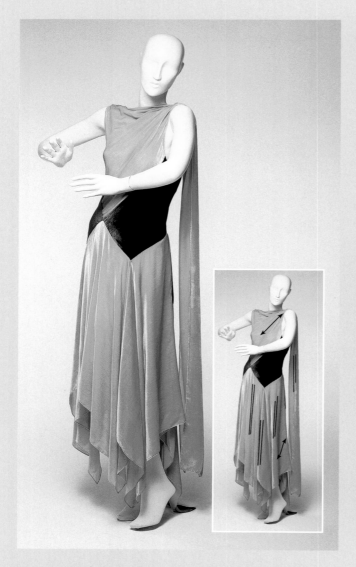

Above: In this classic Vionnet design, c. 1926, the bias cut allows the bodice and green side panel to conform to the figure. The light, airy skirt is made from overlapping square-cut panels, set at a 45° angle so that the bias grain hangs vertically, creating a cascade effect. The straight grain (indicated in the inset by arrows) gives strength to the shoulder area, which supports the weight of the dress. The skirt panels are cut on the bias (indicated by a double line).

Above: Claudette Colbert in *It Happened One Night* wears a bias-cut wedding gown of silk crêpe. This is a heavier fabric than that used in the dress by Madeleine Vionnet (left). Its weight falls in wide, sumptuous folds, following the contour of the hip, and then flows out at the hemline with a lush, fluid finish.

The name of designer Madeleine Vionnet (1876–1975) has become synonymous with the bias cut. The first designer to widely utilize this cut, Vionnet took advantage of the flexibility and fluidity of the bias grain to contour dress shapes in a new way, highlighting the natural curves of the feminine form. She created a collection of groundbreaking work in the 1920s, when corsetless dressing finally became established.

Vionnet often used the purity of the simple, draped square in her work, sometimes referencing the ancient Greek peplos, a square of fabric held at the shoulders and belted at the waist. The miniature mannequin was an indispensible tool for Vionnet's technique. There are many photos of the designer sitting with her doll-sized wooden mannequin on a spinning piano stool as she worked out just how the bias fabric pieces would fit together. She would then make diagrams to pre-cut the fabric into the shapes she needed before draping them onto the full-size mannequin, or onto one of her many private clients.

The bias cut naturally requires larger pieces of fabric to accommodate the tilted pattern pieces. But if they are cleverly seamed, the pieces will wrap the body in a spiral, and the pattern will fit with just as much economy of cut as a straight-grain garment.

Traditionally, softer fabrics are used for bias cuts — georgettes, crêpes and chiffons. Used often in lingerie for its ability to conform to the figure, silk charmeuse is a contemporary fabric favourite. Of course, any fabric can be cut on the bias. Even heavy woollen garments incorporate the use of bias to help a collar roll better or to give some stretch to a specific area.

The bias cut has remained popular throughout the twentieth and into the twenty-first century, the 1930s in particular. In the costume-design studios of Hollywood's Golden Age, extravagance was the rule. Designers employed an army of experts to create some of the extraordinary clothing cut on the bias seen in the films from the 1930s through the 1950s.

Here, a length of silk crêpe, similar to that of Claudette Colbert's gown, is draped with the true bias aligned with the centre front of the mannequin. Study the way the fabric falls as it stretches over the mannequin.

Exercises
Bias-draped camisole

This camisole takes advantage of the bias cut with both the easy drape of the silk mesh overpiece and the cut of the pattern pieces. The front and back are basically squares tilted on the diagonal, the bias grain falling straight down the centre front and back. The bias silk charmeuse fits by allowing the fabric to stretch gently over the bust and shape to the figure over the waist and high hip.

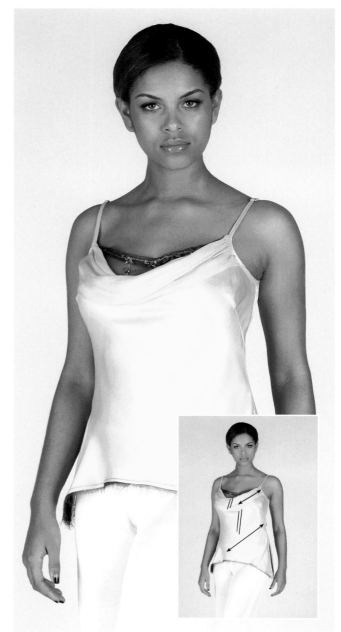

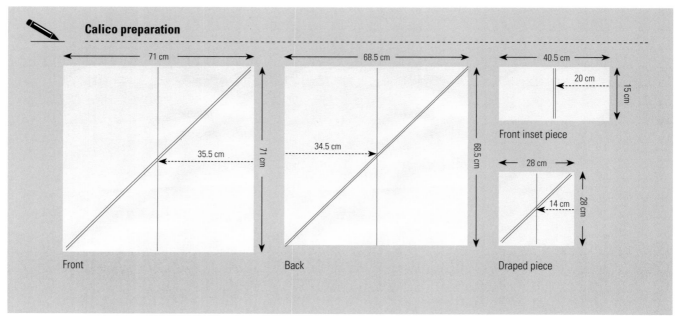

✏️ **Calico preparation**

Front
71 cm
71 cm
35.5 cm

Back
68.5 cm
68.5 cm
34.5 cm

Front inset piece
40.5 cm
20 cm
15 cm

Draped piece
28 cm
14 cm
28 cm

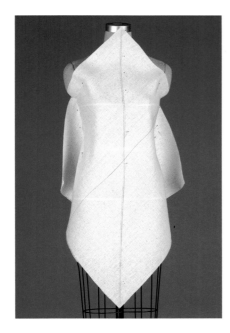

Step 1

- Pin CF bias line to CF of mannequin.

- Smooth calico to the sides of mannequin and pin as closely as you can without allowing it to pull or twist.

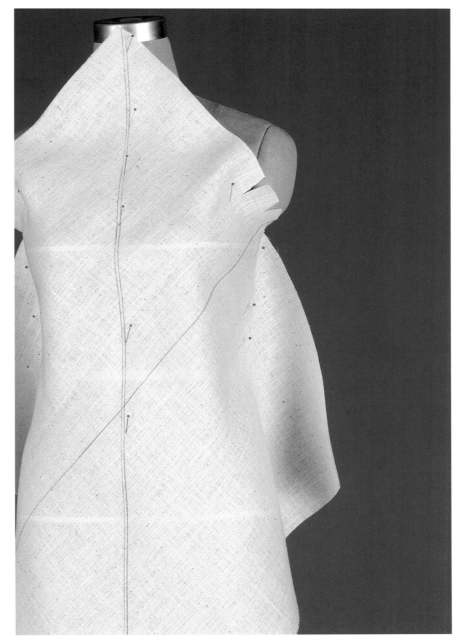

Step 2

- Clip at armscye where necessary. Note that when fabric is pulled tightly, ease forms above and below bust point, but the shape of the mannequin is still visible, as the bias grain tends to mould itself over the mannequin.

Step 3

- Form a side bust dart to pull fabric even closer to the mannequin.

- Repeat from Step 1 for the back.

- Pin the sides together right sides out and trim excess fabric.

- Twill-tape the hem.

- Twill- or sticky-tape the bust line where lace will meet bodice fabric. This will be the point at which the bust ease can no longer be shaped to the body.

Step 4

- Centre bias line of lace inset piece to CF.

- Trim excess where lace will meet top edge of the front piece.

- Tape the upper edge. Trim excess above the tape.

Step 5

- Think of the lace inset as a sort of yoke. As it meets the top of the front edge, it absorbs that extra ease there, and allows a smooth fit from CF to mid-underarm area.

- Turn under lower edge of lace piece along this line.

- Turn down upper edge of lace piece.

- Turn side seams front over back.

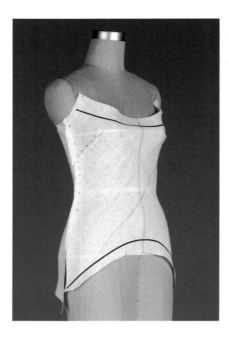

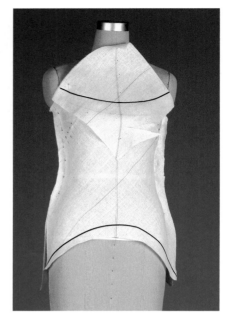

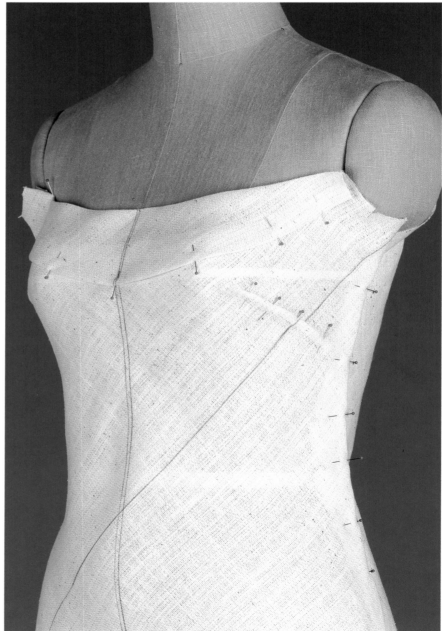

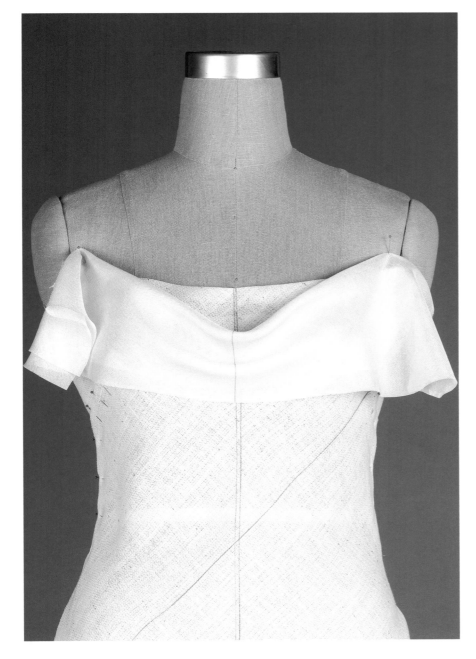

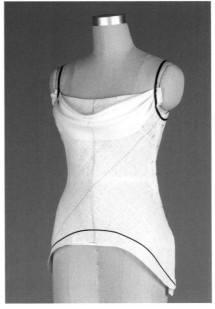

Step 7

- Trim side edges of draped piece and set the straps.

- Remember that the side bust underarm area needs to remain high at the armhole to cover the side of the bust line.

Step 6

- Align bias line of bodice overpiece to CF and determine amount of drape or 'cowl'.

- Here, a silk gauze is used to indicate a softer fabric. It would be good practice to try draping with a piece of softer fabric such as chiffon or georgette here, but if it is not available, the same fabric as the body drape will still work.

- Pin at the sides and again check the depth of the CF drape. Because the lace is sheer, you need to cover the bust line, but you also want the lace still to show.

Fitting on the bias

With the bias, if you want a particular area to be more tightly fitted, it is not always that area that needs to be taken in. Try following the straight grain up to the edge of the piece and pulling in there.

Bias chemise with princess line

The bias cut is perfect for lingerie, softly moulding to the shape of the body. As with the bias-draped camisole, the heavier hemp/silk blend will be used. With the bias, the weight of this fabric will give and stretch in a way that is more similar to the silk that will be used for the final garment. Also, it is easier to see the actual grainlines with this more loosely woven fabric.

Draping in full for the bias

For this chemise the front and back sections will be draped not just from the CF to the princess-line seams, but with a full front. It is necessary when working with the bias to have the support of the larger piece. If it is cut on the bias line, it will stretch too much.

Calico preparation

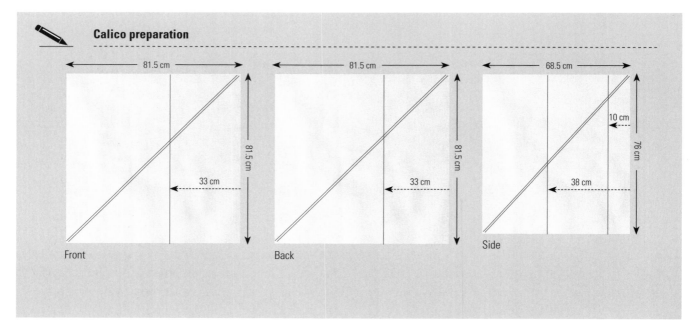

Front — 81.5 cm / 81.5 cm / 33 cm

Back — 81.5 cm / 81.5 cm / 33 cm

Side — 68.5 cm / 76 cm / 10 cm / 38 cm

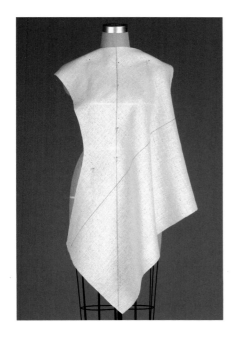

Step 1

- Set front section by first aligning bias line with CF of mannequin.
- Trim along the style line, which is about at the princess line.
- Trim away the excess, leaving at least a 2.5 cm (1") seam allowance.
- Repeat for the back.
- Join the shoulders and pin wrong sides together.

Step 2

- Set side panel piece by centring bias grainline on side seam of mannequin.
- Anchor it around the armscye and then allow it to fall freely.
- At this point the bias will begin to stretch. Let it fall naturally; when it seems to have stopped stretching, pin it lightly along the side seam to keep the grainline vertical.

Step 3

- Pin the three pieces together, wrong sides out.
- Find the balance, experimenting with pulling and fitting as closely as you can. Try pulling from different areas of the same section and see what happens.

Step 4

- Turn front and back over side panel, trimming and clipping where necessary. Turn front over back at shoulder.
- Stand back to check the silhouette: it should skim the body, not have a tight fit.
- Pin up the hem. Check the waist again; pull in as close as possible with the fabric still falling smoothly (not shown).

Step 5

- Place godets by opening up front and back princess seams and inserting godet sections behind the other sections, pulling godets out until you get the flare you want.
- Turn seams to the inside.
- Tape the neck and armhole.

Draping project

Gilbert Adrian designed this bias-cut satin slip dress for 'blonde bombshell' Jean Harlow to wear in the 1933 film *Dinner at Eight*.

The dress became Harlow's signature look and helped to cement her enormous popularity. The spiral dynamic of the bias is perfect for the attitude of this dress; Harlow is bursting with energy, held in only by the close fit of the thin silk.

To arrive at a preparation diagram for a garment that uses this type of spiral design, first drape the dress roughly on the mini-mannequin to determine where the fabric will be cut. Then take the drape apart and see how the pieces might fit together on the fabric most economically. The measurements of the mini-mannequin are half the size of the full mannequin, so you just need to double the specifications to work out the size of the pieces.

This bias dress will be very close fitting. Different types of fabrics will all stretch in varying degrees on the bias, so it will be best to drape in the final fabric.

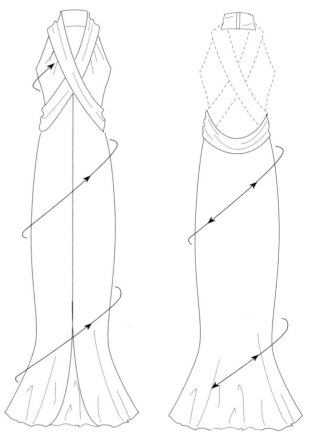

Using a mini-mannequin

- The amount of fabric in the dress is about 3.2 m (3.5 yards). The fabric being used is 137 cm (54") wide.

- Prepare a piece of fabric, or calico, half the size of this estimate – 1.4 m (1.5 yards) long and 68.5 cm (27") wide.

- You can see in the photograph that the dress has a CF seam, so start with the bias line going straight down the CB.

- Wrap the fabric to CF to see if there is enough width to make the dress with no side seams.

- It appears that the fabric will be just wide enough, although it might be short in the front. Bias dresses often use godets to fill in missing corners; with that knowledge you can proceed.

- Pin around hip level, which is the tightest part, keeping the bias running straight up and down the whole way around the mannequin.

- Cut away triangles in the front.

- Cut below bust and to the back on grain.

- It will be difficult to get a close fit at the back high hip area, so put an inset in the lower CB area.

- Use a strip of bias for the wrap-style neckband.

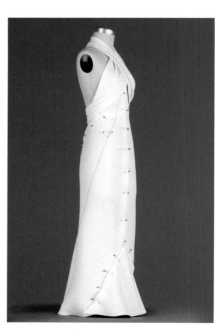

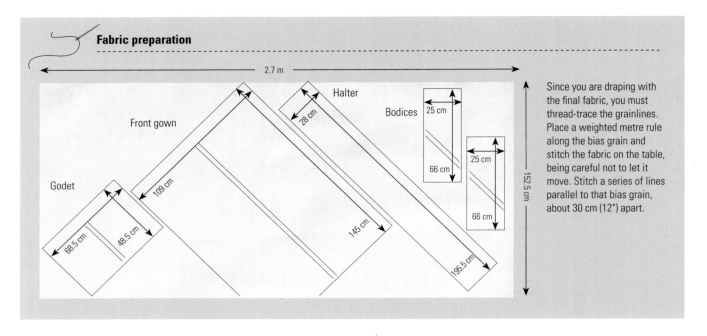

Fabric preparation

2.7 m

Front gown

Halter

Bodices

25 cm

28 cm

109 cm

Godet

25 cm

66 cm

66 cm

68.5 cm

48.5 cm

145 cm

195.5 cm

152.5 cm

Since you are draping with the final fabric, you must thread-trace the grainlines. Place a weighted metre rule along the bias grain and stitch the fabric on the table, being careful not to let it move. Stitch a series of lines parallel to that bias grain, about 30 cm (12") apart.

Step 1

- Align one of the bias lines with CF of mannequin and wrap it towards the back. CF needs to be high enough to reach bust line at CF.

- In order to keep bias line straight, angle fabric up towards shoulder. Pin at right shoulder.

- Set the piece at the CB and CF.

Step 2

- Wrap the fabric around to the back, keeping bias grainlines vertical.

- Pin along the hip line to CB.

- Release the pins on the right shoulder.

- Pin excess fabric at left shoulder.

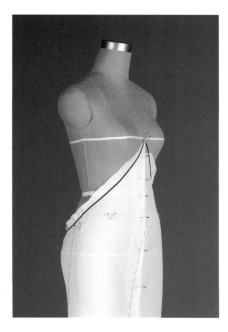

Step 3

- Continue to drape fabric all the way around to CF and pin a vertical seam from underbust to hem.

- Cut away excess at CFs – basically, the two large triangles.

- You have now established the main body of the dress. Continue to cut away excess from the hem and back lines.

Step 4

- Pin CF seam to inside, continuing to refine the fit of the dress. The tightest part will be at the hip. Pull in as much as you can at the waist.

- Note that the look of the dress is pulled up at the CF; the more you pull up at that point, the more fitted the waist becomes.

- Tape the hip line where it stops being able to fit the mannequin and where you see excess is being created. This is where you will need to seam in an inset piece at the back.

- Continue taping up to CF bust point.

- Trim away excess fabric.

Step 5

- Set bodice and back piece. To do this, take a section of fabric that has been cut away and place straight grain along side of bust. Using the strong straight grain here will create less give and keep the area from stretching out. It is always good to support the bust from the side, pushing it towards CF.

- Create two tucks at the top of the neckline area, as in the photograph, to accommodate the bust ease.

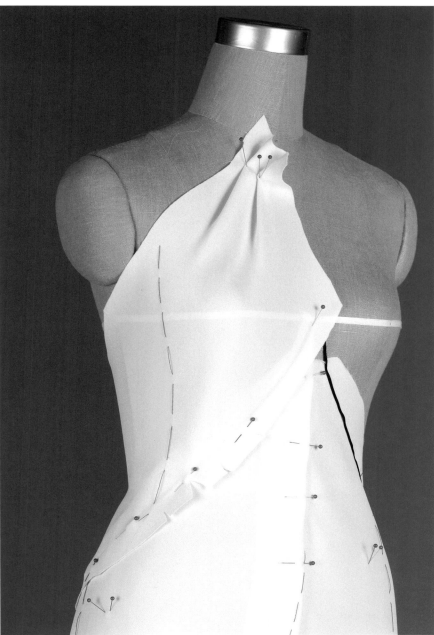

Step 6

- Continue draping front bodice piece by wrapping it around to the back and attaching it to high hip line of skirt piece.

- Pin under the seam allowance where it attaches to the main dress piece, taking in the ease created at that seam.

- Drape the godet at the hem by placing a large triangular piece over the lower CF seam where it is missing fabric. Pin it evenly to the two front sections, allowing it to drape out in the centre, which will give a little more walking room.

Step 7

- Drape the bias halter strap by starting at the CB waist and wrapping it around the front, as in the photograph.

- The strap will have a closure at the CB neckline.

Step 8

- Adjust the strap over the bust area, as in the photograph.

- Turn up the hem.

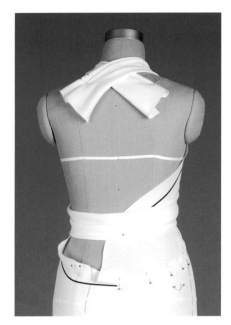

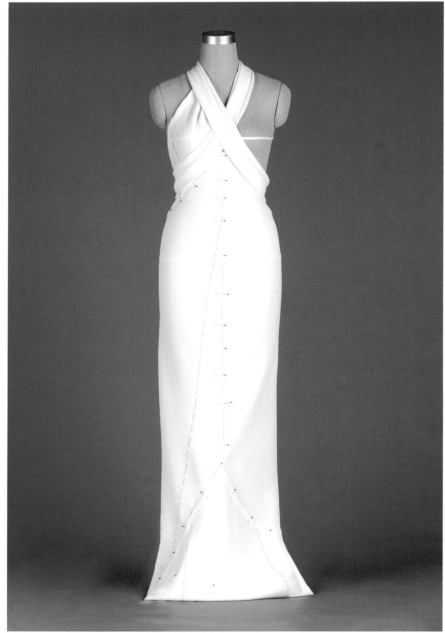

Marking and truing

- Mark the fabric by using a contrasting thread to outline each piece.

- First, thread-trace along all the sew lines.

- On the join between bodice and skirt section, sew a thread-traced line on both sides of the seam so the line will be marked on each piece when the garment is taken apart.

- Crossmark at least once on each piece so it will be easier to join the seams when you true the lines.

- Tailor-tack the tucks (not shown).

- On the bias halter strap, mark where it hits the CB and the side seams, and where it crosses over itself in the CF.

- After thread-tracing, unpin, clip the tailor tacks and press out very gently.

- Study the shape of your pieces and note any lines that look wobbly or unbalanced.

- At this point it is important to discern whether a wavy line is the subtlety of your drape, or whether it is an error. Do not smooth out a line until you are sure which it is. If you are not sure, re-pin the fabric and put it back on the mannequin to check it.

- If you want to save your pattern, use a tracing wheel to copy it onto a piece of drafting paper. If not, since you have draped the dress in the actual fabric, simply trim and sew the dress back together along the sew lines that you have marked.

- You can do this by either:

1. cutting the seam allowance to equal widths so that you can line up your pieces edge to edge and sew them together; or

2. lining up the two thread-traced lines and carefully hand-basting the two pieces together first, before machine sewing.

   The second method is more accurate, the first is faster.

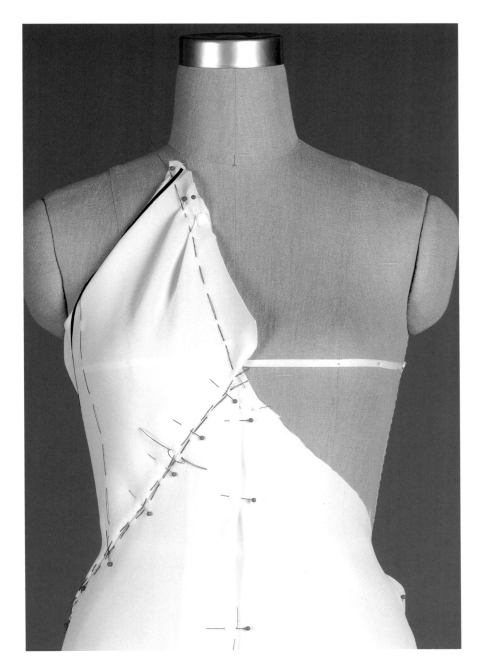

Analysis

- Compare your drape with the dress in the photograph. Before analysing the details, assess the general feeling of it. Try to identify the spiral energy of the bias. It should look like the fabric is wrapping tightly around the body (the straight grains). Held up by the halter strap, the bias grains should be moulding to the curves of the bust, waist and hips.

- Jean Harlow's dress caused a sensation in its time. More than just communicating an attitude, it made a larger statement, creating a new consciousness that women were confidently in control of their sexuality. Does your drape communicate that? Is it extreme enough? Can it be tighter, the proportions more exaggerated?

- Now, starting at the top of the dress, follow the contours of the dress. Start with the negative space at the neckline and shoulder. Does the shape of the areas of bare skin seem to be the same as in your drape? Does the width of the strap look like the right proportion? Check the direction of the tucks. Do they aim towards the bust point correctly?

- The side silhouette is important. In the photograph, the dress has a definite S-curve as it travels out at the hip and in at the knee.

- If necessary, adjust your drape and then thread-trace the corrections in a different coloured thread.

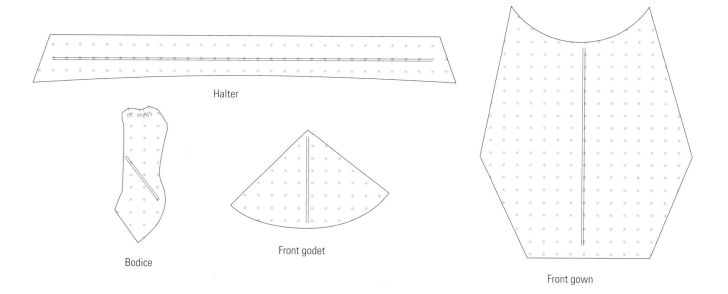

Halter

Bodice

Front godet

Front gown

3.4
Improvisational Draping

History

Improvisation is the act of creating in the moment. In draping, this means working directly on the mannequin on a new design without having a sketch or blueprint to follow.

In this final chapter of the book, having covered the complex techniques of darting, seaming and sculpting shapes, you are back to draping on mannequins with simple panels of woven cloth. Since you are not working from a flat sketch or visualizing a final outcome, you need some reason, motivation or inspiration as a starting point.

Eskimos' furs serve a practical need for warmth and protection. In fashion, inspiration often comes from a beautiful fabric that instils a desire to see it sewn. Experimenting with its drape and flow generates ideas about how to best highlight its particular qualities.

Invention can be triggered by connecting with a muse. Visualize a specific person. How would you like her to look? What unique qualities does she exhibit? How much space does she take up when she enters a room? What kind of impact would you like her to have on those around her? Will she stand out as a star attraction? You help define the reality.

Sometimes, writing notes in a journal about what you want to express helps to ignite the creative process. Inspiration can come from other artists' work or the attitudes and styles of a particular historical era. Designers often say that a collection was inspired by the colours and tone of a particular painting, or the silhouettes of a specific era.

'Classic' fashion design refers to styles of clothing that have stood the test of time. Chanel's tailored suit jacket still works today; the classic two-front-pleat trouser continues to reassert itself. In this chapter you

Chögyam Trungpa's *Abstract Elegance* represents balance and beauty in asymmetry. The same configuration of energy, space and form can be translated into a three-dimensional sculpture, such as a draped fashion design.

302

will diverge from these classic forms to appreciate the beauty and balance in asymmetry and the unexpected.

In costume design, the personality of the character dictates the emotion that the clothing needs to communicate. In making the costume for the Exiled Goddess (right), the first step was to gather the collection of colours and textures to be used. The base of the costume is a hemp/silk loose-fitting tunic top. First, the large blue section was draped from the shoulder, then the contrast raw-silk neckline was draped. The look needed to be ragged, as the character has been exiled for twenty years, so the neckline drape is asymmetrical and twisted. An artist herself, the character has ornamented this part with shells and fringe. Despite her poverty, she has a sense of dignity. Her long shoulder drape is bold and elegant.

Being spontaneous, intuitive and willing to experiment are key to improvisational practice. It is more important than ever to have mastery of your draping techniques. When the designer can rely on these core skills, the intuitive mind can emerge and creativity is free to bring the design to fruition.

'The Exiled Goddess', a costume design by Karolyn Kiisel for a stage production of *Thyestes' Feast*, made of weathered linen and silk, hemp and mussel shells.

Exercises
Asymmetrical draped neckline

This dress, with its simple fitted bodice and full skirt, needs an interesting neckline. Use the intense flourish and long, smooth, tapering brushstroke of Chögyam Trungpa's *Abstract Elegance* (see p. 302) as inspiration.

Approximating the required width, prepare a bias panel, as that will flow the most smoothly of all the grainline choices. This improvisational drape will not be planned out, but the flat sketches below will help you translate the energy flow of the calligraphy into a neckline.

In the drape, the flourish will be created at the back left shoulder. The change in direction at the top of the calligraphy will correspond to the centre front. The uninterrupted drape across the back represents the long brushstroke on the right, and the finish point will be at the left shoulder in the front.

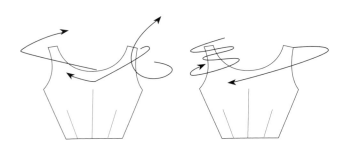

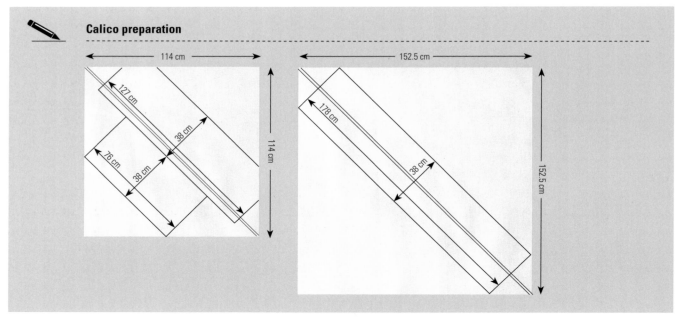

Calico preparation

114 cm

127 cm

76 cm

38 cm

38 cm

38 cm

114 cm

152.5 cm

178 cm

38 cm

152.5 cm

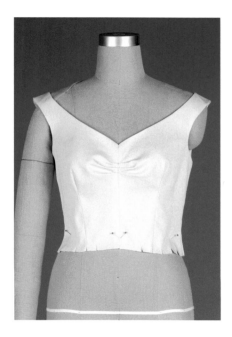

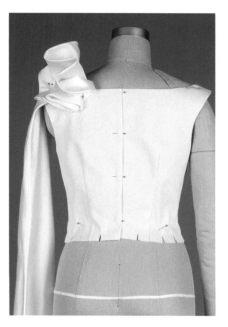

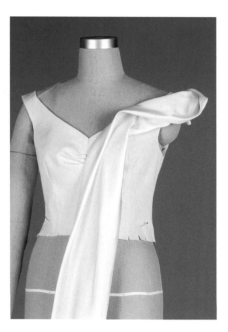

Step 1

- First, create the bodice to use as a base for the new neckline.

Step 2

- The calligraphy in the inspirational image has a flourish at the beginning so, starting at the back, build volume with the bias panel by working in some layered tucks, securing them with pins as you go.

Step 3

- Creating a twist, bring the bias panel around to the front.

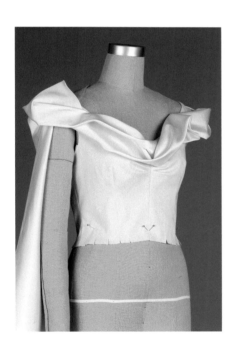

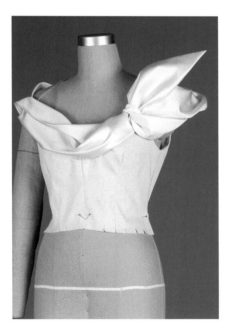

Step 4

- Form CF neckline and right shoulder area, keeping the neck open and low.

Step 5

- The back will have a long, smooth area of visual relief, taking inspiration from the long, rounded part of the calligraphy.

Step 6

- Finish with the pointed end of your piece by echoing the line of calligraphy that tapers off into space.

Draping project

Vivienne Westwood is the grande dame of improvisational draping. Throughout her career, she has taken current trends one step further by doing the unexpected. Her wildly creative silhouettes have challenged our conventional view of beauty for decades.

In doing an improvisational drape of this Vivienne Westwood dress, the goal is to capture the essence of the look without being too literal about the construction. If you are doing a truly improvisational drape, you are starting with only your own idea or concept. Creative inspiration can come from anywhere.

In either case, begin by mapping out the energetic flow of the piece through the grainline configuration. If you are clear on the mood and tone you want to express, this can be something very simple (see the neckline schematic on p. 304).

Without thinking about specific seaming, decide on some parameters for the scale of your garment. This will help you to determine the size of the calico pieces to prepare. Mark the straight grains on each piece. Mark bias grains as well if you think that some areas of your piece will utilize the specific benefits of the bias, such as a cowl or draped section.

If you are draping in calico, consider the final fabric you will be using. Familiarize yourself with the hand of it so that you can use your skills of visualization to understand how the outcome will differ from that of the toile.

When you are ready to begin, relax into your environment and feel the confidence that your skills have become second nature. By anchoring your vision or inspiration foremost in your mind, your own unique style of expression will surely emerge in your work.

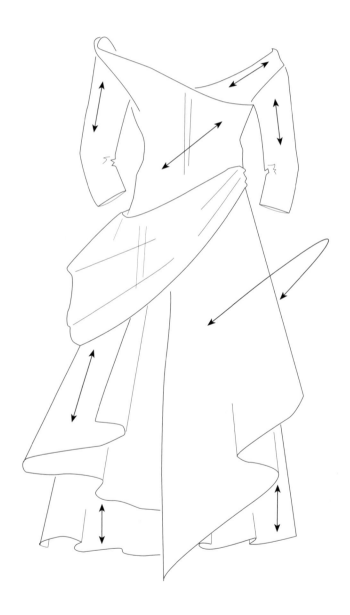

Step 1

- Drape and sew a foundation garment similar to the Georgian corset in Chapter 1.3 (see pp. 74–77).

- Keep upper edge wide across mid-front to accommodate the wide set of the straps.

Step 2

- Drape the front underskirt by aligning a straight grain with the side front of the mannequin.

- First hold in the amount of fullness and flare to create the look that you want in the skirt, then refine the volume into tucks to keep the waistline flat. Keep skirt section flatter in front with more flare to the sides.

- Cut from the side piece the excess created by the flare – basically, the large triangle that is smallest at hem and largest at waist.

- Cut hem about 7 cm (2–3") off the ground from CF to side seam.

Step 3

- Calculate the length of the skirt and turn up the hem.

- The hem must be very deep as it will show when the folds and drapes are pulled up.

- Pick up the front corner and experiment with placement, watching how the folds change with different positions.

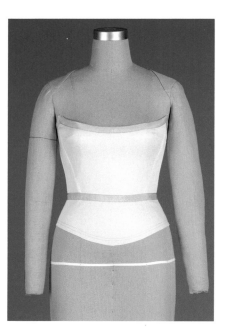

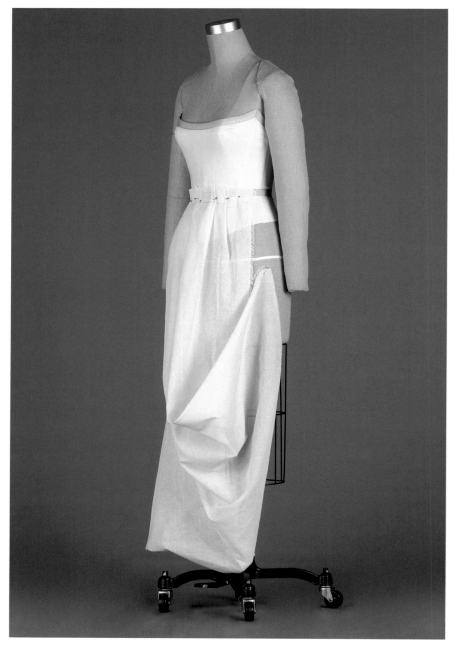

Step 4

- Drape the back by forming tucks in the same way that you did for the front, folding up a deep hem.

Step 5

- Turn up the front hem of the skirt to create the asymmetrical drape.

Step 6

- Attach a long rectangular piece of calico to left side of mannequin, leaving a little more in the back than in the front.

- Hold the centre of the piece and pin it at the waist.

Step 7

- Fold the piece in half lengthwise, bringing the outside edge underneath, and pin it to the foundation at the waist.

- Create some volume at the waist by holding in gathers at the waist to create fullness at the hip in the front and back. Keep the side seam fairly flat.

- Pin the two long edges of the inside piece together.

- Pin up a hem, at least 7.5 cm (3") deep.

Step 8

- Pin a butterfly-shaped fold by reaching in and picking up some of the pinned side seam and connecting the two pieces, as shown.

Step 9

- Refine gathers at waist until they are flat and the drape falls in a balanced way.

- This is a good time for a perspective check. Look in the mirror from a distance and observe the silhouette closely. The pieces should flow with each other at the hems. Make sure you like what you have; after you add the top sections, it will become harder to make alterations.

Step 10

- Start front upper section by aligning one of the bias grainlines with CF of mannequin.

- The straight grain will follow the torn lower edge.

Step 11

- Fasten the calico corner at the right shoulder of the mannequin.

- Notice the broadness across the front chest and keep the shoulder wide.

- Trim off the top edge.

- Make a tuck at right shoulder, folding it down and aiming ease towards bust.

Step 12

- Wrap lower edge of front piece around to the back, draping some deep folds into the back, emanating from left back of waistline.

- Drape a back bodice section centring the bias line on CB of mannequin.

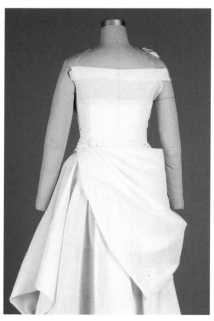

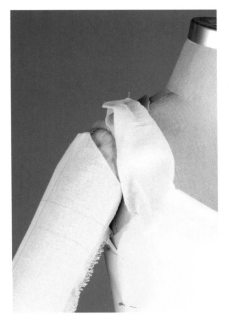

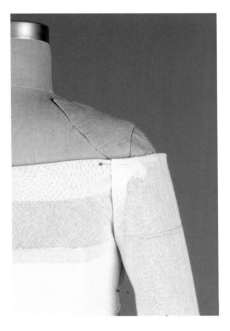

Step 13

- Trim the excess at the left shoulder.

- Wrap fabric around the side to create side seams.

- Clip to the waist at both side seams and pin them front over back.

- Fold over the top edge.

- Cut away excess at the right shoulder, leaving a tail for shoulder wrap.

- Drape left side of bodice by slipping the calico underneath the top edge and creating a strap similar to the right side.

Step 14

- Create sleeves by wrapping rectangular pieces around the arm and fitting them up into the lower armhole. This is an off-shoulder sleeve without a real crown, so a rectangle shape will work.

Step 15

- Pin the back sleeve into the 'armhole', which is actually the side-seam area.

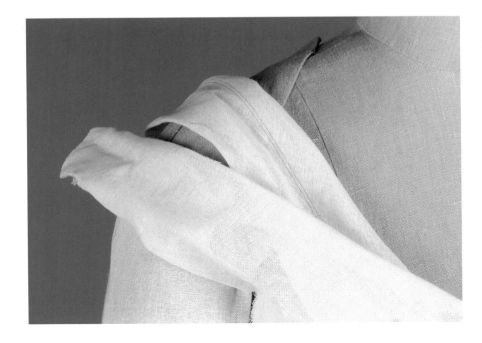

Step 16

- Using an extra piece of bias calico, create a twist effect on the top of the sleeve, as in the photograph. The bodice will be pinned to the foundation, and the off-shoulder treatment should serve to keep the sleeve up.

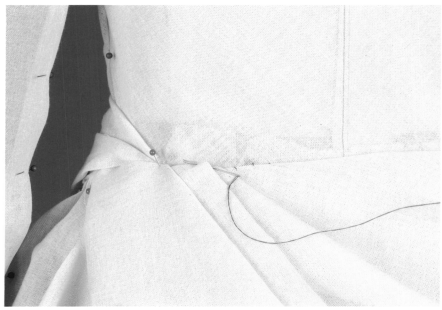

Marking and truing

Step 1

- Tailor-tack all connection points.

Step 2

- Thread-trace and tailor-tack all sew lines and tucks.

Step 3

- If you want to make a paper pattern, disassemble the dress and press it gently. True the lines with your rulers and check the seams against each other.

- Align the grainlines of the calico with the grainlines of the pattern paper.

- Use a tracing wheel to transfer all sew lines and crossmarks to the paper. Add seam allowances.

- If you don't need a paper pattern, check the drape by truing the lines and re-pinning, or simply lay the trued calico pieces onto the final fabric, add seam allowances, cut and sew.

Analysis

- Stand at a distance from the drape and try to discern if it is expressing the emotional tone, attitude or consciousness you were aiming for.

- If it is not quite right, try to assess which elements of the design are not supporting the concept.

- When comparing this calico drape to the Vivienne Westwood photograph, a few areas do not seem to be flowing together well. On the mannequin's left side at the hem, the asymmetrical folds look awkward. Even though it will look lighter and more like the photograph in the final fabric, the drape needs to be adjusted. Sometimes during this process, you will see that suddenly the part you are working on seems to have more life and falls into balance with the whole.

- Part of finding your own unique look is following what proportions you like, what dynamics interest you. When it satisfies your aesthetic, it is done.

A trained eye comes with practice

For designers in all disciplines, excellence is often referred to as 'having a good eye'. This means that one can see and execute interesting composition, balance and proportion. It means being able to recognize when the energetic currents are working together, when design work moves from static to dynamic.

A trained eye comes with practice. Continuing to study the skills learnt in this book will steadily increase your ability to see not just with the eyes of a student, but with those of an accomplished designer who is able to express their own, unique, creative vision.

Glossary

Anchor pin Pin or pins specifically used to firmly secure a calico piece when draping.

Armscye Fabric edge of an armhole to which a sleeve is sewn.

Bateau neckline A high, wide neckline that runs the length of the collarbone and ends at the shoulder. Also known as 'boat neckline'.

Bishop sleeve A long sleeve, fuller at the bottom than the top and gathered into a cuff.

Blouson A woman's long blouse with closely tied waistband, or a style of garment that has extra fabric draping over a waistband or elastic.

Bodice Upper, main, front and back pattern piece(s) of a garment.

Boning A flexible yet firm strip of metal or plastic used to support and maintain shape.

Break point The beginning of the roll line, usually at the first button.

Busk A corset or bustier closure consisting of a piece of slotted stays of steel, bone or wood.

Bust point The highest and fullest point of the bust.

Contour line A line that represents the outer edge of a form.

Convertible collar Rolled collar that forms small lapels when worn open.

Corset A woman's close-fitting undergarment, usually using boning and lacing, designed to support and shape the upper body. Also a woman's tight-fitting, strapless top, usually using boning.

Crinoline A stiff, coarse fabric used to give body and stiffness to a garment.

Crossmarks Lines designating the intersections of fit seams, stylelines, or darts.

Crown The top third of a sleeve, from the underarm line to the shoulder area.

Ease The extra fabric allowed in the fit of a garment. Also the process of sewing a length of fabric into a smaller one without resulting in gathers or puckers, usually in fitting the crown of a sleeve into an armhole or the back of a garment into the shoulder seam.

Fit seam A seam that is used specifically to help create the fit of a garment.

French dart Dart with diagonal intersecting lines that taper at the apex.

Gathers Folds or puckers of extra predetermined fabric that create fullness.

Grommet A short, circular, metal tube applied to a garment for a lace-up opening designed to give a flat, rimmed finish.

Gusset An extra section of fabric set into seams to give fullness.

Intake Amount of fabric taken in when sewing a dart.

Interlining Fabric placed between main outer fabric and lining used to give specific degree of weight or stiffness to the fabric.

Jewel neckline Circular neckline that sits at base of throat.

Knit Fabric constructed by means of interlocking loops between weft and warp yarns.

Loom Machine that weaves fabric by interlacing horizontal and vertical yarns.

Negative space The areas around or outside the positive shape of a garment that share edges with the form.

Peg, pegged Pants and skirts whose side seams narrow towards the hem.

Petersham ribbon Ribbed ribbon used in hats, corsets, and waistbands designed for reinforcement. It can be steamed into curves to fit the shapes of the garments.

Pivot point In a sleeve, the exact point of intersection on the armhole where the seam of the sleeve falls toward the underarm.

Prototype A sample garment using actual fabrics designed to test a design for fit and proportion.

Racer-back armhole An extended and exaggerated back armhole cut-out.

Rib knit Fabric constructed with knit and purl wales (diagonal lines) running crosswise, resulting in an unbalanced plain weave with noticeable ribs on the surface of the fabric.

Roll line The line on a coat or jacket indicating the fold of the lapel from the roll and stand of a collar to the first button.

Selvedges The long finished edges of a bolt of fabric.

Side bust dart A dart that extends towards the bust, originating at the side seam.

Silhouette An outline of a specific shape or form.

Sponge To moisten calico creases with a damp cloth before pressing.

Style line A seamline that runs from one point of a garment to another, used specifically for style rather than to help with the fit of a garment.

Tailor's tacks Loose and temporary double-thread stitches with unknotted ends indicating construction details.

Thread trace Temporary, hand-sewn stitches indicating seams, darts, grainlines and other construction lines.

Truing The process of correcting and equalizing any discrepancies in sew lines created during draping.

Tunic Loose or close-fitting garment that extends over the hips, historically made of two rectangles of cloth.

Underbust Area under bust curve along the upper rib cage.

Weft Continuous yarns that run crosswise in woven fabric. Also known as 'filling yarns'.

Warp A series of yarns that run lengthwise and parallel to the selvedge in woven fabric. Also known as 'ends'.

Yoke An upper, fitted piece of a skirt, a blouse or shirt, or pants that supports another, usually fuller section of fabric.

Resources

Books

Helen Joseph Armstrong, *Draping for Apparel Design* (3rd edition). New York: Fairchild Books, 2013.

Helen Joseph Armstrong, *Patternmaking for Fashion Design* (5th edition). Upper Saddle River, New Jersey: Pearson Prentice Hall, 2009.

Michele Wesen Bryant, *Fashion Drawing: Illustration Techniques for Fashion Designers*. London: Laurence King Publishing/Upper Saddle River, New Jersey: Pearson Prentice Hall, 2011.

Michele Wesen Bryant and Diane DeMers, *The Specs Manual* (2nd edition). New York: Fairchild Books, 2004.

Kathryn Hagen, *Fashion Illustration for Designers* (2nd edition). Upper Saddle River, New Jersey: Prentice Hall, 2010.

Kathryn Hagen and Parme Giuntini (eds), *Garb: A Fashion and Culture Reader*. Upper Saddle River, New Jersey: Pearson Prentice Hall, 2007.

Kathryn Hagen and Julie Hollinger, *Portfolio for Fashion Designers*. Boston: Pearson, 2013.

Sue Jenkyn Jones, *Fashion Design* (3rd edition). London: Laurence King Publishing, 2011.

Gareth Kershaw, *Patternmaking for Menswear*. London: Laurence King Publishing, 2013.

Abby Lillethun and Linda Welters, *The Fashion Reader* (2nd edition). London: Berg Publishers, 2011.

Dennic Chunman Lo, *Patternmaking*. London: Laurence King Publishing, 2011.

Hisako Sato, *Drape Drape*. London: Laurence King Publishing, 2012.

Hisako Sato, *Drape Drape 2*. London: Laurence King Publishing, 2012.

Hisako Sato, *Drape Drape 3*. London: Laurence King Publishing, 2013.

Martin M. Shoben and Janet P. Ward, *Pattern Cutting and Making Up—The Professional Approach*. Burlington: Elsevier, 1991.

Basia Skutnicka, *Technical Drawing for Fashion*. London: Laurence King Publishing, 2010.

Phyllis G. Tortora and Keith Eubank, *Survey of Historic Costume* (5th edition). New York: Fairchild Books, 2010.

Nora Waugh, *The Cut of Women's Clothes*. London: Faber and Faber, 1994.

Supplies

Corsetry (fabric, boning, ribbon, etc.)

Farthingales Corset Making Supplies (worldwide)
farthingalescorsetmakingsupplies.com

Richard the Thread (worldwide)
www.richardthethread.com

Dress forms

Kennett & Lindsell Ltd (UK)
www.kennettlindsell.com

Morplan (UK)
www.morplan.com

Siegel & Stockman (Paris)
www.siegel-stockman.com

Superior Model Form Co. (US)
www.superiormodel.com

Wolf Dress Forms (US)
www.wolfform.com

General

Ace Sewing Machine Co. (US)
www.acesewing.com

B. Black & Sons (US)
www.bblackandsons.com

Borovick Fabrics Ltd (UK)
www.borovickfabridsltd.co.uk

Britex Fabrics (US)
www.britexfabrics.com

MacCulloch & Wallis Ltd. (UK)
www.macculloch-wallis.co.uk

Manhattan Fabrics (US)
www.manhattanfabrics.com

PGM-PRO Inc. (worldwide)
www.pgmdressform.com

Patternmaking

Sew Essential Ltd. (worldwide)
www.sewessential.co.uk

Whaleys (Bradford) Ltd. (UK)
www.whaleys-bradford.ltd.uk

Eastman Staples Ltd. (UK)
www.eastman.co.uk

Patterns

Karolyn Kiisel
www.karolynkiisel.com
Patterns for all garments draped in the book are available to purchase; specific sizes on request. Order by page number and title of garment.

Websites

La Couturière Parisienne
www.marquise.de
Period costume, from the Middle Ages to the early 20th century, with patterns

Fashion-Era
www.fashion-era.com
Fashion, costume, and social history

The Museum at FIT (Fashion Institute of Technology), New York
www.fitnyc.edu/museum

Fashion Museum, Bath, UK
www.museumofcostume.co.uk

Center for Pattern Design
www.centerforpatterndesign.com
Free resources related to patternmaking and design

The Cutting Class
www.thecuttingclass.com
Online analysis of key haute couture and ready-to-wear collections

Fashion Net
www.fashion.net
Global fashion portal

Index

Credits

All dress forms used in the book are by Wolf Forms Company, Inc. http://www.wolfform.com/

7 (top) Lawrence Alma-Tadema (1836–1912), *The Frigidarium*, 1890, oil on panel. Private Collection/The Bridgeman Art Library; 7 (bottom) © Eric Ryan/Getty Images; 8 © B&C Alexander/Arcticphoto; 18 Huipil from the Triki, a mountain-dwelling tribe from outside Oaxaca, Mexico. Model: Elaine Wong; 19 Spa-wear tunic by Karolyn Kiisel for Tara West. Model: Chelsea Miller; 24 © Anthea Simms; 26 Gold-stenciled tunic by Karolyn Kiisel, costume for Mesopotamian Opera's *Thyestes' Feast*. Model: Vidala Aronsky; 31 The Bridgeman Art Library/Getty Images; 40 Modern traditional Tibetan chuba, worn by the Sakyong Wangmo, Khandro Tseyang, Queen of Shambhala; 41 (top) Domenico Ghirlandaio, *Birth of the Virgin Mary* (detail), 1485–90, fresco. Cappella Maggiore, Santa Maria Novella, Florence. © Quattrone, Florence; 41 (bottom) *At the Dance*, fashion plate from *Art, Gout, Beaute* (Paris, 1920s). Private Collection/The Bridgeman Art Library; 44 Side dart plaid blouse designed by Karolyn Kiisel. Model: Ellie Fraser; 46 Photo by Frazer Harrison/Getty Images; 48 Swing dress designed by Karolyn Kiisel. Model: Ellie Fraser; 51 © Sunset Boulevard/Corbis; 58 © Anthea Simms; 60 Courtesy Los Angeles County Museum of Art: www.lacma.org; 64 Photo by Art Rickerby/Time Life Pictures/Getty Images; 68 Photo by Fotos International/Hulton Archive/Getty Images; 69 (top) © Philadelphia Museum of Art/CORBIS; 69 (bottom) Photo by Time Life. Pictures/DMI/Time Life Pictures/Getty Images; 74 © Anthea Simms; 79 © Thierry Orban/Sygma/Corbis; 72 Princess-line bustier designed by Karolyn Kiisel. Model: Julia La Cour; 90 © Michael Freeman/Alamy; 91 © Prasanta Biswas/ZUMA Press/Corbis; 92 Modern traditional kilt in the Fraser Hunting Tartan plaid. Model: Ellie Fraser; 94 © SuperStock/Alamy; 96 Skirt designed by Karolyn Kiisel. Model: Michelle Mousel; 98 Skirt designed by Karolyn Kiisel. Model: Claire Marie Fraser; 100 Photo by SNAP/Rex Features; 103 Photo by Mark Mainz/Getty Images for IMG; 110 Skirt designed by Karolyn Kiisel. Model: Julia La Cour; 114 Carpaccio, *Healing of the Possessed Man* (detail), 1494. Accademia, Florence. © CAMERAPHOTO Arte, Venice; 115 (top) Max Tilke, *Oriental Costumes: Their Designs and Colors*, trans. L. Hamilton (London: Kegan Paul Trench, Trubner and Co., 1923); 115 (center) © Victoria and Albert Museum, London; 115 (bottom) Vintage peasant blouse. Model: Ellie Fraser; 118 Catwalking. com; 122 Author's own collection; 131 Photo by Mark Mainz/Getty Images for IMG; 142 Bell-sleeve tunic top designed by Karolyn Kiisel for Tara West. Model: Michelle Mousel; 146 Vintage mandarin collar blouse. Model: Vidala Aronsky; 148 Photo by Joseph Kerlakian/Rex Features; 150 Peplum blouse with bishop sleeve designed by Karolyn Kiisel. Model: Michelle Mousel; 158 (left, top and bottom) Max Tilke, *Oriental Costumes: Their Designs and Colors*, trans. L. Hamilton (London: Kegan Paul Trench, Trubner and Co., 1923); 158 (right) Fitzwilliam Museum, University of Cambridge, UK/The Bridgeman Art Library; 162 Photo by Apic/Getty Images; 166 Traditional Japanese hakama, worn in *kyudo* practice by Alan Chang; 170 © Bettmann/CORBIS; 177 © Corbis. All Rights Reserved; 187 UPPA/Photoshot All Rights Reserved; 193 © Corbis. All Rights Reserved; 198 Knit top with batwing sleeves designed by Angela Chung. Model: Michelle Mousel; 206 (left) Charles Robert Leslie (1794–1859), *Queen Victoria in Her Coronation Robe*, 1838, oil on canvas. Victoria & Albert Museum, London, UK/The Stapleton Collection/The Bridgeman Art Library; 206 (right) Max Tilke, *Oriental Costumes: Their Designs and Colors*, trans. L. Hamilton (London: Kegan Paul Trench, Trubner and Co., 1923);

207 (left) Max Tilke, *Oriental Costumes: Their Designs and Colors*, trans. L. Hamilton (London: Kegan Paul Trench, Trubner and Co., 1923); 207 (right) © Mary Evans Picture Library/Alamy; 209 (top) Vintage Japanese kimono owned by Shibata Sensei, Imperial bowmaker to the Emperor Emperor of Japan. Model: Elaine Wong; 209 (bottom): Getty Images; 210 © 2003 Topham Picturepoint/Photoshot; 211 Chanel-style jacket designed by Karolyn Kiisel. Model: Ellie Fraser; 223 Photo by Kevin Mazur/Wirelmage; 234 Vintage-inspired brocade jacket designed by Karolyn Kiisel. Model: Julia La Cour; 240 © Anthea Simms; 246 Swing coat with shawl collar designed by Karolyn Kiisel. Model: Claire Marie Fraser; 252 Catwalking.com; 260 © Victoria and Albert Museum, London; 261 (top) THE KOBAL COLLECTION/COLUMBIA; 261 (bottom) © Victoria and Albert Museum, London; 262 akg-images/MPortfolio/Electa; 263 © Sony Pictures/Everett/Rex Features; 264 Wedding dress designed by Karolyn Kiisel. Model: Claire Marie Fraser; 265 Photo by Steve Granitz/WireImage; 266 (top) Everett Collection/Rex Features; 266 (bottom) Photo by MGM Studios/Courtesy of Getty Images; 271 Photo by Ke.Mazur/Wireimage/Getty Images; 280 ODD ANDERSEN/AFP/Getty Images; 284 (left) © THE BRIDGEMAN ART LIBRARY; 284 (right): THE KOBAL COLLECTION/COLUMBIA; 286 Bias camisole designed by Karolyn Kiisel for Jacaranda. Model: Chelsea Miller; 290 Bias lace-trimmed chemise designed by Karolyn Kiisel for Jacaranda. Model: Michelle Mousel; 293 Photo by George Hurrell/John Kobal Foundation/Getty Images; 302 Chögyam Trungpa, *Abstract Elegance*. Calligraphy by Chögyam Trungpa copyright Diana J. Mukpo. Used by permission; 304 Gray silk dress with asymmetrical neckline designed by Karolyn Kiisel for Jacaranda. Model: Julia La Cour; 306 Catwalking.com.

Author's acknowledgments

Thank you to:

Greg Lubkin for helping me with the original proposal and giving me the confidence to do it.

Peter Wing Healey for the initial inspiration that, as a Los Angeles–based costume designer, I should use costumes from films for draping lessons.

Victoria Allen and Russell Ellison for tireless work in researching images and information about costumes and vintage and historical clothing.

Marty Axelrod for his generous help in text critiquing and editing.

Sia Aryai, my amazingly talented photographer, for all his patience while I prepared the draping steps.

Designer P'lar Millar for being my 'beginning draping test-trial student'.

Eddie Bledsoe for costume history research and information.

Aiko Beall, my teacher and mentor for over 30 years.

Helen Rochester, Anne Townley and Jodi Simpson, my email friends at Laurence King, for guiding a first-time author through the strange labyrinth of completing a finished book.

My two daughters, Claire and Ellie Fraser, for their help with computer issues and for their time in trying on clothes constantly and modeling for the book.

My mother for being a great listener and support throughout the process.

About the DVD

The enclosed DVD contains 32 video tutorials in which Karolyn Kiisel demonstrates different draping techniques and skills.

DVD contents

Part 1: Beginning Draping

1. Tearing the Muslin (Calico) (see p. 20)
2. Blocking the Muslin (Calico) (see p. 21)
3. Pressing the Muslin (Calico) (see p. 21)
4. Marking the Grainlines – Pencil (see p. 22)
5. Marking the Grainlines – Thread Tracing (see p.22)
6. Draping the Three Grains (see p. 23)
7. Aligning the Grainlines (see p. 27)
8. Pinning Two Pieces of Muslin (Calico) Together (see p. 28)
9. Turning Up and Pinning the Hem (see p. 29)
10. Pinning, Marking, and Turning Seams (see p. 33)
11. Trimming and Clipping (see p. 45)
12. Side Bust Dart (see p. 45)
13. Turning Front Over Back (see p. 45)
14. French Dart (see p. 47)
15. Long Vertical Darts, Front and Back (see p. 52)
16. Taping the Stylelines (see p. 54)
17. Marking (see p. 55)
18. Truing (see p. 55)
19. Fitting the Dress (see p. 56)
20. Transferring the Muslin (Toile) to a Pattern Paper (see p. 56)
21. Marking the Grainlines – Pulling a Thread (see p. 71)
22. Adding Sections of Fabric (see p. 76)
23. Turning the Seams of a Fitted Garment (see p. 76)

Part 2: Intermediate Draping

24. Draping the Bias Circle Skirt (see p. 101)
25. Draping the Sleeve (see p.133)
26. Draping the Convertible Collar (see p. 137)
27. Draping the Crotch (see p. 164)
28. Fitting the Pant (Trousers) (see p. 182)

Part 3: Advanced Draping

29. The Two-piece Sleeve (see p. 215)
30. Draping the Gown (see p. 274)
31. Fitting on the Bias (see p. 289)
32. Improvisational Draping (see p. 303)

DVD credits

Featuring
Karolyn Kiisel

Director
Kyle Titterton

Producer
Kyle Titterton

Editor
Kyle Titterton

Boom Mike Operator
Fernanda Starling

Lighting
Sia Aryai

Draping Model
Claire Fraser

Make-Up for Draping Model
Naomi Camille

Make-Up for Karolyn Kiisel
Yoko Kagaya, Chinatsu Watanabe, Haruyo Sawada

Key Grip
Alexander Dumitru

Set Designer
Mallory Michelle

Production Assistants
Saori Mitome, Cory Miller, Russel Ellison